# THE CRISIS OF
# BRITISH UNIONISM

'. . . in political life controversy is of its essence. Even if some of it is fictitious and conventional, even if men in active public life have to subordinate some aspects of their personal views to party cohesion, or are influenced by mixed motives, it is still the element of genuine conviction . . . that gives it interest and the spark of divine fire'.

L.S. Amery, introduction to Anthony Trollope's *The Prime Minister* (O.U.P., 1973), p. ix.

# THE CRISIS OF BRITISH UNIONISM

## Lord Selborne's Domestic Political Papers, 1885–1922

edited with an introductory essay by

GEORGE BOYCE

**British Library Cataloguing in Publication Data**

Selborne, William Waldegrave Palmer, *Earl of*
  The Crisis of British Unionism: The Domestic Political Papers of the
  Second Earl of Selborne, 1885–1922.
  1. Selborne, William Waldegrave Palmer, *Earl of*
  2. Statesmen—Great Britain—Biography
  I. Title    II. Boyce, George
  DA565.S4/    941.081′092′4

ISBN 0–9508900–2–2

PUBLISHED BY THE HISTORIANS' PRESS,
9 DAISY ROAD, LONDON E18 1EA.

Produced by Alan Sutton Publishing Limited
30 Brunswick Road, Gloucester GL1 1JJ
Printed in Great Britain

# CONTENTS

## ACKNOWLEDGEMENTS

I am grateful to the following for permission to quote from manuscripts of which they hold the copyright: The Earl of Birkenhead (Lord Birkenhead); Beaverbrook Trustees and the Clerk of the Records, House of Lords Record Office and Lord Coleraine (Bonar Law); the University of Birmingham (Austen and Joseph Chamberlain); the Hon. Sir Edward Carson (Sir Edward Carson); the Earl of Elgin (Lord Elgin); Baron Fisher of Kilverstone (Sir John Fisher); the Librarian, Lambeth Palace Library (1st Earl of Selborne); the Earl of Lansdowne (Lord Lansdowne); the Viscount Long (Walter Long); the Warden and Fellows of New College (Lord Milner); the Earl of Midleton (Lord Midleton); the Marquess of Salisbury (third and fourth Marquess of Salisbury, Lord Hugh Cecil and Lord Robert Cecil). I have endeavoured to trace all copyright holders, I think successfully, but I apologise to anyone whose copyright I have inadvertently infringed.

I also thank Dr. John Turner of The Historians Press for his initial encouragement, and his willingness and patience in inducting me into the new technology; the Earl of Selborne, who made his grandfather's important archive over to the free use of scholars; Mr. Neville Masterman, formerly of the History Department in Swansea, without whose help there would be no Selborne manuscript; and Marilyn Watts of Oxford, who undertook the responsible and difficult task of preparing my manuscript for typesetting.

I am grateful to the Twenty-Seven Foundation; the British Academy; and the University College of Swansea Research Grants Committee for the financial support which made this publication possible.

# INTRODUCTION

William Waldegrave Palmer, second Earl of Selborne (1859–1942)[1] was born into the world of high politics. His father Roundell Palmer[2] read for the bar, entered parliament as a Peelite Conservative in 1847, became a Liberal, and made for himself a highly successful career, serving as Solicitor General, Attorney General and twice as Lord Chancellor, becoming Viscount Wolmer and Earl of Selborne in 1882, and earning the respect of his contemporaries as a man of industry and high principle. When he died in 1895 he left to his son a title, a fine estate – 'Blackmoor' – and a tradition of public service. William Waldegrave Palmer's political career was equally distinguished. He worked as a private secretary in three important offices of state, and was elected Liberal M.P. for Petersfield, Hampshire, before he was 27. He held Cabinet office twice, as First Lord of the Admiralty, 1900–1905, and as President of the Board of Agriculture, 1915–16; was a chief whip, an under-secretary of state, sat on committees, chaired royal commissions, and was a prominent political figure of his generation until his retirement from active politics in October 1922.

Lord Selborne was possessed of all the advantages enjoyed by members of the hereditary ruling class:

> A young patrician grew up in the world of the great house where the intimate affairs of state were dinner table gossip; he went into parliament as a young man, became private secretary to father, uncle or cousin, and gained the parliamentary and administrative experience prerequisite to high office if he was willing to learn.[3]

But despite early lessons from his family about duty and obligation – when he was ten his mother[4] urged him not to forget 'our family motto "To do my duty in that state of life into which it shall please God to call me"'[5] – young Palmer did not seem particularly willing to learn. He performed ably enough at Winchester (where Edward Grey, later Viscount Grey of Fallodon, was his fag); he took a first in history at Oxford in 1881; but, in his own words, at university 'I hunted and played cards and cricket and tennis and ragged – I took no part in politics'.[6] However, his wild oats sown, he soon, to his father's gratification, 'showed a worthy ambition to seek for opportunities of usefulness, and was active in following them when found'.[7] His activities were those which befitted a man of his station: he served on the commission of the peace for Hampshire, and he qualified for and joined the Hampshire militia. Indeed, he considered making the army his career, but his father persuaded him to try politics, and he quickly gained valuable administrative experience when in 1882 he was appointed private secretary to H.C.E. Childers, first at the War Office and then at the Exchequer, and then in 1884 served as private secretary to his father in the Lord Chancellor's Office. In 1883 he married Lady Beatrix Maud Cecil, eldest daughter of the third Marquess of Salisbury, a family and political connection that was to establish important links in his Unionist career. Within two years of leaving university he was adopted as second Liberal candidate for Coventry, and in 1885 he stood as Liberal candidate for the Eastern or Petersfield division of Hampshire, and was elected.

Lord Selborne's path into politics was smooth. It was true that he had a stiff fight in Hampshire, and only won because of a split in the Conservative vote between two rival Conservative candidates; but the world of politics which he entered in December 1885 was, despite the reform of the electoral system which took place between 1883 and 1885, the kind that catered for the able son of a highly placed Peer. The entry of David Lloyd George, a man of very different social background, into the House of Commons in 1890 may have shown that the era of the 'cottage-bred man' had arrived; but the entry of William Waldegrave Palmer into that same House five years earlier demonstrated that the era of the estate-bred man was far from over.

Hardly had Selborne settled into his seat than, in June 1886, he was obliged to defend it, this time as a Liberal Unionist, in opposition to Gladstone's policy of home rule for Ireland. But to Selborne the issue was not at first clear cut; not only did he hesitate, he even went so far as to suggest to his father in January 1886 that home rule might not, after all, be the devil's work, since there seemed no other alternative save 'the government of Cromwell'.[8] He voted for Jesse Collings' motion which turned out Lord Salisbury's Conservative administration on January 27 because in his election speeches he had called on the Liberal party to take steps to 'multiply the owners of land'.[9] And, to complete the confusion, despite the fact that he stood as a Liberal Unionist in June 1886, he found himself supported by Gladstonian Liberals and opposed by Conservatives.

Nevertheless, between January and June 1886, the Liberal Unionists were sorting themselves out as a separate party. On 22 April Lord Goschen informed Selborne that 'Liberals opposed to Gladstone's Irish measures are organising', with a headquarters at Spring Gardens.[10] Not all dissident Liberals supported this move, Joseph Chamberlain and his radical followers remaining for the time being aloof; but although Liberal Unionists were offered seats in the administration which Lord Salisbury formed following the election of June 1886, none accepted,[11] for the Liberal Unionists were determined to play an independent role in politics, supporting the Conservative government on the great issue of the Union, but opposing it, if necessary, on other grounds. And while Selborne declared that 'we place . . . this question of the Union before every other question of current politics', he warned that 'it will rest with the Government whether we shall continue to support them. We cannot entirely abandon our Liberal principles, and support them in reactionary legislation'.[12]

From 1886 until his father's death in 1895, Selborne sat in the House of Commons, first as a member for East Hampshire, and then, from 1892, as member for Edinburgh West, a seat he contested mainly because he did not like to stand again for his Hampshire seat where he would be standing on Conservative and Liberal Unionist votes against Gladstonian Liberals who had been loyal to him in 1885 and 1886.[13] And if it is true that there is a 'single crucial distinction between politicians who just did their particular jobs, and politicians who took it upon themselves to create the general situation',[14] then for the first ten years of his political life Selborne undoubtedly falls into the former category. There are several reasons for this. He was a young M.P., finding his way round the complex and fragmented politics of the period; he appears moreover to have been very much under his father's influence, often seeking (though he did not always follow) his father's advice on controversial matters; and from 1886 to 1892 he was chief Liberal Unionist whip, a job which required skilful, patient, but essentially background work. Nevertheless, he looked back on his ten years in the House of Commons as 'the making of my political opportunities'.[15] The great domestic issues which confronted his mature political career: Ireland; the House of Lords; social reform; and the character of the Unionist party – were all foreshadowed or defined in the ten years of his political apprenticeship.

On his father's death in 1895 Selborne attempted to retain his seat in the Commons, honouring a compact which he made with his friend St John Brodrick,[16] that whoever lost his father first would fight a 'test case'.[17] When Selborne entered the House on 13 May 1895 the radical M.P. Labouchère called attention to 'the presence in this House of a nobleman . . . who has since become a Peer of the Realm', and after an inquiry his West Edinburgh seat was declared vacant.[18] The new Earl of Selborne, however, was not fated to while away his time in comparative idleness in the House of Lords, for when Lord Rosebery's Liberal government fell in June 1895 the Liberal Unionists ended their 'independence' by accepting office in Lord Salisbury's new administration. Joseph Chamberlain, since 1891 the leader of the Liberal Unionists in the Commons, became Colonial Secretary; and, on 30 June, Lord Salisbury offered Selborne the post of Under-Secretary of State for the Colonies.

For the next fifteen years Selborne's career was centred on imperial and international politics: his five years at the Colonial office, followed by a decade divided equally between the Admiralty (as First Lord) and the Governor-Generalship of South Africa, almost wholly diverted his attention from domestic concerns; and his papers covering this period will be the subject of a second volume: a few items only are printed here. But his experience was important for his general political convictions. It was gained at a time when the empire was undergoing a series of crises: the Jameson Raid and the South African war; the increasing burden of defence expenditure and the necessity to maintain British naval strength in a world dominated by Russia, the United States of America and Germany; above all what he regarded as the often misguided policies of the Liberal government towards the South African constitutional question between 1905 and 1910, when the 'importunate and insane House of Commons' all too often had its way.

Lord Selborne believed that a House of Commons dominated by what he disparagingly called the 'Home-Rule-Pro-Boer-Little-England-Socialist party' was quite unfit to take key decisions about imperial matters. His misgivings were sharpened by the growing tension between the House of Commons and the House of Lords following Lloyd George's 'People's Budget' of 1909, and the danger that the Liberals would 'request the King to create enough Peers to pass an "Emasculation of the House of Lords and Establishment of the House of Commons as a Single Chamber Tyranny" Bill', which would give the Commons power to 'reverse our policy on Tariff Reform, to denounce the Preference given by us to our Colonies, most surely to disrupt the Empire'.[19] When Lord Selborne returned home to an atmosphere of political crisis in 1910 he was, despite his cordial relations with individual Liberals such as Lord Crewe and Sir Edward Grey, prepared to throw himself heart and soul into the great struggle between the Liberals and the House of Lords which was the watershed of Edwardian politics.

History has not been kind to those Unionist Peers who, in Lord Selborne's words, preferred to perish in the light, slain by their enemies than perish in the dark, slain by their own hand, who refused to toe the official party line and, in the last resort, abstain from voting on the Parliament Bill. Roy Jenkins has portrayed them as fox-hunting backwoodsmen, political dinosaurs, who could not see that the process of constitutional evolution had passsed them by;[20] and a less partisan observer, the American historian G.B. Adams, remarked in bewilderment that 'to an outside student of English history, the constitutional importance of the parliament act seems to have been a good deal exaggerated, especially by its opponents'. The bill, Adams wrote, merely took away the Lords' power to delay for more than two years a measure sanctioned by the people.[21] And if the Unionist 'die-hards' were nothing more than backwoodsmen, then Lord Selborne and his like were indeed blind and foolish opponents of democracy and reform.

But this was not how Selborne, for his part, saw the issue. He based his case against the Liberals on his interpretation of the British constitution. 'The theory of government of the United Kingdom', he wrote is a partnership between the Crown and the people. The sphere of the Crown is rule; the sphere of the people is policy. As it would be impossible for the people always as a whole to express their opinions on matters of policy, they do so through representatives elected to the House of Commons; and, because it is possible that a temporary and discredited majority in the House of Commons might abuse the trust committed to them, a Second Chamber is necessary to insure the people against the usurpation and abuse of their authority.[22]

Thus the legislature as a whole was 'self-checking. As in a watch, the main-spring neutralised the inertness of the hair-spring and the hair-spring neutralised the explosiveness of the main-spring. There was little probability of the organism as a whole ever doing a wild action, or even going utterly to sleep'. But with the Parliament Bill, the 'concept of checking' was lost: there was a 'single chamber with no rival to fear, and open to all the temptations that have beset every despot since the days when David numbered the Children of Israel'.[23]

The destruction of the checks and balances of the British constitution was made all the more serious by the growth of power of the executive, buttressed by the party machine, in the early twentieth century. The influence of the people's representatives in parliament was 'steadily waning' and 'the power of the Cabinet, a body of some twenty ministers who exert their influence over the members of Parliament by the machinery of the caucus, is steadily waxing'. The party managers in the constituencies might not represent the average opinion, even of the adherents of the party in their constituency, 'much less that of the constituency as a whole, but they can make it impossible for a man to remain a member of Parliament if he quarrels with them'.[24] Thus, the second chamber, after the Parliament Bill, would be a 'sham second chamber', since 'the House of Lords is not in form to be abolished but gradually deprived of all power';[25] and the lower House, for its part, was firmly in the grip of the government and the caucus. What emerged from the 'wreck of the two Chambers' was 'an inner junto of the Cabinet directing the party machine and practically uncontrolled in administration and legislation'.[26]

It was to defend the prescriptive functions of the King, Lords and Commons that Lord Selborne became a 'die-hard' in 1911, and refused 'any responsibility for the revolution, direct or indirect, and to see that it is only consummated by the creation of Peers'.[27] He collaborated with Lord Willoughby de Broke (who, to be sure, did hunt foxes[28]), and George Wyndham, to concert opposition to the Liberals; and when he and his fellow 'die-hards' were defeated in August 1911, he played a leading part in organising the Halsbury Club, a pressure group within the Unionist party, pledged to stiffening the leadership against further concessions on the constitutional issue, and to speaking with one voice on other important political issues, such as home rule, disestablishment, and trade unionism. Selborne identified the struggle of his own class for restoration of its political rights with the best interests of the British people. The Liberals, far from defending democracy, were bent on destroying it, and Selborne had faith in British democracy, which he described as 'the least unfit . . . to wield power of which the world has yet furnished example'.[29] The power of the people must be invoked to check the tyranny of the single chamber, and Selborne aimed to do this by introducing into the British constitution the device of the referendum, which would ascertain the people's will on important political and social questions, a will only imperfectly expressed through the general election, in which the issue was 'a bewildering complication of rival policies, diverse bills, and personal considerations . . . overshadowed by . . . the "cup-tie" aspect of the giant struggle between the great political parties'.[30] A referendum of the people on great single issues such as disestablishment or tariff reform would be a court of appeal from the tyranny of the caucus. 'I would far rather argue before the electors, who themselves were about to give a vote on a definite concrete proposal . . . than I would argue to a tyrannical majority in a Single Chamber dominated by the caucus'.[31]

One of the chief examples cited by Unionists of 'single chamber tyranny' in operation was the Liberals' attempt to put an Irish home rule bill on the statute book following their victory over the Lords in 1911. The details of such a bill had not been disclosed to the electorate in the general elections of 1910, and Unionists argued that the electorate had therefore been denied any real expression of its wishes on this crucial matter. But what were they to do in face of a Liberal-Irish Nationalist alliance which could pass a home rule bill through the Commons, and the Parliament Act which ensured its passage after two years through the Lords? Lord Selborne, despite his firm stand against the Liberals in 1911, approached this second great constitutional crisis with a profound sense of realism. In September 1911 he confessed that he regarded it 'as quite certain that an Act conferring Home Rule on Ireland is going to pass into law', and that Unionists would 'not be able to repeal the Act'.[32] Selborne disavowed any attempt to resist this inevitable process by unconstitutional or extra-parliamentary means. 'I will never say', he wrote in 1913

> that it is always wrong to take up arms. I should myself take up arms without any hesitation for the Monarchy against a republic . . . But civil war is the ultima ratio and the last party in the world that ought to turn to arms if it can possibly avoid it or go outside legal and constitutional forms is the Conservative and Unionist Party. If they did so lightly it is likely that it would mean the breaking up of our society and the end of the Nation, for it would remove all restrictions on Radicals and Socialists who are blinded to the value of tradition and authority.[33]

And although he believed that the Ulster protestants who were preparing themselves to resist by force of arms the imposition of home rule had right on their side, he did not believe that an Irish settlement could be achieved simply by cutting Ulster out of the home rule bill, and letting the rest of Ireland go its own way. Instead, the problem of Anglo-Irish relations must be reconsidered as a whole, and with regard to the welfare not only of the Irish, but of the English, the Scots, the Welsh, and indeed of the empire.

The answer was to re-cast the United Kingdom constitution in a federal mould, to establish federal legislatures in the various parts of the kingdom, and to make them subordinate in certain respects to a common United Kingdom parliament: and this system might even be incorporated within a federal system for the whole empire.[34]

But 'home rule all round' involved a constitutional change of the utmost magnitude; and time was running out for a peaceful resolution of the Anglo-Irish crisis on such ambitious and far-reaching lines. The Ulster Unionists were by 1914 armed and ready to resist; the Liberal government was pressing on with its home rule bill, though not without misgivings and some tentative feelers about partitioning Ireland; and Lord Selborne could only watch helplessly, and warn that 'in Ulster you are up against that most uncompromising historical fact, a community which is ready to suffer any consequence rather than submit to what it believes to be a wrong and an evil'.[35] But just when civil war seemed inevitable, and matters were passing out of the hands of the politicians at Westminster – ('Talk of Nero and Rome and fiddling', Selborne exclaimed in disgust in June 1914[36]) – the Irish crisis was overtaken by the greater crisis of Europe which broke in August.

The danger of civil war receded as Irish Nationalists and Unionists rallied to the colours, but the outbreak of European war did not ease the difficulties confronting the Unionist Opposition. On the contrary, it exacerbated them, for Selborne and his fellow-Unionists were dismayed and angered by the Liberals' decision to place the home rule bill and a bill for disestablishing the church in Wales on the statute book. Their frustration was increased by the government's ineptitude in conducting the war, and Selborne was particularly irritated by the fact that to draw attention to the government's shortcomings would appear unpatriotic, would lay the Unionists open to the charge of raising party issues, and might seem like pressing the government to divulge secret information. The upshot of it all – the formation of a Liberal and Unionist coalition in May 1915 following a series of crises which rocked the Asquith administration – was not one that Selborne welcomed, although he accepted a place in the new Cabinet: 'It is very difficult', he wrote to his sister Sophia, 'to sit down and work with the men we have been fighting bitterly for years'.[37].

Lord Selborne entered the Cabinet as president of the Board of Agriculture and Fisheries, a post which suited his lifelong interest in farming and the land. It was also, his great friend Lord Milner pointed out, an important post, one 'vitally affecting our power of endurance in the long stuggle'.[38] Home food production in a prolonged war in which the submarine made its first effective appearance could certainly prove an essential part of the battle for national survival; and Selborne tackled his task with his customary enthusiasm, vigour, and administrative ability. Within a few weeks of taking office he had persuaded Milner to chair a sub-committee to examine the possibility of stimulating an increase of foodstuffs in Britain; and by July 1915 an interim report, recommending a guaranteed minimum price for wheat, was ready.[39] It was then that Selborne had his first taste of the frustration which eventually drove him out of Asquith's Cabinet. Despite his strong support of Milner's report, it was shelved; and his grave warnings about the effects of the German submarine menace were wafted aside by the Prime Minister. 'We cannot conceal from ourselves the fact', Selborne wrote feelingly to his son Robert Palmer, then serving in Mesopotamia, 'that in a life and death struggle such as this intelligently directed autocracy has an immense advantage over democracy'.[40]

Selborne's dismay at the Cabinet's failure to act on Milner's report was increased by its reluctance to introduce an adequate measure of military conscription. In September 1915 Selborne declared to Lord Kitchener that he was 'profoundly convinced that the army cannot be kept up to strength through 1916 without compulsory service', and he urged Kitchener to use his great prestige in the country to press for a bill to be brought into operation should the number of voluntary recruits fall below the necessary level.[41] But his appeal met with blunt refusal, and this, combined with the Cabinet's slowness in establishing an effective co-ordinating body with the allies, and other defects in the machinery for waging war, nearly drove Selborne to despair. Then in October 1915 came a German invasion of Serbia, which the government failed to prepare for. 'What I should like to do', he wrote to Austen Chamberlain, 'is to say to Asquith that I am quite willing to continue a member of the government and look after turnips to show that there is no breach of unity, but I think the best contribution I can make now is to reduce the size of the Cabinet by resigning from it'.[42]

Selborne, however, stayed for the time being, perhaps mollified by the government's acceptance of the principle that, if a last canvass for voluntary recruits organised by Lord Derby should fail by 12 December 1915, it would acquiesce in the introduction of a limited measure of conscription; but his departure, as it turned out, was delayed for only a few months. He was still deeply unhappy about the government's lack of interest in the problem of home grown food supplies; and he blamed the Liberal Chief Secretary for Ireland, Augustine Birrell, for Dublin Castle's failure to anticipate the rebellion which broke out in Dublin on Easter Monday, 1916. Finally, when Lloyd George concluded negotiations with John Redmond and Sir Edward Carson for a Irish settlement, based on the exclusion of Ulster, to come into effect at once, Selborne's cup was full, and on 16 June he extricated himself from an increasingly impossible position by sending Asquith his resignation.[43]

Asquith once described Selborne as lacking both in insight and in foresight.[44] Yet Selborne had the insight to comprehend that the undemanding methods used by the Prime Minister in running his wartime government were quite unsuitable, and the foresight to grasp that if these methods were continued, the war would be lost. Patriotism alone kept

Selborne at his post until June 1916; and after he resigned he composed some notes on his War Cabinet colleagues, pinpointing what he regarded as the strengths and weaknesses of Asquith and his team of ministers.[45] The Prime Minister, he acknowledged, was 'intensely patriotic and cared with his whole soul for England's victory, but he never acted except to get out of a grave difficulty into which he ought never to have got'. Selborne paid full tribute to Asquith's qualities: his cleverness, his wisdom, his imperturbability; but 'for the rest he was quite hopeless as a war P.M. He had no vision . . . no power of leadership of any sort or kind'. Lloyd George, on the other hand, had 'driving power and courage in wonderful combination'. But he was also a 'born intriguer', with whom, Selborne commented, 'I would never wish to go out tiger hunting . . . not because I doubt his courage but because I know that he would leave anyone in the lurch anywhere if he thought it suited his purpose'. Selborne reckoned that 'if George's vision and drive could have been combined with (Bonar) Law's business habits and straightness, the results would have been doubled'. This was, in fact, the political combination, made in December 1916, which was to see the nation through to victory: but by the time it came about Lord Selborne was out of office, and he was never to hold Cabinet rank again.

Lord Selborne's remaining years in politics revealed a growing alarm at the direction of public affairs. Although he admired Lloyd George's qualities as a war leader, he profoundly distrusted his ambition to continue to lead a Unionist-Liberal coalition, and pressed Austen Chamberlain to take the leadership of the Unionist party. When this failed, Selborne associated himself with a group of Unionist critics of the post-war coalition, including Lord Salisbury and Lord Willoughby de Broke, but he was not sanguine about the chances of bringing the party back to the straight and narrow path. More deep-seated than his disappointment at the shape of party politics was his concern over what he regarded as the failure to tackle the main problems confronting his country: Ireland, India, the House of Lords, the trade unions.

Selborne was deeply involved with the first three of these problems. His resignation from the government in 1916 did not mean that he was opposed to any attempt to settle the Irish question; on the contrary, he was as determined as he had been before the war that a settlement must be made, but that it must be one compatible with the safety and security of the United Kingdom and the empire. The aims and aspirations of Irish nationalists, Ulster Unionists and the British people could be reconciled by jettisoning the home rule act passed by Asquith's government in 1914, and substituting an overall reconstruction of the government of the United Kindon on federal lines.[46] Selborne found a willing ally in F. S. Oliver, amateur historian, pamphleteer, and political manipulator, with whom he had corresponded on constitutional questions before the war. Together they drafted a pamphlet, privately circulated in 1917, *A method of constitutional co-operation*, in which they explained their plan for federal reform, involving the establishment of parliaments for Ireland, Scotland and England, with a single central United Kingdom legislature to manage matters of common concern; and they canvassed their scheme among British and Irish politicians, including Sir Horace Plunkett, Sir Edward Carson, Lord Salisbury, Austen Chamberlain and Walter Long. But despite converting some leading Unionists to the federal idea, Selborne and Oliver were forced to admit failure. Lloyd George was never seriously interested in such a far-reaching reform of the constitution; public opinion in Great Britain and Ireland remained apathetic; and by the spring of 1918 the initiative was lost, when the government decided to take powers to apply conscription to Ireland.

The failure of federalism was a bitter disappointment to Selborne, not only because it left Ireland unsettled, but because it left the United Kingdom parliament over-burdened with work and thus unable to cope with running the country and the empire. Selborne was certain that unless parliament were reformed and modernised, disenchantment with parliamentary government would grow, and more and more power would accrue, on one hand to the Prime Minister, and on the other to extra-parliamentary bureaucratic organisations;[47] and he warned Austen Chamberlain that, if federalism and second chamber reform were both allowed to 'slide', 'I should regard the position of this country as very dangerous – I should regard revolution as very possible'.[48] Selborne was finding the post-war world an increasingly uncomfortable one, menaced by the two great modern scourges, nationalism and socialism. Only his strong sense of duty compelled him to serve as chairman of a committee examining a bill for the reform of Indian government, for he questioned the whole premise on which the bill was based: that the kind of political institutions which suited England would invariably take root in an oriental country as well. 'I see no way out of the mess . . . except by bloodshed – bloodshed if we sit still, bloodshed if we graft any western form of government on to any eastern civilisation'.[49] Irish Sinn Feiners were on the move, wresting independence from Britain by force, probably in alliance with the Bolsheviks of Russia;[50] and the Triple Alliance of railwaymen, miners and dockers, 'these modern predatory barons', was threatening the livelihood of the nation.[51] Demands for nationalisation of industry would complete the downfall of the British system of government, turning the House of Commons into 'nothing but a wage auction'.[52]

It is not surprising that Lord Selborne, in his own words, 'gradually slid out' of this uncongenial political world, which differed so markedly from that which he had entered as an enthusiastic young Liberal M.P. in 1885. Lord Salisbury kept him closely informed of political events, and especially of the fate of Selborne's arch-enemy, Lloyd George, in 1922. But Selborne was not prepared to take part in politics if he was not also willing to shoulder the burden of responsibility, and he requested Bonar Law not to consider him for a place in the Conservative administration which Law was forming after the fall of Lloyd George in October 1922. Anyway, he wished to devote his remaining energies to saving his estate and house for his children and grandchildren.

It might appear that the political life of Lord Selborne and of like-minded Unionists was dedicated to frustrating the 'progressive' forces of modern British and Irish history. But Lord Selborne once declared that the secret of success in politics was to 'believe something wholeheartedly and to avow it. Men will always follow a steady consistent and fearless lead'. Unionism, he was convinced, could be 'a living creed . . . one which inspires faith and courage'.[53] He had boundless confidence in the genius of the Anglo-Saxon race, provided it was properly led by the aristocracy, and more than a little contempt for those races which did not have the good fortune to be Anglo-Saxon. The Unionist leadership's decision to join a coalition under Lloyd George in 1918 brought him near to a despair; and his belief that such an alliance could not last, but must prove unpopular with the Unionist rank and file, was vindicated in 1922. But that coalition experience exposed the Unionist dilemma. For what was the meaning of Unionism in the post-war world? In September 1916 Selborne upbraided the Marquess of Salisbury for defining the purpose of the Unionist party as 'to defend certain capital institutions and in everything else to go slow'. There was 'no more inherent merit in going slow than there is in going fast', and the party's purpose, Selborne argued, should be to 'defend certain capital institutions' and 'in everything else to see that the changes which are made are made in conformity with the tradition of the past and made in the interests of the nation and not of a section of the nation'.[54] Unionists, he declared

are opposed to unbridled collectivism because it is incompatible with the liberty of the nation, and to uncontrolled individualism because it is incompatible with the happiness of the nation. They know that all men are not equal and that a political system founded on the theory of equality must fail, but they believe that all men and women have a right to the best opportunity which can be afforded them of using their gifts to the best advantage, and therefore they are prepared to use the power of the nation to assist the individual and thus adjust the balance between individualism and collectivism.[55]

In *The Working Constitution of the United Kingdom* (1905), Leonard Courtney divided British political parties into 'two camps of progress and of caution.' While admitting that 'the gradations of temperament must be infinite' he argued that 'there are always two masses, the one characterised by attachment to things as they are and by hesitation to change; the other, by a strong sense of existing shortcomings and defects, and by a readiness to entertain plans for their amendment'.[56] Liberal Unionists always saw themselves as belonging to the camp of progress rather than that of caution. In 1891 Jesse Collings claimed that they stood for

Maintenance of Unity of Kingdom and one Parliament of United Kingdom, Local Government, District Councils, etc., Allotments, Small Holdings, Sanitary Reform, Rural measures, Free Education, Technical Education, Reduced Taxation, Relief of Local rates, Factory legislation, etc, etc, etc, . . .

Liberalism, by contrast, stood for home rule 'to which everything else is to be postponed'.[57] But in the event it was the Union, 'to which everything else is to be postponed' that became the identity of the party after 1886, despite the influence of Joseph Chamberlain, while progressivism seemed to be the prerogative of the Liberals (however 'unprogressive' many Liberals might in fact be). The frustration felt by Selborne at the predicament in which he believed the Liberal Unionists found themselves – a frustration which in 1912 provoked him into declaring that 'the present flabbiness lies mainly with the Tories by origin'[58] – was the understandable reaction of a Liberal Unionist who despaired of capturing the Tory party for his ideas. The disasters of the 1910 elections, following the Unionist split on Tariff Reform, provoked the revival of the Irish question in an acute and uncompromising form, and placed Selborne in a 'die-hard' camp in which he did not really belong. It has been said that the wartime and post-war coalitions enabled the Unionists to emerge from the political wilderness and reassert their control over the political process;[59] but this occasioned great stress and strain in the party, for if it was to modify or even abandon its Irish identity, then it ran the risk of becoming, as Selborne feared, an adjunct of Lloyd George's new centre/right grouping against the 'bolshevist menace'. Selborne and his colleagues played some part in averting this fate; but it was hard for him and his like to stand in the progressive tradition when their only role was to find and destroy fusion of the Liberal and Unionist parties. By 1920 Selborne no longer even sounded like a Liberal Unionist; his increasingly sterile comments were more reminiscent of the crusted, inert Toryism that he had not long ago despised. And the Liberal Unionists became the forgotten party of British politics.

What, then, was the crisis of British Unionism? Oscar Wilde suggested that it was the absence, rather than the presence, of politics:

Lady Bracknell (sternly): . . . What are your politics?
Jack: Well, I am afraid I really have none. I am a Liberal Unionist.
Lady Bracknell: Oh, they count as Tories. They dine with us. Or come in the evening, at any rate.[60]

This jibe was less than truthful (though containing elements of truth) in Wilde's day, nor was it justified in 1912; but it was vindicated after 1916 when Liberal Unionists abandoned their commitment to the Irish Union and thereby found themselves bereft of a distinct political identity. For the party was a far from homogeneous group of Whigs and Radicals, and despite their perfectly sound claim to be as progressive as anybody else, and Selborne's frustration at their failure, as he saw it, to impart this political mentality to the Tory party, the fact remained that the Irish

Question was the issue that kept the Liberal Unionists, and the Unionists as a whole, from disintegration. It is fashionable nowadays to regard Ireland as an incubus; but Selborne's career demonstrates that it was essential for the unity of a great British political party. And once the Union was compromised by its very defenders, Liberal Unionism (and Unionism generally) could not for long survive the departure of Ireland from the centre of the British political stage. But at least Selborne, in his political retirement, could reflect on the irony of political life as he witnessed the triumph of his 'living creed' in the era of Stanley Baldwin and Neville Chamberlain. Only now it was called 'Conservatism'.

Selborne was a man of solid rather than brilliant parts. Yet his early departure to the Lords, and his long periods as an administrator rather than a politician, did not deprive him of influence in the Unionist party. On the contrary, his strong sense of public duty, his reputation as a man of integrity and principle, and his wide circle of important political acquaintances (not to mention relatives) ensured him a central place in British politics between 1906 and 1922, a place fully documented in his extensive archive. He was a devoutly religious man with a fervent belief that morality must have a place in politics, even if it proved inexpedient; he was invariably fair-minded, and earned the respect of political friends and foes alike. And his correspondence bears out his faithful adherence to the advice given to him by his father when he first decided to make his bid for a place in public life: 'It is not worth while to eat dirt, for the sake of a seat in Parliament'.

There is no biography of the second Earl of Selborne. The documents printed here are selected mainly from his own papers. The Selborne archive, which was given to the Bodleian Library by the Viscount Wolmer (now the Earl of Selborne) in 1970, comprises 222 volumes of manuscript and printed material, with a further 12 volumes of estate and legal documents. I have also examined some 20 other collections, by way of detective work, to track down letters of which Lord Selborne did not keep a copy, but which are worth including.

All documents are printed as the originals, with the following exceptions: I have expanded some contractions and initials; thus 'Yrs' becomes 'Yours', and G.P., when first cited, becomes Gallipoli Peninsula, but in obvious cases (e.g. Mr. G., for Mr Gladstone), I have retained the original; I have standardised dates, thus August 7th 1914 becomes 7 August 1914; and I have indicated breaks in the text by three dots.

Apart from the introduction and footnotes, there is no additional material. I have provided brief biographies of all the characters mentioned in the text, with a few unimportant exceptions.

John Brooke has remarked that 'One of the difficulties university teachers have experienced in preparing courses on nineteenth-century political and constitutional history has been the lack of reliable editions of political correspondence which could be placed in the hands of students'.[61] I have prepared this edition of Lord Selborne's papers in the hope that it will prove useful to students of late nineteenth and early twentieth century British history, and will serve as a full and reliable edition of one of the most complete modern collections of British political papers.

## References

1. For a brief outline of Lord Selborne's life see the article by the Reverend J.S. Brewis (at one time Selborne's intended biographer) in the *Dictionary of National Biography*, 1941–50, pp. 647–50. The family lineage is traced in *Burke's Peerage*.
2. Roundell Palmer (1812–1895), Baron Selborne, 1872, Earl, 1882, Solicitor General, 1861, Attorney General, 1863–66, Lord Chancellor, 1872–4, 1880–85. A brief character-sketch is provided in A.B. Cooke and John Vincent, *The governing passion: government and party politics in Britain, 1885–1886* (London, 1974), pp. 122–3.
3. J.C. Cornford, 'The parliamentary foundations of the Hotel Cecil', in Robert Robson (ed.), *Ideas and institutions of Victorian Britain* (London, 1967), p. 269. Selborne never doubted the ruling gifts of the landed class; see his *Mr. Lloyd George and the land* (1912?), p. 9.
4. Lady Laura Waldegrave, second daughter of the eighth Earl Waldegrave, whom Roundell Palmer married in 1848. She died in 1885.
5. His mother to Selborne, 7 March 1870, 93/7.
6. Lord Selborne's reminiscences, 191.
7. Roundell Palmer, *Memorials: personal and political* (privately printed, Edinburgh, 1892), p. 544.
8. Selborne to his father, 29 Jan. 1886 (RP 1869/143).
9. *North and East Hants Herald*, 3 Oct. 1885.
10. 13/5.
11. Though George Joachim Goschen in Jan. 1887 replaced Lord Randolph Churchill as Chancellor of the Exchequer.
12. *Parl.Deb.*, 3s., vol. ccx, col. 364, 31 Jan. 1887.
13. Reminiscences, 191.
14. Cooke and Vincent, *The governing passion*, p. 136.
15. Reminiscences, 191.
16. Later the Earl of Midleton.
17. Reminiscences, 191.
18. *Parl.Deb.*, 4s., vol. xxxiii, col. 1058, 13 May 1895.
19. Selborne to Joseph Chamberlain, 20 Dec. 1909 (9/177).
20. R. Jenkins, *Mr. Balfour's poodle* (London, 1968). But for a more objective view see P. Clarke, 'The Edwardians and their Constitution', in D. Read (ed.), *Edwardian England* (London, 1982), pp. 45–7.
21. G.B. Adams, *Constitutional history of England* (London, 1971 edition), p. 486.
22. *Rights of citizenship*, (London, 1912), p. 198.
23. Lord Selborne, *The state and the citizen* (London, 1913), p. 161.
24. *Rights of citizenship*, p. 199.
25. *H.L. Deb.*, 5s., vol. ix, col. 845, 8 Aug. 1911.
26. *Morning Post*, 12 Aug. 1913.
27. Selborne to A.J. Balfour, 24 Dec. 1910 (1/139).
28. His autobiographical fragment, *The passing years*, is a finely balanced admixture of sport and politics.

29. Selborne to Robert Palmer, 16 April 1912 (109/49). In his early campaigning days, Selborne stated his faith in an 'educated democracy' (*North and East Hants Herald*, 3 Oct. 1885).
30. *Rights of Citizenship*, p. 226.
31. Ibid., p. 224.
32. Selborne to Austen Chamberlain, 4 Sept. 1911 (AC 9/3/58).
33. Selborne to T.C. Platt, 19 Sept. 1912 (77/18).
34. Selborne to Austen Chamberlain, 4 Sept. 1911 (79/71).
35. Selborne to Sir Edward Grey, 3 April 1914 (77/96).
36. Selborne to Lady Selborne, 16 June 1914 (102/126).
37. Selborne to Sophie Palmer, 28 May 1915 (114/98).
38. Milner to Selborne, 6 June 1915 (12/246).
39. Selborne to Hankey, 13 June 1915 (80/14) and to Asquith, 15 July 1915 (81/53).
40. 109/61.
41. *Selborne to Kitchener, 17 Sept. 1915 (80/42).*
42. Selborne to Chamberlain, 30 Oct. 1915 (AC 13/3/91).
43. 80/194.
44. G.B. Pyrah, *Imperial policy and South Africa, 1902–1910* (Oxford, 1955), p. 160.
45. 80/285.
46. Selborne to H.A. Gwynne, 5 Aug. 1916 (84/4).
47. *H.L. Deb.*, 5s., vol. 33, cols. 512–521, 5 Mar. 1919.
48. AC 12/214.
49. Selborne to Lady Selborne, 11 June 1919 (103/110); see also his speech in the Lords, 12 Dec. 1919, vol.37, col.1005.
50. Selborne to Lady Selborne, 22 Mar. 1921 (104/50).
51. Same to same, 5 April 1921 (104/50).
52. *H.L. Deb.*, 5s., vol. 33, col. 485, 4 Mar. 1919.
53. Memorandum by Lord Selborne, July 1912 (79/80).
54. 6/185.
55. 79/80.
56. *The Working Constitution of the United Kingdom* (1912 ed.), pp. 16–17.
57. S.S., No.40.
58. Selborne to Bonar Law, 19 Dec. 1912 (B.L. 28/1/64).
59. Not the only occasion on which they did so; see R. Jay, *Joseph Chamberlain* (Oxford, 1980), p. 344.
60. *The Importance of Being Earnest* (1895).
61. *John Brooke, The Prime Ministers' Papers, 1801–1922 (London, H.M.C., H.M.S.O., 1968).*

*Abbreviations*

| | |
|---|---|
| *A.* | *Asquith Papers, Bodleian Library, Oxford.* |
| *A.C.* | *Austen Chamberlain Papers, Birmingham University Library.* |
| *B.L.* | *Bonar Law Papers, House of Lords Library.* |
| *CAB.* | *Cabinet Papers, Public Record Office, London.* |
| *D.* | *Eighth Duke of Devonshire Papers, Chatsworth House.* |
| *J.C.* | *Joseph Chamberlain Papers, Birmingham University Library.* |
| *J.S.S.* | *Sandars Papers, Bodleian Library, Oxford.* |
| *L.G.* | *Lloyd George Papers, House of Lords Library, London.* |
| *R.P.* | *Roundell Palmer Papers, Lambeth Palace Library, London.* |
| *S.S.* | *3rd Earl of Salisbury Papers, Christ Church Library, Oxford.* |
| *4th Salisbury* | *4th Earl of Salisbury Papers, Hatfield House, Hertfordshire.* |

# Chapter 1

## 'Criticise me mercifully, dearest father': The Making of a Unionist, 1885–1895.

1. From Roundell Palmer

30 Portland Place, W.
16 May 1885

My dearest Willie,

After considering the information contained in your letter, I am not unwilling that you should accept the invitation which you have received to stand for the Division,[1] if you are satisfied, in your own mind, on the three following points:–

1. That there is a *reasonable* chance of success.

2. That the expectations which have been formed, as to the limit of expenditure and as to assistance from the constituency towards meeting it, may be (within reasonable bounds) relied upon.

3. That the contest will be conducted with good feeling, and in a kindly and generous way, (so far as you and your friends and supporters are concerned) without interfering with private friendship or neighbourly relations; and without any intervention of agitators from without, who might use language tending to set chap against chap.

To this last point, the mere fact, that your uncle thinks it right to take part on the other side, (as he is most justly entitled to do, according to the opinions which he has always held), is enough to give even more importance, than it might under other circumstances have had. But, under *any* circumstances whatever, I should have thought it essential. It is not worth while to eat dirt, for the sake of a seat in Parliament![2] God bless and guide you! Believe me ever, my dearest son, your most affectionate father.

Selborne

96/119

1.   The Eastern or Petersfield division of Hampshire.
2.   Viscount Wolmer was elected Liberal M.P.; the results of the contest were:

|  |  |
|---|---|
| Wolmer: | 3,414 |
| W. Nicholson (C): | 3,253 |
| D. Henty (Ind.): | 179 |

The 'Independent' candidate, Henty, was put up by some dissident Conservatives in the division who resented the choice of William Nicholson (a former Liberal Member for the borough of Petersfield) as official Conservative candidate.

## 2. From Roundell Palmer

Blackmoor
Petersfield
21 December 1885

Dearest Willie,

. . . What a scare we have had about the 'Home Rule' question. I should think that foolish person Herbert Gladstone has, probably, been the cause of it all.[1] It is evident, from the form of his father's disclaimer,[2] that *something* has been under consideration (though not determined upon) which *somebody*, who ought not to have betrayed any confidence reposed in him, knew *something about*, and translated into the definite and astonishing form, in which it appeared in the newspapers. Perhaps it may not be a bad thing, that it *did* so appear. I hope we may conclude, from Lord Hartington's letter,[3] that Liberals in general would exercise their own judgement, in the public interest, on *any* measure for the Government of Ireland, which *any* of their leaders may propose . . . Ever your affectionate father

Selborne

96/125

1.  In December 1885 Herbert Gladstone leaked a statement that his father was about to tackle the question of home rule for Ireland. This disclosure was known as the 'Hawarden kite' and it was made by Herbert Gladstone in order to force his father to take the initiative on Ireland and thus ensure that he would remain the controlling influence over Liberal policies. The statement appeared in the press on 17 December. Michael Hurst documents the incident very thoroughly in *Joseph Chamberlain and the Liberal Reunion* (London, 1967), pp. 30–1, fn. 2.
2.  W. E. Gladstone issued a disclaimer stating that no accurate representation of his views was to be found except in his own public utterances, and that the 'kite' was not an accurate representation of his views, but a speculation upon them. He added that his son's statement had been published without his knowledge or authority (John [Viscount] Morley, *Life of Gladstone* [1906 ed.], vol. ii, p. 505).
3.  On 20 December 1885 Lord Hartington wrote to his chairman in Lancashire informing the public that no proposals of Liberal policy on home rule had been communicated to him, and that, for his part, he stood by what he said at the election. (Ibid., p. 506).

3. To Roundell Palmer

9 John Street
Berkeley Square
23 January 1886

*Private*

My dearest Father,

I think you will like to hear what I gather to be the political situation in the House on the Irish question. In the first place the Irish, especially Parnell, have been mildness and moderation itself in their speeches. 'Let the land question be settled first in all fairness to the landlords (presumably with English money), and then all difficulties will disappear – we are ready to give all the solid guarantees possible for the integrity of the Empire, the supremacy of the Imperial parliament, and the protection of the so called Loyalists. We will accept Home Rule on these terms.' In the private conversations of the Irish members in the writing and other rooms, (where they talk very openly), to which I have listened they use just the same language. You would think that no more moderate men existed.

Gladstone evidently leant in his speech[1] towards Home Rule; but he did insist very strongly on the necessity of preserving the integrity of the Empire through the supremacy of the Imperial Parliament, and on the duty of protecting the minority.

I had an opportunity of talking yesterday with Lord Northbrook and he was kind enough to speak his mind fully. He is not, I gathered, much alarmed at Gladstone's attitude; but he thinks, that, although Mr G. has not yet fully made up his mind, he leans to this solution – To adopt Mr Giffen's scheme and buy out the landlords. To keep all the garrisons in our hands. Not to give the Irish power to return to protection;[2] but short of this to give some assembly at Dublin entire control of purely Irish affairs. And, what is most important, to retain in the hands of the Imperial Parliament the sovereign power, i.e. power to pass a law concerning Ireland over the heads, if necessary, of the Irish Parliament. The most objectional feature in this scheme seems to me that he contemplates retaining the Irish members in the Imperial Parliament. If it was a condition that *no* Irish members remained in the Imperial Parliament I cannot help thinking that solution a good one. Please give me your views upon it especially with regard to two points –

1.   Do you think that the Irish would really accept it?

2.   Do you believe that conditions could be attached, and *enforced*, to prevent the Irish levying troops, under the guise of volunteers for instance?

There is evidently a large section of the Liberal party, which will resist any measure of Home Rule of any sort or kind. At least they say so now. The independent extreme Radicals lean apparently towards giving Parnell almost all he wants. The bulk of the Radicals who look to Chamberlain and Dilke to lead them have given no apparent signs whatever of what line they intend to take. I have a suspicion that they would not be sorry to see Gladstone make a false move, and take that occasion to strike out a line for themselves. The Tories are acting weakly. 'Mr Smith is to go to Ireland to report. *If* he thinks coercion necessary, they will bring in a bill. They *may* be able to bring in a local government bill for Ireland &c &c'.[3] In fact they are trying to get themselves turned out.

The whole is a game between the Irish, Gladstone, Radicals and Tories. Each wants the other to move first. The first step must apparently be a false one. In this most difficult time, give me dear Father the benefit of your advice.

At present I incline to this course.

1.   *Coercion*. It would be my duty to support the Executive if they ask for fresh powers, supposing of course that the powers demanded should be reasonable and likely to effect their purpose. I sincerely hope that they will ask for such powers, not temporarily, but as permanent additions to the criminal law of the land.

2. *Home Rule*. Even though I might approve of such a definite scheme as that laid down in the earlier part of the letter, not to support any *vague resolution* on the subject, unless the details are before us and satisfactory. Your very loving son

Wolmer

R.P. 1869/127

1.   In the debate on the address, 21 January 1886. The election of 1885 resulted in the return of a minority Conservative government under Lord Salisbury. The figures were: Liberals 334; Conservatives 250; Parnellite Nationalists 86.
2.   To erect tariff barriers against the United Kingdom. For Giffen's scheme see *Nineteenth Century*, Vol. 19 (1986), pp. 329–45.
3.   W. H. Smith, Viscount Chilston (1825–91), became Chief Secretary for Ireland in December 1885. In the debate on the address on 21 January 1886 it was announced that Smith had gone to Dublin to investigate whether Irish disorder could be handled by recourse to ordinary law or required exceptional measures. On 26 January the Conservative government announced its intention of asking leave to introduce a coercion bill and a land bill (Viscount Chilston, *W. H. Smith* [London, 1965] pp. 201–5).

4.   From Roundell Palmer

Blackmoor
Petersfield
26 January 1886

My dearest Willie,

. . . To go at once to the points on which this Irish question really turns; I have not carefully studied Mr Giffen's scheme for buying out the landlords: but Mr Giffen is an able and an honest man, and I should not set aside, off-hand, any scheme, which he advocates as really practicable. It is obvious, however, that, before the ground is prepared, for those who have any conscience in this matter to entertain at all any project of an Irish Parliament, *this* part of the matter must be dealt with, in such a way as *to settle it*; and that not on paper only, but practically. I am afraid that this would take more time, necessarily (even if it were clear that it could be done at all), than what remains in the life of a man in his 77th year, who thinks he has had a Divine call to give up a long-cherished hope of retirement and rest before leaving this world, in order that *he* may give Ireland peace under a domestic government. It follows, that no such preliminary measures as would really take the land-owners out of the power of the Parnell faction, could be passed and brought into practical operation, before the more perilous and questionable parts of the ulterior measure were determined upon.

I will assume, that we might keep the garrisons in our hands. But to enforce (I suppose) the laws, which Parnell and his nominees might make! That is the only thing they could do, except in case of a rebellion, or foreign invasion. Mr Gladstone and others are not the men I take them for, if (under the circumstances which their contemplated measure would introduce) they would not reduce those garrisons to a numerical strength so low, as practically to make them nothing but an outward sign and symbol of Imperial power; which might possibly be irritating to the dominant party, but would afford little security against them, if the measure failed to produce great harmony and good will.

As for such a limitation of the legislative power, as would prevent the Irish Parliament from returning to protection, I will simply say; that I do not believe it would or could be insisted upon, consistently with (what I suppose to be) the general principle of any scheme intended to give satisfaction to Parnell and his followers. To retain the general power of taxation, as to Ireland, in the Imperial Parliament, would not be consistent with any such scheme; to give it to an Irish Parliament under fetters, which might prevent them from raising an Irish revenue for Irish purposes in whatever way they might think best, and also alleviating (according to whatever might be their own ideas), Irish distress, could never be a final or an acceptable settlement.

You seem to be struck with the idea of retaining a soverign power of Imperial Legislation, capable of over-riding any Irish Legislation, as very important. I am not. *That* power must *necessarily* exist, as to any, and every, dependency of the Empire: it exists now, as to *all* our Colonies. But its exercise under any circumstances but those of insurrection, a general public confusion, would be against the principle of the whole constitutional arrangements; which it would practically upset: and therefore it does not take place as to any of our Colonies under Parliamentary Government; and it would not (unless in the contingencies mentioned) take place as to Ireland. I myself look upon the suggestion of this, as if it were (for any but those exceptional purposes) a practical and important matter, as little more than a *blind*; and an excuse for the (*to me*) wholly intolerable and inadmissible proposal to leave the Irish members in the British Parliament, at the same time that they have one of their own.

I cannot help thinking, that this proposal recommends itself to the mind, or minds, which seem to favour it, for one or other of *two* reasons, than which I cannot imagine any worse:– the one, as a mode of *seeming* to satisfy engagements to maintain the integrity, and resist the dismember-ment, of the Empire, which may be *represented* as more substantial than a Repeal of the Union, which would make the Monarchy the only constit-utional bond:– the other (base and discreditable in the last degree, if it were consciously entertained, but which may possibly exercise some latent influence even over minds which would reject the open suggestion of it with indignation) – as an instrument for securing to one political party a preponderance, in the British Parliament, over its opponents. I dismiss the last idea, without saying more:– it is by no means certain that the attachment of a (really) foreign element in the British Parliament would be greater, in the long run, to one British party than to another: – what is more probable is that it would be an element, naturally tending to ally itself with those politicians and measures, which might seem most likely to lower their country in the scale of nations.

To return to the first idea. Does it really mean that, while Irish affairs are to be managed by Irishmen in Ireland only, *British* affairs are *not* to be managed by Britons without the interference of Irishmen? If it means anything else, I shall wish to know what the new constitution of the Imperial Parliament is to be:– how Imperial are to be separated from British affairs; what limits are to be placed, and how, upon the Irish veto in the British Parliament; and why Irishmen should have a power, denied to our Colonies, in Imperial affairs.

Let me strongly advise you to attach no more weight than they deserve to any Parnellite professions:– and to *follow no leader* against your own judgement, in these vital matters. Ever your most affectionate father

Selborne

96/127.


5. From Roundell Palmer

Blackmoor
Petersfield
28 January 1886

My dearest Willie,

I am glad you mean to be here on Saturday: *perhaps* there may be time for a little talk about things in general. I am not going to blame you, for thinking (as I suppose you did) that what you had said in your election speeches about Allotments obliged you to vote for Mr Collings' motion.[1] But I myself, even if I went as far as Chamberlain himself in the Allotment question, should have seen in Mr Collings' motion nothing but a move to turn out the Government, and bring Mr Gladstone in; and, unless I had thought *this* desirable, in the actual position of the Irish question, I should certainly have voted as Lord Hartington, Sir H. James, and Arthur Elliot did. It is most unusual, according to my experience, to put any such expression of the opinion of the House, upon all sorts of questions omitted from the Speech from the Throne (whatever the House may think about them) into the form of an amendment of the address; and, if often done, it would make the debate on the Address (even more than it is at present) an opportunity for mere waste of time, and for airing everybody's ideas, reasonable or the reverse, *de omnibus rebus*. To decline to vote for pledging the House to an abstract resolution on such a topic, by amendments to the Address (unless one's real object were to vote no confidence in the Government), would be perfectly consistent with such an opinion as I suppose yours to be on the merits of Mr Collings' proposition, and also with any engagements, in that sense, which you might have undertaken to your constituents. And to do so, in the actual circumstances of the debate and the division, would scarcely have seemed to me consistent with the policy (which`I, at least, decidedly hold) that a Crimes Act is really necessary for Ireland.

My regard for some of the outgoing Ministers, and for the characters of public men in general, made me glad that they *spoke out* on *this* point; even though it *was* at the last moment, and when it might have been attributed to the motive of rallying the 'Liberal' friends of order in Ireland, and opponents of concession to Parnellism, in the coming division. That they (the late Ministers) played their cards very ill, by their hesitating and temporizing language in the Queen's Speech, followed by the explanation that they were *waiting for Mr Smith*, – and then, at last, speaking out *without* waiting for him, when it was (as they so often told *us*) 'too late' – is undeniable. Still,`I should not have voted for their turning them out of office.

And now, I have to tell you, *confidentially*, that Mr Gladstone wrote to me yesterday (after the division, and in anticipation of his being called upon to take office) a letter honourable (as I think) to both of us; in which he invited an explanation of my views, with the *desire*, – as I cannot be wrong in understanding him – though not with the *expectation*, that they might be compatible with my serving again with him. I will shew you his letter, and my answer;[2] which (as you may suppose) was conformable rather to his expectation, than to his desire: and it may, therefore, be taken (between you and me) as settled, that I shall have no part in the new arrangements, whoever else may. I think you will approve of *both* letters; and I trust that mine to him was in a tone not less friendly, than his to me. Believe me ever, dearest Willie, your affectionate father

Selborne

96/135

1.  One of the amendments to the address was a motion by Jesse Collings, Liberal M.P. for the Bordesley division of Birmingham, regretting the omission from

the Queen's speech of measures for benefiting the agricultural labourer. A division on 26 January resulted in the defeat of the government, the Parnellites voting with the Liberals. Home rule was not discussed, but Gladstone followed up his victory by forming a government ostensibly aimed at enquiring into the Irish situation.

2.   The main text of Gladstone's letter to Lord Selborne is printed in *Memorials: Part ii, personal and political, 1865–1895*, (London, 1898), pp. 203–5.


6.   To Roundell Palmer

9 John Street
Berkeley Square
29 January 1886

My dearest Father,

I was very glad to get your letter. In these most critical times I desire to have your advice and guidance above all things. Probably I shall often act unwisely and perhaps sometimes contrary to what I know to be your views, but it will I pray God only be done conscientiously and because I believe it to be right. I thought a great deal over my vote on Tuesday and gave it very deliberately. Of course if Mr Collings' motion had alone been the point at issue, I should have had no doubt or hesitation. But I knew that the real point was, whether considering the state of affairs in Ireland and the House of Commons, it was wise to turn out the Government. I thought and think it was. I need not remind you of the excessive weakness of their Irish policy during the last 7 months, ending with a theatrical attempt to appear strong. You are not unmindful of that in your letter. But you had to face this fact. The Tories were in a minority of 170 in the whole House. They could not possibly have carried on the government unless nearly 50 Liberals were prepared to support them through thick and thin. A casual, solitary, or occasional vote, would have been of no use. If I had supported them on Tuesday I ought to have been prepared to vote with them *always*. What occurred on Tuesday must have occurred sooner or later with the Tories in such a minority. I and 40 other odd Liberals were not and could not possibly be prepared always to vote with the Tories. I think both conscience and honour forbid such an idea. Surely then the sooner the change of government took place the better; the sooner we were face to face with the situation, which must have arisen sometime or other the better. Was it for the interests of the country either that Mr Gladstone should possess the power and not the responsibility?

But I had to ask myself, what use will Mr Gladstone make of the power, when he has the responsibility? As far as I was in a position to answer the question, I believed he would at once bring in a gigantic scheme of land purchase and then a measure of Home Rule. Was I prepared to support this policy? Yes on two conditions –

1.   That the payment of purchase money to the landlords in no sort of way whatever depends on the men who will have authority in Ireland.

2. That a measure of Home Rule is accompanied by the removal of the Irish members from the English House of Commons. If either of these conditions are unfulfilled, I shall speak and vote against Mr Gladstone's measure for Ireland. My vote then will be worth neither more nor less than my vote on Tuesday was. Then you will say very naturally, 'but law and order must be preserved in Ireland'. Most certainly it must. At this moment the offences against the law are almost entirely confined to boycotting. The course I apprehend that Mr Gladstone will take is this.

He will try and arrive at an agreement with Mr Parnell on the lines of the Irish policy I have previously mentioned. If they agree, boycotting will cease. That would be a sine qua non in the negotiations. If they do not agree Mr Gladstone will not bring in his Irish measures, but must bring in a stringent coercion bill, in the form (let us hope) of a permament addition to the law. Such a bill will have a great deal fairer play and will be much easier to pass, if brought in by Mr Gladstone than if brought in by the Tories. Here are my honest views. I have tried very hard to act honestly and conscientiously and after all the thought I am capable of. My reasons for going in for puchase and home rule is [sic] that the endless round of crime coercion and conciliation seems to me not to amount to government at all. Our relations with Ireland for 600 years have been increasingly dangerous to the Empire. They are now intolerable. I see no other alternative to my policy except the government of Cromwell. I feel assured that this is only possible after Home Rule has failed. Criticise me mercifully dearest father. And believe me, your most loving son

Wolmer

R.P. 1869/143

7.   To Roundell Palmer

9 John Street<br>Berkeley Square<br>9 February 1886

Dearest Father,
The Government is a queer one in some ways.[1]

I cannot help strongly suspecting that they will fall to pieces when they begin to discuss Ireland.

Aberdeen is of course mere paint. I quite expected such an appointment when Morley was made Chief Secretary. He, Morley, will do one of two things if he holds office for any length of time, either solve the Irish question or bring actual civil war upon us in that country. That is of course supposing he acts up to his words and does not become an ordinary humdrum Secretary.

I am not sorry that Jesse Collings[2] and Joseph[3] rule at the Local Government Board. They will now have to put their ideas into the words of an Act of Parliament, and we shall know exactly what they mean.

Harcourt at the Treasury *is* supremely ridiculous.

The riots[4] here yesterday were disgraceful. The heads of the police ought to be dismissed. You see Childers and Broadhurst had not had time to go to the H.O.. Childers I understand was in Edinburgh. What are permanent officials for, if they can't act in such a case? *I* think the Socialist *leaders* ought to be arrested and punished at once, Hyndman and Co. What do you think? . . . Your loving son

W

R.P. 1869/159

1. For some pungent comments by the 1st Earl of Selborne on Gladstone's Cabinet see MS Selborne 96/139.
2. Jesse Collings left the Liberal party over home rule in 1886.
3. Joseph Chamberlain was President of the Local Government Board in Gladstone's ministry.
4. The 'West End riots' of 1886, which arose out of a meeting of the unemployed in Trafalgar Square.

8.   From Viscount Goschen

Seacox Heath
Hawkhurst
22 April [1886]

*Private*

My dear Lord Wolmer,

You will have seen in the papers that Liberals opposed to Gladstone's Irish measures are organizing. We are forming a Committee, (address 35 Spring Gardens). It is still in its infancy. Hartington has asked Brand, Sellar and Grey to look after things in general; and we shall now hope to have a centre whence information can be given, and whither news can be carried.

I do not know whether I told you that I at once let Hartington know what you had said to me, thro' Milner about your views. Both he and I are pleased to think that you will act in this matter, on the same lines with us. In the common cause, I heartily wish you may be able to influence some of your friends among the new members to see things in the same light as you do.[1] Yours very truly

George Goschen

13/5

1. The meeting at Spring Gardens resulted in the establishment of a Liberal Unionist Committee which, Hartington wrote in August 1886, 'shall probably have a paid permanent secretary'. Chamberlain duly joined this committee, though he still retained his own Birmingham Association.

9.   To A. Craig Sellar

Blackmoor
Petersfield
30 July 1886

Dear Craig Sellar,
I do hope that what I see in today's *Times* is not true, viz that we Unionists are to be all mixed up with the Gladstonians in the House.

It is madness.

If we are all mixed with the Gladstonians, we are swallowed up. We shall feel uncomfortable as being out of sympathy with those around us. The influence may be too strong for some of our weaker vessels – others will not attend.

Our speakers will get no encouragement. No volume of cheering. We shall have no sense of being a party, and we shall dis-appear. It is incredible folly to my mind to propose such a thing. Our whole strength, and *only strength*, will be in copying the Parnellites, i.e. in *sitting*, *acting*, *cheering*, and *voting* together.[2]

I do hope you agree with me. I feel it so very strongly. I do not think that our leaders have any right to settle thus without calling us all together and consulting us. Yours very truly

Wolmer

D 340/2031

1.   On 7 June 1886 the House of Commons divided on the second reading of Gladstone's home rule bill, which was defeated by thirty votes. Gladstone thereupon appealed to the country. Viscount Wolmer contested his Petersfield seat as a Liberal Unionist, and was again returned to Parliament. The election resulted in the return of 316 Conservatives, 78 Liberal Unionists, 191 Gladstonian Liberals, and 85 Irish Nationalists. A Conservative government was formed under Lord Salisbury. Liberal Unionists were invited to take Cabinet posts, but none did so. Their party structure was the Liberal Unionist Association, a group of some five hundred financial contributors who had originally supported the anti-home rule Liberals, and a number of local affiliates in all parts of the United Kingdom. Chamberlain's followers were organised into the National Radical Union, which eventually merged its activities with the L.U.A.
2.   The Liberal Unionists eventually did sit on the Opposition side of the House, with the Liberal Unionist Privy Councillors sitting on the Opposition front bench.

10.   From Roundell Palmer

Coldhayes
East Liss
Hampshire
11 April 1887

My darling son,
. . . The crisis[1] is a very serious one; for the conversion of such a man as Mr Gladstone from a Christian Statesman into a Revolutionary demagogue,

prepared to *see*, as well as to *call*, black white and white black, and to sacrifice *everything* to his own political objects is about as dangerous a thing as could happen to any free country. But if it calls out (as it seems to do) *steady* courage and resolution on the other side, I have no doubt of there being enough virtue and common sense in the country to meet the danger and prevail.

The present idea seems to be, to *intimidate* a majority of above 100 into submission. Strange stuff those Englishmen must be made of, who can be so intimidated. Ever your most affectionate

Selborne

97/5

1.  The introduction of a Criminal Law Amendment (Ireland) Bill on 1 April 1887 by A. J. Balfour, Chief Secretary for Ireland, led to a prolonged and angry debate in the House, and the government's use of the new closure rule for the first time. When the closure was carried the Opposition Liberals under Gladstone and the Parnellites walked out of the House. The Liberal Unionists supported the government's measure (see Lord Selborne to Sir Arthur Gordon, 7 and 28 April 1887, *Memorials, part ii*, pp. 261–3).

11.   To S. K. McDonnell

Liberal Unionist Association
1 Great George Street
Westminster
London, S.W.
27 June 1891

Dear McDonnell,

Jesse Collings has drawn up this circular which he is very anxious for me to send to Lord Salisbury in the hopes that he will find time to read it, as he regards the matters contained in it to be very important. Believe me, yours very truly

Wolmer

*Memorandum by Mr Jesse Collings*

The result of the recent by-elections should afford no grounds for a pessimistic view of the political situation provided that full and immediate effect is given to the lessons to be drawn from these elections. The failure of the Unionists at these by-elections is to a great extent accounted for by circumstances which will not exist at a General Election – the suddenness of the vacancies and the consequent haste with which the Unionists had to seek candidates, allowing but a short time for the Unionist candidates and their helpers to speak and to become known to the electors, while on the other hand the Gladstonian candidates had for a long time been nursing the constituencies in a persevering and unscrupulous manner – the special manner in which the divisions were flooded by Gladstonian-Irish orators

. . . Turning from the by-elections to the General Election, the position seems to be as follows. The Gladstonians have adopted the policy, which they are pushing with great vigour, of representing the contest as the old one between 'Liberals' and 'Conservatives', and ignoring the Irish Question altogether, or as far as they possibly can. They are striving to fight on the lines of 1885 with the advantages of an attacking party which they had not then; with an extended programme, and by an unscrupulous outbidding of anything any responsible Government can offer.

They are taking to themselves the credit of much of the good work done by the Unionist Party – and minimising or denying the usefulness of some of the best measures of the Government. The Unionists – especially the Conservative wing of the Party – are unwittingly aiding the Gladstonians in this policy and playing into their hands: Firstly, by conceding to them in the Press and on platforms the names of 'Liberals' and 'Radicals'. In all the elections I have taken part in Conservative Chairmen, Speakers, Agents &c, &c, almost invariably by habit allude to the Gladstonians by these Party names . . .

Secondly, by speeches, leaflets, &c, dealing with the respective action in past years of the 'Liberal' and 'Conservative' parties (before 1886). Instituting historical comparisons between the two Parties and contending for the superiority of the 'Conservative' policy, &c, &c. All this might be very good and true, but it should be avoided now as it assists the Gladstonians in putting Home Rule out of sight and mind, and effectually helping them in their efforts to make the electors believe that the contest is one between 'Liberals' and 'Conservatives'. What we have to do is to convince the electors that the main issue now is precisely the same as it was in 1886. Mr Gladstone was defeated then, if not mainly, to a very large degree by *Liberal abstentions*. These abstainers would not and will not in sufficient numbers vote simply 'Conservative' as such. We are sure of the Conservative vote. Our principle aim and governing idea should be to increase the *Liberal Unionist vote*, or to so impress the so called Liberals and waverers with the gravity of the situation as to induce them to abstain. Unless the issues and spirit of the 1886 election are actively revived; and if by the lapse of time and by Gladstonian action Home Rule is considered to be dead, or no longer dangerous; and if the issue is allowed to be a simple Party one; then too many of those who abstained or voted Unionist in 1886 will vote Gladstonian ('Liberal' they will consider it) in 1892. Therefore all Unionists should on all occasions, in season and out of season, show that Home Rule (always describing what Mr Gladstone [sic] Home Rule scheme was) is only scotched by the defeat of 1886; that it remains as firmly as ever the one point in Mr Gladstone's programme, and for which, if he were again in power, everything else would be put aside; that the Gladstonians are trading on the name of 'Liberal' for the purpose of Home Rule; and that votes obtained on any other question are votes obtained under false pretences, and would be used for Home Rule . . . It should be thus shown that there has not been since 1886, and is not now, any issue as between 'Liberals' and 'Conservatives'. That there are two new Parties with plain and distinct policies.

*Parties*

| *Unionist* | *Gladstonian, Home Rule or Separatist* |
|---|---|
| Composed of Conservatives, plus a section of the old Liberal Party. | Composed of a section of the old Liberal party, plus the two Irish factions. |

*Policy*

| *Unionist* | *Gladstonian* |
|---|---|
| Maintenance of Unity of Kingdom and one Parliament of United Kingdom, Local Government, District Council, &c, Allotments, Small Holdings, Sanitary Reform, Rural measures, Free Education, Technical Education, Reduced Taxation, Relief of local rates, Factory legislation, &c, &c, &c. Giving full particulars of these. | *Home Rule* (Explaining Gladstonian scheme and further Irish demands) to which everything else is to be postponed. |

If possible it would be a great advantage if candidates would call themselves 'Unionist' without any qualifying term . . . This would probably be more difficult to bring about now because though the great bulk of the Conservative Party realise the gravity of the crisis and are ready to make any sacrifices to avert disaster, yet there are some I find in most divisions who regard the contest from a Party point of view and and speak of 'Conservative victories' and 'Conservative gains' and by whom Home Rule is regarded as only an incident in a Party fight . . .
S.S./40


12.   From Charles A. Cooper

Office of *The Scotsman*
Edinburgh
27 July 1892

Dear Lord Wolmer,
I need not tell you how sorry I am to hear that you are to resign as Whip.[1] At the same time I feel that it is necessary for your political present and future that you should take an active part in the House itself. It is satisfying

to hear that you and Mr Chamberlain have made provisional arrangements for your retirement.

The question you put as to the place the Liberal Unionists should take in the House is one of great difficulty. Still I have a clear conviction that they should be on the Opposition side. It will be said that by doing so they identify themselves with the Conservatives. Can anything more be said on that point than has been said during the elections? Will the Liberal Unionists be disunited if more is said? I do not believe they can. They are in opposition on the very groundwork of the Gladstonian party – Home Rule. All other questions are as nothing so far as the incoming Government will be concerned. Clearly we are in opposition, and there is to my thinking, no good reason why we should not adopt the outward and visible sign of it.

But there is another and a deeper reason operating with me. I believe the old Liberal Party to have finally disappeared. We are its heirs. Its principles and policy are ours. How are we to give effect to them? I believe we can best do so by helping to build up and consolidate the Unionist party. Call it by that name if you like. It will be Liberal. It will shed some of the old fashioned Tories. It will not be joined by the Laboucheres and other extremists. It will be cursed by the Nationalist agitators. But it can be made strong; and it will gather to itself all that is moderate in Gladstonianism either in Parliament or the country. The first step is pronounced and obvious opposition to Gladstonianism and that will be shown by sitting on the opposite benches.    If it be considered undesirable to build up a new party, or reconstruct old parties, there still remains the Parnellite example. They have always sat on the Opposition side, and they have not sacrificed their independence.

Your forecast was wonderfully good.[2] I did not expect we should be beaten by so many. I am, dear Lord Wolmer, faithfully yours

Charles A. Cooper

13/124

1.  As chief whip of the Liberal Unionists. In 1892 Wolmer was elected M.P. for West Edinburgh. He decided to stand for the new seat because, he wrote in his reminiscences, 'Politics became very bitter between 1886 and 1892 and I found that, if I stood again for East Hants, I should be standing on Conservative and Liberal Unionist support against the Gladstonian Liberals who had staunchly supported me in 1886 as well as in 1885. I did not like doing this: and besides I was ambitious and I was determined to try and wrest West Edinburgh from the Gladstonian Liberals. So about 1888–9 I announced that I would not stand again for East Hants and became candidate for West Edinburgh which I won in 1892 after a tremendous fight by 500 votes' (MS Selborne 191, pp. 22– 23a).
2.  Wolmer forecast that the election of 1892 would result in a home rule majority of forty seats, which proved to be exactly right, though mistaken in detail. A

booklet containing his predictions is in the Selborne papers, MS Selborne 13. The actual results were:

| | | | |
|---|---|---|---|
| Gladstonians: | 269 | Conservatives: | 269 |
| Labour: | 5 | Liberal Unionists: | 46 |
| Irish Nationalists: | 81 | | |
| | – – – | | – – – |
| | 355 | | 315 |

13.   From Roundell Palmer

Blackmoor
Petersfield
22 February 1893

Dearest Willie,

. . . The Irish Government Bill is a much better piece of *workmanship*, than that of 1886, and presents, in my judgement, fewer *secondary* points for attack. But, of course, the new Parliamentary constitution, which it gives to *Great Britain and the Empire*, opens an entirely new field of principles and probable consequences, and is much worse than the simple exclusion of Irish members, proposed in 1886.[1] As for the land question, the three years' delay is nothing, unless there is British legislation upon it during the interval: which (I presume) is in view. The provision that the Irish Parliament is not to take away men's property *without compensation* is really nugatory; as the *measure* of compensation would be in their power. Ever your most affectionate

Selborne

97/45

1.   One of the most controversial questions about home rule was the retention of Irish M.P.s in the Westminster Parliament. In the home rule bill as originally presented Irish representation was to cease. It was argued, however, that in that case it would be difficult to justify the British Parliament's retention of extensive authority over Irish affairs, and Gladstone agreed that the question should be reconsidered. The second home rule bill in 1893 provided that Irish representation at Westminster should continue though decreased in number and restricted in powers.

14.   From Roundell Palmer

Blackmoor
Petersfield
2 March 1894

Dearest Willie,

. . . It seems to me, that nothing could less justify Mr Gladstone's declaration of war upon the House of Lords[1] than their action upon the Local Government Bill.[2] If a second Chamber is of any use at all, one, *at least* of its necessary and most ordinary uses must be (as it has always been) to make amendments in the details of Bills, which it accepts in principle.

The House of Lords, on this occasion, has yielded a great deal which it had good reason for thinking desirable, and the amendments last sent down by it to the Commons and which were accepted with such a bad grace yesterday, were so manifestly within their legitimate province as to make the attempt to found a quarrel upon them preposterous:– *both* being upon lines which in earlier stages of the Bill had commended themselves – the one to the Government generally and the others to the Minister in charge of the Bill – with this difference only, that the 'charity clause'[3] is now made more elastic as to number than Mr Fowler[4] proposed to make it.

I did not myself vote for the line of 300 instead of 200 in the last very narrow division on that subject in the House of Lords; because it did not seem to me to be a point for the sake of which the contest should have been prolonged. But, being now so settled, I have no hesitation in saying that I think 300 is the best line – better than either 500 or 200.[5]

As to the Charity clause, my chief doubt is, whether its practical operation will not more nearly coincide with that of Cobb's clause,[6] than might be desirable. We have been told that the disposition recently of the Charity Commission has been towards giving ecclesiastical trustees a majority when they bring them in:– I doubt whether this is quite accurate:– but there is no doubt that they have sometimes, perhaps not seldom done so: and they are a body, who stand very much in awe of the House of Commons, and are likely to be much influenced in their action under this Bill by what has passed in that House.

If the Bill had come back to the House of Lords with Lord Salisbury's amended clause rejected,[7] I should myself have acquiesced in what I may call the *Belper-Camperdown* amendment[8] (what it was at first proposed to *me* to move) rather than imperil the Bill. But, while the difference, as to probable numbers of the new ecclesiastical trustees is not likely to be practically great, the clause as it now stands seems to me sounder in principle; and in one respect a decided improvement, as getting rid of the restriction of the ecclesiastical trustees to parochial electors.

I think the House of Lords has come badly out of the whole business. If they had insisted upon nothing they would have been open to the charge of being frightened at what they had done on the other Bills, and behaving in a cowardly way upon the Bill, which was primarily one on which they were capable of forming a final judgement. And their enemies would have thrown this in their teeth; as was apparent from the tone of such of the Radical papers as I saw, after their giving way (as far as they did) when the Bill first came back from the House of Commons. If any one thinks, that they have unnecessarily made Mr Gladstone show his teeth against them, I cannot agree. He had proof enough before he spoke last night that the Radicals, on whom he depends, would do all in their power to bring the House of Lords into popular odium, and to destroy it if they could whether it yielded more or less on this particular question: and, if we *are* to be attacked, we may meet the attack, not only with a better conscience but with a better prospect of repelling it also, by doing our duty according to the best of our judgement than by shrinking from it.

*If* Gladstone now retires it seems to me that Rosebery *cannot* succeed him, and that *Harcourt must* – assuming the party to remain in power. But will Gladstone go before the dissolution? I do not think they will let him, – and I do not think he will resist their will. Ever yours

Selborne

97/83

1. On 1 March 1894 Gladstone, in his last speech in the House of Commons, declared that the repeated rejection of the government's bills by the House of Lords, raised a question of the gravest character, and had reached the stage at which the Lords showed itself ready, not to modify, but to annihilate the work of the Commons. 'In our judgement', he stated, 'this state of things cannot continue' (Henry W. Lucy, *A Diary of the Home Rule Parliament 1892–1895* [London, 1896], pp. 308–9).
2. The Parish Councils' bill (which became an act in 1894) established 6,880 district and parish councils. It received its first reading in March 1893 and its second on 2 November. It was finally passed only after many amendments by the House of Lords.
3. The 'charity clause' was clause 14 of the bill, which related to the appointment by the parish council, or the election, of members to governing bodies of non-ecclesiastical charities.
4. H.H. Fowler (1830–1911) later Viscount Wolverhampton, President of the Local Government Board in 1892 and mover of the Parish Councils' bill. He originally proposed that the elective element on the body of trustees should be one third.
5. It was originally proposed in the bill to give councils to all parishes over 300 inhabitants, and to group smaller ones together.
6. H. Cobb, Liberal M.P. for Rugby. His 'clause' (which Fowler adopted) proposed that the number of trustees elected by the ratepayers or appointed by the parish council should be a majority of the whole body (*Parl. Deb.*, 4s., vol. xix, col. 702, 7 Dec. 1893).
7. Lord Salisbury proposed to restore something like Fowler's original intention of making the number of additional trustees not exceed one third of the whole number of the governing body (Ibid., vol. xxi, cols. 893–987, 23 Feb. 1894).
8. An amendment moved by Lord Belper on 23 Feb. 1894 and supported by the Earl of Camperdown, that the power given to the parish council to elect a majority of trustees should be permissive and not obligatory, and that the council should have the right to appoint as trustees any of the officers acting at present (Ibid., cols. 990ff).

15.　To Roundell Palmer

49 Mount Street
W.
3 March 1894

My dearest Father,

You see it is all true. Gladstone has resigned and Rosebery is to succeed him. I think one must be very thankful that Rosebery is to be the future leader of that party, but Labby is simply furious[1] and may turn him out by resolutely sulking. It will be most interesting to see how Rosebery will use his opportunity.

He is bound by his party to proceed on three special lines of policy
Social Reform
Home Rule
Anti House of Lords
On Social Reform I think he is prepared to go to very great lengths experimentally, and therefore will not I expect meet with internal party difficulties in that quarter. But how on earth he is going to manage on the other two questions passes my comprehension. He is a convinced Imperialist and therefore cannot favour Gladstonian Home Rule. He is surely not a one chamber man, and therefore cannot desire to abolish, though he understandably wishes to reform, the House of Lords.

Query, will he get out of both these difficulties at once by going in for a Quasi Federal system? I say 'Quasi Federal' because while the powers of the Irish, Scotch, English and (?) Welsh legislatures [sic] would be limited by statute, the Imperial Parliament would remain as now nominally sovereign.

My forecast is that he will bend his policy in this direction . . . Ever your loving son

Wolmer

R.P. 1871/295

1. Labouchere proposed a strong anti-House of Lords motion in the Commons, which was passed, partly because of resentment against the choice of Rosebery as Prime Minister instead of Harcourt.

16.   From J. Powell Williams

House of Commons Library
4 March 1894

Confidential
My dear Wolmer,
. . . I confess truly that I am anxious about this cry 'Lords v People', and that I consider it dangerous. I do not think that we have done all that might reasonably have been done to check-mate the G.O. Madman. If Lord Salisbury, on Wednesday last, had given way, as many Conservative peers wished him to do, Gladstone would have been landed in the mud without the ghost of a reason for a war-cry concerning the Parish Councils' Bill. Lord Salisbury's action gave him his chance, and, like a cunning old General, he fastened on it.

The action of the Peers about the Employers' Liability Bill has landed us in this sweet position[1] – an enormous number of workmen have failed to get what they want owing (as they say) to the House of Lords, whilst a comparatively few workmen, having escaped from a danger which menaced them, are contented, remain tranquil, and cannot be got to attend a meeting, or to stir a foot either for the House of Lords or for the Unionist leaders! The effect of the loss of the Bill on the North is very bad indeed, and this is as well known to Sir Henry James as it is to me. This is not an opinion. I can give you *proof*. Look at the enclosed letter from McLachlan,[2] e.g. of course we can explain things, but what I dread is an outrush of the latent *feeling* against the House of Lords which all who know great cities are aware exists.

And we have not heard the last of it. Gladstone is certain to blow, somehow or other, a final blast of the trumpet before he goes quite out, and is seen no more.

Leaflets are in hand headed '*What the H of L did to the Employers' Liability Bill*' and '*What the House of Lords did to the Parish Councils' Bill*'. They come out very well, and we must circulate them widely, and otherwise do our level best, under conditions less favourable to us than they might have been. Yours very truly,

J. Powell Williams

13/140

1. The Lords had made considerable amendments to the government's Employers' Liability Bill, the most important of which was a 'contracting out' clause.
2. Not attached.


17.    From Joseph Chamberlain

Highbury
Moor Green
Birmingham
12 October 1894

My dear Wolmer,

. . . If you have an opportunity of full discussion with Lord Salisbury, will you ask him from me to consider whether it might not be possible for the House of Lords to spoil the game of the Gladstonians by itself dealing with some of the more important social questions by means of Bills?

In order to do this effectively the House of Lords must be prepared for something in the nature of the reforms suggested in my speech last night.[1] I believe that in principle Lord Salisbury is not opposed to any of them; and I suggest as especially worthy of attention the House Purchase Bill,[2] the extension of the Artizans Dwelling Act,[3] the establishment of Courts of Arbitration,[4] Compensation for Injuries and Accidents, and Alien immigration.[5]

If the House of Lords sent down a batch of Bills liberally conceived and dealing with these subjects the Government would be in a difficult position. If they refused to consider them and put them aside for Welsh

Disestablishment and other constitutional reforms, I think we should have them in a trap. If, on the other hand, they attempted to deal with them, they would have no time for Irish or Welsh measures and there would be a revolt of their supporters.

I do not know whether the House of Lords is capable of rising to the occasion, but I am sure that if they were they would utterly confound the politics of their opponents and prevent the raising of a cry at the General Election, which although it has failed up to the present time, may be revived with more chance of popular support after the rejection of, say, the Welsh Disestablishment Bill. Believe me, yours very truly

J. Chamberlain

JC 5/74/23

1. In Birmingham, reported in *The Times*, 12 October 1894.
2. The idea of a house purchase bill was put forward by Chamberlain as a means of enabling the working man to become the owner of his dwelling 'on comfortable terms'.
3. The Artizans Dwelling Act was passed by Disraeli's government in 1875, and was the first major attempt to tackle the problem of working class housing in the great towns. Municipal authorities in London and the large towns were empowered to draw up improvement schemes, to purchase the land involved, compulsorily if necessary, and to let or sell it for the provision of working class housing.
4. To arbitrate between employers and workers in strikes.
5. To regulate the inflow of foreign labour.

18.   To Joseph Chamberlain

Hatfield House
Hatfield
Herts.
15 October 1894

Private

My dear Mr Chamberlain, Lord Salisbury is much interested by the suggestions made in your letter to me and generally sympathises with the line of tactics therein sketched out, subject of course to the discussion of details and to the possibilities of the case.

For instance, while he sees his way pretty clearly to the introduction of an Aliens Immigration Bill and of an Arbitration Bill into the House of Lords, he is afraid that any attempt to deal with the question of the purchase of Working Men's dwellings, in which the main element is a financial one, would be held to be an infringement of the privilege of the Commons. As regards the Employers' Liability Bill Lord Salisbury's sympathies are, I gather, distinctly and definitely, in favour of your solution of the problem. Two difficulties, however, which would not be very serious ones for a government to deal with, appear to him to render caution very necessary in our present position of opposition.

The first of these difficulties is the 'domestic servant' one. The second is the susceptibilities of the Employers generally. He fears that, while they might be willing to acquiesce in the solution of this question on your lines by a responsible government, which they supported, they might resent the same proposal from the same quarter in opposition, as uncalled for, and in a manner which might make itself seriously felt at the general election.

These reflections apply to the broad principles of the policy. There are, however, also minor difficulties to be surmounted, such as the question of personnel. It is not easy to pick out exactly the right men in the Lords, to whom to entrust the handling of such very important social questions, and their solution would require much care and consideration. The Aliens Bill Lord Salisbury is willing to continue to father himself, and this point applies therefore to the remainder of the Bills on your list only. I have shown this letter to Lord Salisbury and he bids me expressly assure you that these criticisms are not to be taken as indicating any want of sympathy on his part with your general views on these subjects. Believe me, yours sincerely

Wolmer

JC 5/74/24

19.  To the Marquess of Salisbury

49 Mount Street
W.
7 April 1895

My dear Papa,

On Thursday last Arthur[1] called me and dwelt on how serious was the present situation. He said that Chamberlain's vote on the Welsh Church,[2] which would otherwise have passed as expected and inevitable, coming on top of the Warwick[3] business and punctuated by the venemous and mischievous articles in the *Standard* and *New Review*, had really affected the attitude of many Conservative M.P.s headed by Beach towards the Unionist Alliance, and that the situation was fraught with grave peril. What he wanted was to emphasise all this to Chamberlain and to impress upon him the absolute necessity of elasticity being observed in respect of the compact, and of avoidance of all suspicion of aggressiveness in such negotiations in the future, and the absolute necessity of the greatest tact being used by all L.U.s in their speeches and votes and public letters during the next ticklish few weeks. I did this and more. I told Chamberlain that in my opinion Warwick, as to which I hold exactly opposite opinions to what I do about Hythe,[4] has resulted in a grave miscarriage of equity and reason; that, if I had been Whip, I should have advised that the local conservatives should have admitted that the call lay with the Liberal Unionists and that the Liberal Unionists should then have proceeded to call Nelson. Chamberlain took it as nicely as possible and practically admitted the justice and expediency of my views. He then proceeded in a strain, which fairly made me lumpy in my throat. In justification of my sensations I may add that he has privately and separately poured forth the same confession to Arthur and to Douglas, and that they under the influence of the same feelings both confess to having played the part of Balaam.

This is what Chamberlain said. That he was a man of great ambitions; that the dream of his life had been to be Prime Minister; that he had had great ideas, which he had looked forward to carrying out as Prime Minister; that, for what he consistently believed to be the safety and welfare of his country, he had sacrificed all his ambitions, all his hopes, all his dreams; that they had gone for ever to limbo; that consequently he had been abused by his old friends, now his opponents, as no public man before had ever been, and that that abuse represented a positive deadly hatred; that he confessed to not being insensible to the influence of a hatred which would 'rejoice if I lost my wife'; but that he was prepared to face that through, now and always; that, however, he was human and required friendship, honourable consideration and trust from those he worked with; that he had always received these from you and Arthur; that he had hoped that the rank and file of the Conservative party, however much they might naturally and consistently object to certain views of his, were disposed to accord him similar sentiments, as he had come fully to accord to them; that he had been wholly unprepared for the venemous and malignant attack on his honour and character, obviously preconcocted, which had just proceeded from the *Standard* and *New Review* and which he understood not a few Conservative M.P.s avowedly sympathised with; that if the Conservative party distrusted, not his opinions or judgement, but his honour and honesty, he would have nothing more to do with them or political life; that he had laid all these considerations before his wife and children and was really seriously considering whether he would not at the general election retire altogether from public life and so on.

Arthur, Douglas and I are all of one mind that this is perfectly genuine. It is evidently a great mistake to suppose he is wholly pachydermatous. He kept repeating, 'from my enemies anything but to be stabbed in the back by my friends!!' What he wants at this moment is sympathy; and Bob at my suggestion is going to suggest to some of your representative men like Wharton or Harry Northcote who have been shocked at these attacks to let him know their sentiments; but the fact remains that he yearns for sympathy from the Conservative party.

I thought you would be interested to learn this singular confirmation of your view of the impulsiveness of his nature. If you did not see the attacks on him I have mentioned, you will not readily guess how bad they were.
Yours affectionately

Wolmer

P.S. Of course I answered him in the manner which would naturally occur to anyone in such circumstances.
S.S./60

1. Arthur James Balfour
2. Chamberlain voted for a Welsh Disestablishment bill on its second reading.
3. The resignation of the Speaker, Arthur Wellesley Peel, in 1895, resulted in a vacancy in Warwick and Leamington. The seat was considered by the Liberal Unionists to be theirs, and they nominated the former Speaker's son, George Peel. This was endorsed by A. J. Balfour in a public letter, but did not have the approval of Akers-Douglas or of Captain Richard Middleton, Chief Conservative Party Agent. Local Conservatives put up a candidate of their own, and Chamberlain was heavily criticised in the *Standard*, the official Conservative organ in London.
4. Hythe was becoming vacant due to the retirement of Sir Edward Watkin, who had sat as a Liberal in the 1880s but had asked for the Conservative whip in 1880. Akers-Douglas maintained that his original application for the Conservative whip had decided the question of which party Hythe would belong to.


20.   From the Marquess of Salisbury

Beaulieu
13 April 1895

*Private*
My dear Willie,
Many thanks for your most interesting account of Chamberlain's emotions. I sincerely pity him – if that is not too big a word to use – for he has got himself into a peck of troubles. That unlucky letter over the Welsh Church and his speaking in favour of the death duties last year – were proceedings better suited to the innocence of the dove than the wisdom of the serpent. If he wishes for a following – which is purely a question of taste – he has no chance now except to put as far into the shadows as he honestly can his anti-Church and anti-land opinions. I think he has got himself into trouble largely from a very common defect of earnest men – he cannot believe in earnestness on the other side. He does not believe in a convinced Churchman, or a squire who retains his opinions honestly and he does not – or rather did not – realise that they would be impervious to his powers of persuasion.

I do not, however, look upon this part of his troubles as serious. Undoubtedly, if he means to shape his political life on the Birmingham view of Church and squire those two authorities will in the long run refuse to take him for one of their leaders. But, if he will put that philosophy in the lumber-room for the present, as Pitt did his views on reform, or Canning and Castlereagh their views on Catholic emancipation, this little breeze will very speedily be forgotten. The compact is a much more urgent question – and may be a much more dangerous one. I hope as you have put your hand on to the guidance of this matter that you will not entirely withdraw it: for we are in a rather serious mess. We have been perhaps all to blame for assuming that the difficulties of the compact would arrange themselves as they arose – instead of trying to avert them. I confess that till these two cases – Warwick and Hythe occurred, I did not realise what these difficulties were. We looked at the matter purely from a Parliamentary point of view. We saw that the continued existence of the Liberal Unionist party was probably desirable, and certainly inevitable: and therefore we pledged Conservative support, to assure certain number of seats to it. For this we were amply paid by support in the constituencies, and still more in the House of Commons. It never occurred to us to ask how the Conservatives in the constituencies might like it. We were imitating the statecraft of the potentates at the Congress of Vienna, who strove to establish the balance of power, by exchanging slices of territory certified to contain so many million souls. As Jefferson observed at the time, these marketable souls would in the end have the deciding voice, whether the bargain of which they were the subject should endure or not. We were guilty of the same miscalculation. Consider how the 'compact' looks to the eyes of a keen Conservative in Leamington or Hythe. Under it it is the destiny of him and all his fellows, to speak and spend, to labour and to intrigue in the less lovely details of a party struggle, with a knowledge that the result of the exertion can never be that any Conservative should be returned to Parliament. If he were in a Radical borough, in however small a minority, he would not be without hope. He might always expect, or dream, that political exertion would end in a political victory. But in a Liberal Unionist borough, hope must be left behind. He belongs to a political tribe which happen what may can never win. At the moment of success the prey will be taken by his own leaders out of his mouth. Now this state of self-denial might have been possible for a short period – one or two parliaments. But it is against human nature that men should go on working and speaking permanently, with no other prospect with which to encourage each other except the hope that if they only work hard another political section may win. At all events, we have no right to count upon such a resolution, unless we have in each instance an assurance to that effect, from those whose interests are affected. I see no way out except a list, each item of which shall be based on consultation with the local Unionist politicians. But I am not wholly sanguine that we shall be able to construct that list. It is a case in which the interests of the whole Unionist party are on one side, and the interest of parts of it on the other. In such a conflict of interests the whole ought to prevail: but it very seldom does. I have troubled you at so much length in order to impress upon you that the matter is much too thorny and difficult to be left to Middleton and Williams. They are men of great intelligence – but their natures are not pacific. If the matter could be handled by you and Akers Douglas I should have more hope . . . Ever yours affectionately

Salisbury

5/21

21.   To the Marquess of Salisbury

Blackmoor
Petersfield
18 April 1895

My dear Papa,

I sent on to the Duke[1] a letter Henry Northcote had had from Chamberlain and which he invited me to send to you.

I was writing to the Duke; and, as I thought it extremely probable that he knew much less about Chamberlain's present frame of mind than you did, I took it upon myself to send him the letter asking him to pass it on to you. If the present trouble blows over without Chamberlain taking any hasty step, such as announcing an intention to leave public life, the experience may prove useful to him and all of us, except that he is so buoyant and wears past experience so lightly.

As to the compact I am afraid I do not much believe in the possibility of making a list, which will have any binding value. The conditions of each case are not fixed, but very fluctuating conditions; and the turn of mind of the local people depends quite as much upon the individuality of the candidate as upon his particular shade of colour. I do not much believe in the 'hopeless outcast' frame of Tory mind you suggest to me. When a hitch arises like the one in Leamington, that theory naturally occurs to the aggrieved party, but, if it had been a practical reality, surely the compact never could have lasted as a working system for 10 years.

The fact is that in the majority of L.U. cases the local Conservatives regard their L.U. member both for local and parliamentary purposes as a thoroughly sound Conservative completely identified with themselves.

It is the occasional exception, which causes the trouble.

Of course I put the seats of the Birmingham class in a separate category. In their case I expect the feeling you refer to has a real existence.

I doubt, moreover, if you would find the local Conservatives willing, however reasonable and loyal, to inscribe their constituency on a L.U. list as a permanent division of seats. They would consider they were pledging themselves too much to an unknown future.

No, I do not think that there is any way out of it except a general understanding at headquarters, and the fixed rule that no individual candidate is ever to be put forward, publicly or adopted, by the leaders till *after* he has been accepted locally by both the local C and L.U. associations. I can never remember any exception to this elementary rule, till Douglas wrote an official letter to the Conservative candidate at Hythe (a very small matter comparatively, but still the first breach of the principle) and Chamberlain and Arthur made this colossal blunder about George Peel at Warwick. Neither of them knew anything whatever about the constituency and neither of them consulted anybody who did.

Although I think the compact has more solidity in it still than you do, if properly worked, yet I regard it of course as only a temporary expedient, and whatever fate befalls us after the General Election, in my opinion the union between the two sections must be made formally and officially closer.

I do not think that Hythe will prove as serious a case nearly as Warwick.

At Warwick the rank and file of the Tories are evidently solid with their leaders. My information is that this is by no means so at Hythe, and that the Liberal Unionists turn out to be very much stronger than the Conservatives supposed. If that information is correct, it will probably lead to a mutual and bona fide agreement to arbitration of some sort.[2] Believe me, yours affectionately

Wolmer

S.S./61

1. The Marquess of Hartington.
2. Eventually, George Peel withdrew his candidature but the seat remained in Liberal Unionist hands, with Alfred Lyttleton being elected as a compromise choice.


22. To Joseph Chamberlain

7 May 1895

My dear Mr Chamberlain,

I cannot express to you easily the value I attach to your truly kind letter of yesterday, nor the pleasure it has given me.

Believe me when I tell you that all you say of your regard and esteem for my dear father was reciprocated by him to you. It is not once nor twice but many times that he has spoken to me of you in words corresponding exactly to what you write of him.

I cannot pass over your allusion to myself. It has been an equal pride and pleasure to me to be your follower in the House of Commons and to be admitted to a share of your friendship and confidence.

What the wrench will be to me if I am forced from the Commons[1] to the Lords you can I think estimate; but there will be no use in sulking, these things are sent to try a man, and probably some work will turn up for me to do[2] . . . Believe me, yours sincerely

Wolmer

JC 5/74/27

1. On the death of his father in May 1895, Wolmer succeeded to the title of Earl of Selborne, which necessarily involved relinquishing his seat in the House of Commons. He had earlier made an agreement with the Marquess of Curzon and St John Brodrick, later Earl of Midleton, that whoever lost his father first should test the constitutional issue of relinquishing his seat. For a wry discussion of his future elevation and its effect on his political prospects see an article by Lord Wolmer, 'The Bitter Cry of the Eldest Sons', in *National Review*, June 1888, pp. 441–5.
2. On 24 June 1895 the Liberal government resigned, following a defeat in a vote taken in committee on the Army Estimates. On 8 July Parliament was

dissolved and at the ensuing general election the Conservatives and Liberal Unionists obtained a majority of 152 seats over all other parties combined. The Liberal Unionists at last accepted office under the Conservatives, but they still retained their separate party organisation until 1912. Lord Selborne became Under-Secretary of State for the Colonies under Joseph Chamberlain.

# Chapter 2

# 'A movement towards schism, and some atmosphere of intrigue': Unionist Politics, 1903–1911.

1. From Henry Hobhouse

15 Brinton Street
W
23 June 1903

Dear Selborne, I don't know if you quite realise how this new departure of Mr Chamberlain[1] is likely to split our party from top to bottom, just as Mr Gladstone's new departure did in 1886. As then, it is possible (or probable) that the anti-reformers will be in a minority. But that minority is sure to contain many thoughtful and sensible men, whose removal will weaken the party for years to come.

I do not think there would have been any serious opposition to a proposal to investigate the very difficult economic questions involved in a closer commercial union with our colonies or in a system of retaliation against foreign countries. But we are suddenly asked to follow a powerful minister in adopting a scheme which appears to many of us to be scarcely distinguishable from Protection. *Or* we are told to deliberate and sit on the fence, until he is ready to take to the platform and preach his new doctrines.

My special object in writing to you is to ask you to see that the enquiry now being conducted by the Cabinet is an absolutely fair one *to both sides*, and that its results are not allowed to be published piecemeal or unfairly.

You will easily understand that the position of the L.U. Association is an extremely critical one and it will require as great tact as yours used to be to keep it together.

Forgive my troubling you with this letter. Believe me, yours sincerely,

Henry Hobhouse

73/1

1. In a speech in Birmingham on 15 May 1903 Joseph Chamberlain made tariff reform a major issue in British politics. This involved establishing a commercial union of the empire, to abandon Britain's nineteenth century policy of free trade with all nations, to erect tariff barriers, and to lower those barriers in

favour of empire trade. In this way Chamberlain hoped to accomplish a number of aims: to hold the empire together and keep Britain a great world power; to provide revenue for social reform; and to give the government the means of safeguarding British industry. Chamberlain's Birmingham speech obliged the Cabinet to take account of the issue; he even went so far as to hint that tariff reform would be an issue in the next election: 'Our opponents may, perhaps, find that the issues which they propose to raise are not the issues on which we shall take the opinion of the country'. On 9 June 1903 the Cabinet met and discussed tariff reform, but decided simply to collect further information before committing itself to any course of action.

2.   From A. J. Balfour

10 Downing Street
Whitehall
S.W.
26 June 1903

*Private*
*Dictated*
My Dear Willy,
Hobhouse is, from Chamberlain's point of view, one of the irreconcilables, and I think he would shed him without the smallest scruple.

Of course, as you know, I have exhausted every device in my power to prevent a party split. But I think Hobhouse is a little unfair in the passage in which he describes himself as 'being requested to sit on the fence until Chamberlain is ready to take the platform and preach the new doctrines'. As a matter of fact, the difficulty is to prevent Chamberlain preaching the new doctrines *now*, in their most aggressive form, and, if Hobhouse is asked to 'sit on the fence', it is in the interests of that very unity which he desires to maintain. Yours affectionately

AJB

34/29.

3.   From A. J. Balfour

North Berwick
11 September 1903

Copy Private
*Dictated*
My dear Willie,
The enclosed correspondence[1] shows that the Duke, after having apparently wavered a good deal, has finally resolved to go, and that all the waverers will go with him.[2]

In the light of this, please read Chamberlain's letter. Common sense appears to indicate that if the Duke and the so-called Free-Fooders go, there is all the more reason for doing everything possible to make Chamberlain stay. But, after such reflection as I have been able to give to the matter in the few hours since receiving the latter's communication, I feel moved in the opposite direction. What I have been striving to do is to keep the cabinet together. But, if the right wing insist on going, it is not so certain that we should not do better without the left-wing also . . .

I think it possible that we might find a way of conferring 'preference' without touching corn: but I am disposed to think that I must make it quite clear at Sheffield[3] that, though a Corn Duty may be right, and (as I shall publicly state) would, under certain circumstances, be expedient for the commercial interests of the working classes, it is not, owing to historic causes, within the sphere of practical politics, and forms no part of our plan.

If Joe goes on this very ground, this will emphasize the position, and make it extremely difficult for our opponents to declare that this is merely the old 1846 controversy[4] in a 20th century dress.

Of course, I am assuming that Joe goes *en amité*, and that Austen stays. I am also assuming that the Duke and *his* lot go: I could not let Joe go if they stay. On the other hand, if they go, the difficulty which Joe will feel in keeping within the limits of which I should approve will be increased, since he will have lost one of the chief motives for moderation of statement, and will feel more than ever driven to rely upon Protectionist support.

He will of course, be a great loss, both administratively and in debate; but, in the House of Commons at all events, the new Government ought, in its higher offices, to be better equipped than the present one.

The above policy may startle you at first, but, before rejecting it, think it over . . . Yours affectionately

Arthur James Balfour

J.S.S.

1. Not attached.
2. The Duke of Devonshire led a group of Unionist free traders in the Cabinet. Balfour was particularly concerned to retain his support, and he tried to persuade the Duke to treat the fiscal question as an open one for the time being. Selborne was also anxious to keep the Duke. The Duke accepted Balfour's compromise, but again expressed unease when he became acquainted with the Blue Paper which Balfour circulated to the Cabinet, together with his 'Economic Notes on Insular Free Trade', on 5 August, because the Blue Paper advocated not only retaliation but also preference and food taxes. On 9 September Joseph Chamberrlain offered his resignation to Balfour, and on the same day the Duke offered to resign.
3. Where the annual meeting of the National Union of Conservative Associations was to be held.
4. The controversy over the repeal of the corn laws.

4.   From Ernest Pretyman

Orwell Park
Ipswich
18 September 1903

My dear Selborne,

This is a terrible break up,[1] but I do not see what other course Chamberlain could take. To have gone to the country on the question of preference by food tax would have meant a debacle and Balfour's decision seems to be absolutely the right one as to choice of battle grounds except from the agricultural point of view.

Retaliation[2] means an increase in price of machinery and other manufactured goods, a rise in the price of Labour, but no rise in anything the farmer has to sell. What are we to say to them?

Also can you tell me what you privately think as to whether we can carry on into next year. No worse moment than this could be chosen for a General Election from our point of view and I sincerely hope it may be postponed for some time.

If we only have time to educate the electors I believe 'Retaliation' is a very strong platform and will draw many from the *Radical* Camp, certainly in the towns . . . Yours very sincerely,

E. M. Pretyman

73/3

1.   Joseph Chamberlain's resignation, which was made public on 18 September.
2.   Retaliation i.e. the protectionist aspect of the tariff reform policy, which laid stress on the fact that other nations were protecting themselves and erecting tariffs against British goods, and urged that Britain needed to do the same.

5.   To Ernest Pretyman

Blackmoor
Liss
19 September 1903

My dear Pretyman,

I am confident that Balfour and Chamberlain have done the right thing. The more I study the question the more I am convinced that, if this country is to maintain itself in the years to come in the same rank with U.S., Russia and Germany, the unit must be enlarged from the U.K. to the Empire. Therefore I am sad to see preference dropped for the moment; but I bow to the inevitable. Balfour's plain duty was to keep the party together as much as possible so that when we are beaten at the next general election we may come back a strong and not a weak opposition. Chamberlain's duty to the Empire is to try and convert *it*, i.e. colonies *and* mother country. *Hinc illae lacrimae.* I do not think you need have the very least fear of a general election this year, nor do I see now any reason why we should be put in a minority next session. I only dread one topic from that point of view, Army Reform. If I am right, then Balfour will be able to choose his own time for a dissolution. The unknown quantity is the measure of success that Chamberlain, freed from the trammels of office, will have with the constituencies. I think it is quite on the cards that this time twelve months things will be wearing a very different complexion. Have you read the supplement of the National Review for September?[1] If not, do so at once. It is a very able piece of work.

I do not think you need be afraid of retaliation raising prices to the agriculturists. It would if it meant an all round minimum tariff. But that is not Balfour's plan. The basis is to be the present tariff. He would commence a negotiation say with Germany for better terms for our exports with the threat of retaliation behind him. I do not believe Germany would hesitate to make a bargain. She would now refuse; but she would not hesitate if after a General Election Balfour had a mandate to this effect. But suppose she did refuse. Then it is not proposed to put a duty on all our imports from Germany but to select those articles which will hurt Germany most *and* us least. For the sake of argument suppose it was machinery which was selected, a very unlikely choice in my opinion, then the duty would go on German machinery but all other machinery would be coming in free, why then should the price be raised?

Tell me what you think of Balfour's 'Economic Notes'.[2] Yours sincerely

Selborne

73/5

1. 'The Economics of Empire' by the Assistant Editor.
2. A.J. Balfour's 'Economic Notes on Insular Free Trade', 25 July 1903. This, and a commentary on it, was circulated as a Cabinet Memorandum on 5 August 1903. Copy in 119/152.


6.  From J.S. Sandars

10 Downing Street
Whitehall S.W.
21 September 1903

*Confidential*

My dear Willie Selborne,

I telegraphed to you this morning that the Duke stays on.[1]

This was finally settled at a lengthy but satisfactory interview at Devonshire House on Wednesday evening, when the chief returned radiant. He left the next day for Balmoral, and in the course of the afternoon the Duke came to see me, and we had a lengthy, confidential talk. You may count upon it that his mind is now absolutely made up. His only difficulty really after the departure of Chamberlain was his attitude towards those with whom he ought never to have been associated. He dwelt emphatically on this cardinal error of his, but he has since seen Ritchie and although our late

Chancellor of the Exchequer was furious at the turn events have taken, he nevertheless absolved his distinguished friend from those charges which he of all others was most likely to feel. B of B[2] was of course in the same category; G. Hamilton in a somewhat different position. But when I told the Duke or rather when I read to him the letter which he (G.H.) had written to AJB in which he spoke of other circumstances determining his course, the old boy was quite relieved. He has written to them (the free traders) relieved his conscience, and is now comfortable. The Duchess telegraphed to him from Balmoral – she had been over there for the day – beseeching him to hold firm! He laughed when he told me, and said that he supposed the Duchess had not realised that Chamberlain was going. This is the situation on this head . . . Ever yours

J. S. Sandars

1/20

1.  Sandar's jubilation was premature. At Sheffield on 1 October Balfour outlined his policy of retaliation. He asked the party to support him in urging the people to give future governments the power of imposing tariffs to be used in bargaining in order to lower foreign customs duties. This proved too much for the Duke who resigned on 2 October. However, the Duke's procrastination enabled Balfour to accept Joseph Chamberlain's resignation (A. Sykes, *Tariff Reform in British Politics*, 1903–1913 [Oxford, 1979] pp. 49–50).
2.  Balfour of Burleigh.


7.   From Joseph Chamberlain

Highbury
Birmingham
23 September 1903

*Private*
My dear Selborne,
Many thanks for your kind letter. I know how true a friend you are and I understand that you are making some sacrifice in remaining to support and carry a policy which is not all that we could wish. The really serious point with which I had to deal was the division in the Party. If we had been united, if the timid ones could have seen that boldness was the best policy, I would have gone confidently to the General Election on the whole programme, and although we might have been beaten next time, we should have had a clear run afterwards.

As it is, my resignation will, I hope, appease those opponents in our own ranks who were rapidly becoming personal and violent and who would have made difference of opinion the preface to a permanent breach. In that case, and if you can as a Government meet the overwhelming public demand for a reform of the War Office, I think your position may be stronger than it has been for some time, and that you may have no difficulty in getting through one or even two more sessions. This will give us time for education which is now the most important part of my public work. Believe me, always, yours very truly

J. Chamberlain

P.S. I had hoped that you were going to be my successor,[1] but I gather from the papers that Lord Milner will be invited. He is first-rate in many ways, and his appointment would, I think, entirely satisfy the public.
9/126

1. As Secretary of State for the Colonies. The post went to Alfred Lyttleton, who held it until 1905. Lord Selborne accepted the post of Governor-General of the Transvaal and High Commissioner for South Africa in February 1905.

8. To Austen Chamberlain

1 September 1904

*Private*
My dear Austen,
I entirely share your view that the position of the party is very critical[1] and that the Prime Minister alone can reunite the major portion of it and that he must take his line at the earliest opportunity.

I agree also very strongly that the step he should take is to plump for the summoning of a Colonial Conference:[2] but I dissent from your rider 'with the assured intention of acting upon its conclusions *if* they were satisfactory.' I dissent, because I do not think it compatible with the position, which Arthur has rightly or wrongly taken up. He is absolutely precluded I think from including a tax on food in his programme for the *next* election and that would be including it. It may be that he has not used words which could be shown to fix him to this position; nor am I sure that it was the position he meant to take up; but I am quite sure that that is how the spirit of his pledges is understood by the country at large and by that large mass of the party which stands between the Tariff Reformers and the Free Fooders.[3] Nor do I think such a course would be really consistent with his frequently repeated dictum, with which I identify myself, that the great change of fiscal policy, when it comes, must be a change made with that manifest and overwhelming national assent, which alone can settle these big questions and make reaction impossible. Moreover I should strenuously object to Arthur pledging himself to any such limitation as you suggest (though of course not with favour) of a 1/– duty only on wheat, or against what you call a scientific tariff. Even if I did not think the rider you propose impossible for Arthur for the reasons given, I should object to purchasing it by any such price as a limitation on our discretion, especially as I cannot see what is going to be gained by it. We are not under any circumstances going to win the *next* election, so why fetter ourselves?

The following is my policy.

Plump for the Colonial Conference, refuse to fetter ourselves beforehand about its terms or proposals in any degree whatsoever, but assert that, if we arrive at a satisfactory conclusion, we will take it in our hands to the country instantly and ask them to vote aye or no on it as a whole at a second general election. Understand that this is my policy for the next general election, which we are not going to win. For the general election after that, which we are going to win, I would in opposition have pushed the matter a stage further and matured and hardened national opinion and for that second general election my policy will be – Colonial conference – no fettering pledges – and carry it out if we arrive at a satisfactory conclusion at once and without going back to the country again.

The advantage of this policy is more than keeping Arthur's credit with the utmost scrupulosity and more than saving us from inconveniently fettering pledges. It will keep a much larger party together than yours as I understand it, and that is of *paramount importance* that our party should be as large and as united as possible when we are in opposition. Now I think that a larger, a much larger, portion of the party will unite on my 'nuance' (if I may use such an expression) than on your 'nuance'. I predict nothing about the out and out Free Fooders. They are I think unreasonable and I do not find myself able to enter into their feelings. But they have an important fringe and beyond that fringe is a great mass of Conservative opinion, which because it is Conservative is very cautious and chary on embarking at one step in great changes. Both the fringe and the mass will accept the policy I advocate wholeheartedly. There remains the assured Tariff Reformers of all degrees, which includes the great majority of the L.U.s and a large section of the Conservatives. What will they lose by my policy. Nothing absolutely nothing. They will on the other hand gain the committal of the largest obtainable portion (the great majority) of the Unionist party to the policy of the Conference with the Colonies, and in opposition they will find that united Unionist party mature in opinion and harden into accepting the consequences of the Conference as well as the Conference itself, a second and more advanced step which will become easy and natural to them all when opposing a Home Rule government in power, but for which in my opinion a much smaller number are prepared at this moment. Forgive the inordinate length of this letter. And believe me, yours ever

Selborne

AC 17/3/80

1.   This in reply to letters from Austen Chamberlain, 30 and 31 August, 73/18, 24.
2.   Austen Chamberlain, with other Tariff Reformers in the Unionist Party, was anxious that Balfour should summon a Colonial Conference to ascertain Colonial opinion about tariff reform and preferential treatment; if their views were favourable, then Chamberlain hoped that Balfour would be compelled to

adopt tariff reform as official Unionist policy (see also Austen Chamberlain to Selbourne, 30 August 1904, 73/18).
3. Free fooders were those members of the Unionist party who held to the free trade doctrine.


9. From Austen Chamberlain

Highbury
Moor Green
Birmingham
3 September 1904

Private

My dear Selborne,

... I cannot see what we gain by procrastination, whom we pacify by hesitation or how we can make a good fight on a half hearted programme.

I have already urged the disastrous effect on candidates of telling them that success means a second dissolution. They will (wisely) defer standing till we know our own minds and mean business.

You urge that Balfour is understood to have rejected by anticipation my policy in the declaration he has already made.

I think you are mistaken; certainly he does not himself take that view of his speeches. Please look at the Bristol speech – the most specific of all and one accepted by Beach. He there distinctly confined his restrictions to the circumstances of the moment and reserved full liberty of action for himself and his colleagues if circumstances changed.

Who are the men whom you hope to gain and whom my suggestions will lose? I cannot see them.

We are suffering from weakness and flabbiness which kill enthusiasm. What we need is a great appeal for a great end – an appeal to a cause which touches mens' emotions and rouses their sympathy. Your policy would excite just as much enmity and be assailed with just as much bitterness and lies as mine, but you would kill zeal and dishearten friends without converting foes.

I agree that all my suggested limitations are so many defects. I regret them; I prefer the Birmingham policy; I believe in the whole of it, but I am trying to find a bridge for the weak who are yet willing, and I recognise that there must be some compromise. But I do not see how we can accept your solution, and when a man like yourself is found to propose it, I confess I am filled with consternation. It seems to me a weak and futile evasion, disarming no enemy, discouraging every friend and leaving our difficulties in the future as great or greater than they are now, whilst lessening Balfour's credit and prestige and therefore his power to cope with them.

Yours ever

Austen Chamberlain

P.S. I shall of course tell Balfour that I sent you a copy of my letter to him. I have not communicated with any of our other colleagues though I have some feeling that they too ought to know my views.
73/27


10.  To Austen Chamberlain

Admiralty, Whitehall
6 September 1904

My dear Austen,
It is almost exactly a year ago since I did my utmost to persuade A.J.B. to adopt Preference and a corn tax as part of his immediate programme. I believed I was right at the time and now I am quite sure I was right. Victory might have been achieved a year ago on these lines. Victory cannot now be achieved on any lines at the next general election, and just as my whole mind was directed to achieving victory then so it is now directed to bringing off as large and united an army as possible after that defeat which is inevitable. So only and so best can we be preparing the way for our subsequent victory.

I do not hesitate and I am not the least ashamed to say that our whole tactics should be directed towards securing the largest and most united minority possible while we are in opposition.

With this object in view I am as clear and decided in pressing my policy on you now as I was my policy of twelve months ago on A.J.B.

I do not of course object to your policy in principle. It suits me personally well enough. But I know my policy will produce greater results and therefore I urge it. You ask me who will like it. I reply that great mass of central conservative office feeling which is never seen or heard and which therefore some people ignore. We have been losing bye elections, whether the candidates have been whole or half hoggers[1] because this central conservative influence has not been *working* for us. It may have been voting but it has not been working and it is on its work that we depend. Your policy may rally and unite it largely but mine will do so thoroughly and completely and enthusiastically.

I can understand your preferring your policy to mine on its own merits, but honestly and truly how can you possibly prefer your policy, weighted with limitations about a 1/– corn tax or the nature of the tariff, to mine passes my comprehension. Indeed I find your objections very hard to understand; they seem to me to be so inadequate.

In the first place how an intelligent candidate who knows that his party is not going to have a majority can be discouraged by the prospect of a 'vista of elections' I do not understand. In the second place I do not assent that my policy involves any fresh future difficulty. In the third place I cannot acquiesce in the justice of your epithets. A policy which is attractive to both candidates and electors and which unites the party and gives us a larger minority than any other cannot be justly described as futile. One which is bold frank and simple cannot justly be called evasive.

If you believed we had a chance of winning the next general election I should fully comprehend for what you were contending; but you do not believe that any more than I do and therefore while I of course understand your preference for your own policy I really do not understand your hostility to mine.

You are quite the last person in the world with whom I like having any serious difference of opinion even on a question of tactics. On the question of principle I believe we are in full agreement, but at the present moment tactics have a special importance.

Now a word on the personal aspect of the case, personal I mean to A.J.B.

I do not dispute that AJB has never intended to pledge himself against including a tax on food in any shape or form in his policy for the next general election. But I have received a very strong impression that the mass of plain men have never thus interpreted the spirit of the assurances he has given or which have been given on his behalf and that nothing will persuade them to the contrary. I could not therefore urge on him a course which I fear would have the effect of shaking the confidence of a great mass of his fellow countrymen in his plain dealing. Our people do not like refinements however logically constructed or carefully guarded.

I may be wrong in this. I do not dogmatise I only speak for my own impressions, and if A.J.B. finds himself in this position because he rejected the advice which I (as doubtless others) gave him a year ago, I can certainly claim to be disinterested. Ever yours, my dear Austen

Selborne

A.C. 17/3/83

1.  The 'whole hoggers' were the Chamberlainite tariff reformers who were fully committed to Joseph Chamberlain's fiscal plan which they wished to make the platform of Unionist policy.


## 11.    From Austen Chamberlain

11 Downing Street
13 September 1904

*Private*

My dear Selborne,

I am certainly as reluctant as yourself that there should be even an appearance of controversy between us, and I have been tempted for this reason to leave your last letter without reply. But your views are too important to be left unnoticed and I must say very briefly why I disagree with them.

1.  I do not believe that the doubt and hesitation visible in the party outside the House of Commons are due to any objection to thorough fiscal

reform – least of all to colonial preferences with all that that implies. I think that they are the natural and inevitable outcome of the similar doubt and hesitancy which prevails among the leaders. If the latter were united, I think our present difficulties with the mass of the party would disappear and that there would be no lack of workers or enthusiasm.

2.   You seem to me to attach too much importance to *quantity* and too little to *quality* in the composition of the party in the next House. What is essential is that those of us who are returned should be united and determined. It is differences of opinion which alone would paralyse our efforts. A few votes more or less are of little consequence if all which we are supposed to possess are reliable.

3.   Your policy turns wholly on the difference which you make between the next election and the next but one. But this is a distinction which you cannot explain to the world or the party. In individual constituencies candidates and workers fight to win. If you tell them before hand that defeat is certain, they will not work. Your real intentions must therefore remain secret; and your policy will appear to them as discouraging as it did to me.

4.   As regards Balfour's position I fear he agrees with you rather than with me, but *not* for the reasons which you give. If he thought and told me that his honour was pledged, I should deeply regret it, but I should at once cease to press him. You cannot ask any man to do what he thinks his honour forbids; but that is not Balfour's line. On the eve of leaving I have had a letter from him. He argues the question wholly on grounds of policy and on those grounds both you and I may fairly argue with him if we disagree with his premises or his conclusions.

I fear that I do differ profoundly. I think my position this autumn will be made very difficult, but I will do my best to keep things smooth while this Parliament lasts. But I start today for my holiday greatly depressed by the conviction to which his letter has brought me that when the dissolution comes I shall not be able to see eye to eye with him or to conceal our difference of opinion from the public. Yours ever

Austen Chamberlain

73/31

12.   From the Earl of Midleton

India Office<br>Whitehall S.W.<br>24 November 1905

Private

My dear Willie,

One ultra confidential line to tell you it is all UP with the Government. Arthur spared Joe at Newcastle[1] and briefly asked for Unity in presence of the common enemy. Joe at Bristol[2] made a regular appeal for a charge in which the vanguard alone stand by him. The Times and D[aily] T[elegraph] both *uninspired* then said Arthur had better give it up and a crisis arose. We had a long discussion in Cabinet today. Arthur is for resigning at once, as near New Year as can be so that Elections may be on new registers. Walter Long made a vehement appeal for delay till February – for Ireland; Akers Douglas and Hood both said electorally it was a great mistake to give notice before Christmas and let canvassing go on till January. The Chancellor[3] was against resignation at all. I was strong for delay at all events till January (1) for Long (2) To checkmate G. Curzon's assault on the Military Policy in India[4] (3) To give you a little more time (4) Long Elections never suit us (5) the party would understand dissolution but not resignation (6) Campbell Bannerman might decline to take office now. Lansdowne was for going. A. Chamberlain significantly observed there would be more speeches – G. Balfour does not want to show Redistribution Bill[5] – A. Forster wants more time: he thinks he can conciliate Volunteers![6]

It is a terrible pie but Arthur is sick of it. I have no doubt he will resign before end of December. We shall get hideously beaten, but the nation is tired of us and 'hit high, hit low' there's no pleasing them.

It is a long way back to 1895 and you will remember the high hopes with which we all took office. I am sorry it should flicker out, still more so in January with a 6 months session to face in which it will be difficult to be critical and yet patriotic. They are sure to reverse a good deal. Personally, I know it is right we should go; we are all stale and not doing our best work, though I enjoyed the last 3 days more than any since I came here, for I have felt every telegram I sent may weigh with Minto as nothing did with George . . .

Goodbye old boy. I am so sorry to hear rheumatism is still bad. Did I tell you Hopie's remark 'I've told Acland Hood to ask Arthur not to put silly fellows like Londonderry and me in his next Government. The difference between us is that I know I'm a silly fellow – Londonderry doesn't!' Yours ever

St. J.B.

2/118

1. At the National Union of Conservative and Unionist Associations conference, where Balfour defended his policy of abstention from fiscal debates in the interests of party unity.
2. At the annual conference of the Liberal Unionist Council.
3. Austen Chamberlain
4. Curzon and Kitchener had long been at loggerheads in India, and their feud continued after the former's resignation as Viceroy in August 1905, centred now on Kitchener's plan for the reorganisation of military control which, he argued, should be vested in the Committee of Imperial Defence instead of the Government of India.
5. A bill for the redistribution of parliamentary seats, which Balfour would have introduced had he stayed in office. Unionists were keen on redistribution

which, they calculated, would produce a margin of seats in their favour if the United Kingdom as a whole (including Ireland) were considered.

6.	H.O. Arnold-Forster was seeking to reallocate money available for the Volunteer force (which numbered 249, 611 in November 1905) to allow a greater sum to be spent on the more valuable part of the force (the Volunteers were described by the Norfolk Commission on the auxiliary forces as unfit to face enemy troops). The knowledge that the government was in a decline weakened Arnold Forster's hand in his attempts to gain a reduction in the force.

## 13.	From the Marquess of Salisbury

Hatfield
19 January 1906

My dear Willie,

The catastrophe[1] is so amazing in its completeness that no doubt you will be anxious to know anything that we have to say in explanation of it. But I don't think we can help you much. Arthur professes to think that none of the burning questions which we were struggling over before the Election had anything to do with it. He looks upon the disaster as a mild attack of the revolutionary malady in Russia and the socialist complaint in Germany and Austria. I dare say this is true to a great extent – that is to say the the Labour Movement and Organisation (of the magnitude of which our clever wirepullers never seem to have had a glimmering though it must have been going on under their very noses for months or even years) has been of incomparably greater importance than anything else. But no doubt the other issues contributed. We did not know we were in for a hurricane, but it was a misfortune that at such a moment the crew were fighting amongst themselves. From all sides we hear of the mischief which the Chinese labour question has done us.[2] Misrepresented as the facts were they might not have been effective but for the circumstance that the question fitted in with the labour fever here. Men who were rising against what they consider the tyranny of capital here had no difficulty in believing that capital was guilty of every atrocity in S. Africa. So this issue was merely an expression of the labour movement and as I say the labour movement has left the fiscal question a long way behind in importance. As to this latter no school of fiscal opinion has escaped overwhelming defeat. Linky and Elliott have fared no better than Harry Chaplin and Bonar Law or than Arthur and Gerald. It is evident that amongst those who have voted for us Joe has commanded a great deal of support. In the towns I should think he might reckon on a majority of those who remain our friends, perhaps a large majority. In the country districts I am not so sure. Our candidate here thinks he only succeeded by insisting that he was against any tax on food. But I have only spoken of those who remain our friends. If you reckon those who deserted us and whom we must regain if we are ever to make a show again you will realise the additional weight which Joe has placed on our shoulders. To these workingmen a food tax is probably another example of the indifference of capital to the struggles of the poor; but is only an element and by no means the largest element in their attitude. Still we have moved a long way from the time when Joe thought he would sweep the country! Besides all this Arthur's leadership is much blamed. I think with some justice, though we must all take a share of the blame. We ought to have followed your advice last Spring. At that fatal Cabinet when we decided that we would take no part in the fiscal votes of censure debates.[3] We determined to withdraw on the food tax motion. We ought not to have withdrawn; as we were divided in opinion, it should have been left an open question. We then determined to withdraw on the retaliation motion and you protested. You were quite right and we were wrong. It was the P.M.'s own policy which was involved in this motion and our action plunged us into contempt. Of course we had reasons. Austen would have resigned upon the difference of treatment of the two motions and the dissolution would have been immediate. Personally I had only just gone to the Board of Trade. The whole Fiscal question seemed to me to be a moving quicksand of hypothesis. I did not care about any part of it without more precise data which I had had no time to acquire. I was glad that it should sink into some contempt. Unfortunately it was we who sank into contempt. But you warned us. I think that all this has augmented the magnitude of our destruction. And how!!! I wish to goodness you were home. That we don't quite agree on the fiscal question doesn't matter. We have other fish to fry. Just conceive our position in the House of Lords. We must of course bend before the storm – indeed generally lie flat down. But there are questions of such vital moment that we may have to resist, whatever the consequences. What a decision to have to take! I have not much confidence in Lansdowne except in his own subject and Beach will of course always want to run away. I earnestly hope that nothing upon which we must risk the constitution will arise this year. I doubt whether we could resist *anything* successfully. I have no doubt the Labour Party will insist on payment of members and upon taxing ground rents, etc. Well! one comfort is that on these – be they bad or worse – the Lords have nothing to say. For my part too I dread them much less than some other possibilities. Then after a year or two, the situation will be much easier. The majority in the commons are bound to quarrel and to dread a dissolution and then . . . Yours ever

S

5/110

1.  Following the resignation of A. J. Balfour on 4 December 1905 a Liberal government under Sir Henry Campbell-Bannerman took office, and in January 1906 it went to the country. The result was the 'Liberal landslide', when the Liberals won 377 seats, a majority of 84 over all other parties combined. The Unionists saved only 157 seats, the two Balfours, St John Brodrick and Alfred

Lyttleton losing their seats. The Irish Nationalists won 83 seats, but one of the real surprises of the election was the return of 53 Labour members.

2.   The use of Chinese labourers in the gold mines of the Witwatersrand, and the practice of housing them in compounds, was widely condemned by the Liberals on moral and humanitarian grounds.

3.   In March 1905 Balfour, in the interests of party unity, had recommended abstention on four Liberal resolutions condemning preference and tariffs.

### 14.   To Joseph Chamberlain

High Commissioner's Office
Johannesburg
20 December 1909

My dear Mr. Chamberlain,

H.M.G. are going to appoint Herbert Gladstone first Governor General;[1] so, if we do not win the general election,[2] you will see I shall not be leaving South Africa voluntarily but I shall have seen my task there through as you advised and wished me to do. If on the other hand at the general election victory is ours, as I believe it will be, and Arthur Balfour wishes me to join a Tariff Reform Cabinet, I hope you will agree with me that I should be justified in passing on my work in South Africa to someone else.

I should dearly love to have a place in such a Government; yet I could not join such a Cabinet unconditionally, and it is on this point that I greatly desire to enlist your support. The first task of such a Cabinet must be tariff reform in its fullest aspect; but its second, and to my mind equally essential, task must be to apply a remedy to the constitutional deadlock, which has really arisen.

The relations of the Lords and Commons cannot permanently remain as they are now. If we do not find the remedy, the Home-Rule-Pro-Boer-Little-England-Socialist party will one day surely return to power and they will drag the Crown into the quarrel between the two Houses. They will request the King to create enough Peers to pass an 'Emasculation of the House of Lords and Establishment of the House of Commons as a Single Chamber Tyranny' Bill.

If the King refuses, we shall see the formation of an avowed republican party. If he yields, well, Exit Anglia. It would then be in the power of a House of Commons possessing a majority as bad or worse than the present to reverse our policy of tariff reform, to denounce the Preference given by us to the Colonies, most surely to disrupt the Empire.

Some people may say 'impossible' – I say that there is no depth of malignant lunacy, to which such a majority, if constitutionally uncontrolled, would not sink. Now I come to the remedy. In the first place I am in favour of very considerable changes in the House of Lords itself, but that is a comparatively unimportant matter.

My second point is the one which matters – I plump for the referendum. Now I do not know your views on this matter. I have an instinct, I hope erroneous, that, notwithstanding the essentially democratic principle underlying the referendum, you may object to it.

That many objections can be urged to it I know well, but those objections are objections of detail. I have thought a great deal about the question and I believe that I have found an answer to all these objections and that I have a plan which will work. Now what I ask of you is this – If you do look askance at the referendum, do not finally commit yourself, do not pronounce against it, until I have been able to talk it all out with you.

If you need no conversion, I shall throw up my hat for joy. If your judgment is in suspense, give me the chance to open all my mind to you about it, for my feelings on the subject are very strong and my judgment deeprooted. I believe that between us we could frame such a scheme as would restore stability to the Constitution and so to the Empire and that we could convert our party readily to it.

Arthur Balfour knows my views and has never expressed hostility to them, but he has in no way committed himself to accepting them. I have never discussed the matter with Austen, but I hope to do so immediately on my return and in the meantime I should like him to know my views. Yours,

Selborne

9/177

1. The Union constitution came into force on 31 May 1910; the first Prime Minister was Louis Botha. The emergence of Botha as Prime Minister is described in L. M. Thompson, *The Unification of South Africa*, pp. 448–55.
2. Following the rejection by the House of Lords of the Liberal government's budget on 30 November 1909, Asquith moved in the Lower House that 'the action of the House of Lords in refusing to pass into law the financial provisions made by this House for the service of the year is a breach of the Constitution and a usurpation of the rights of the Commons'. He announced an immediate dissolution. On 23 December 1909 it was announced that writs would be issued on 10 January 1910, and that polling would be spread over the fortnight beginning 15 January. The Unionists were defeated, finding themselves in a minority of 124.

15.   From the Earl of Midleton

34 Portland Place
W
28 April 1910

My dear Willie,

This will be my last letter to you in South Africa,[1] but it ought just to catch you before you embark at Capetown, which you ought to do with the lightest heart possible, for while almost every other Administrator who ever landed in South Africa has come away leaving all sorts of difficulties behind, and most of them with a sense of failure, you are able to look back on a period of almost undiluted triumph. It is really a great delight to see how your work is appreciated, both in South Africa and in this country, and I am very glad you are now turning your back on it and not trusting your luck too long. We shall also value very much your return here. You will arrive, as I ventured to predict three months ago when Bob and others were being recalled in such a hurry and as I think very prematurely, in time for the crisis, which will not really take place until after the middle of June.

Trouble succeeds on trouble at present, and there is no end to it. Since the momentous declaration by Asquith that he would pledge himself to ask for guarantees[2] the desire by the Home Rulers and Labour members to rush a general election is not so great: having got the promise of extreme measures, they are in no hurry to risk their seats again, and the idea just now is that the Government will shove us if possible into an August election, or even dissolve in September, when the working classes can be there, and the holiday makers are absent. To frustrate this, it will be necessary for the House of Lords to deal with the veto[3] by the middle of June, and as Rosebery's resolutions[4] come first we must shorten the former.

A sort of ex-Cabinet was held the other day at which the following were present:– A J B, Lansdowne, G.W., A. Lyttleton, Long, A. Chamberlain, Bonar Law, Cawdor, Curzon, Londonderry, Halsbury, Salisbury.

Opinions were very varied, Curzon, Wyndham and Austen Chamberlain are against any concessions at all, or at least any hint of any alternative, and as Austen said, 'If after all, we only win twenty or twenty five seats at this election, we shall have won on the second round, and a third round will do for them; we must prepare for it.' This shows to my mind, the false reasoning of some people; we may win twenty or thirty seats; this will leave us still sixty to the bad and that will be a knock-down blow. If Asquith declines to go on without creation of peers, and also refuses to go to the country without guarantees, the only alternative is that Arthur should take office, (which Arthur realises), and dissolve at once. The preliminary difficulty as to money must be got over somehow. If Arthur should return as Austen supposes, with sixty majority against him, there seems no alternative to a creation of peers, or the complete surrender of House of Lords for certainly Asquith will not then take office again without a creation, and equally certainly Arthur could not live a week in the House of Commons with a majority of sixty against him, and the Budget to carry.

At the end of the meeting, I pressed strongly that the referendum should now be trotted out as an alternative, not in so many words, but to be discussed so as to accustom people to it. I believe it will be the final solution and the only possible one. I think it would be reasonable for the King, who will have to make a great appeal to both sides, to say to Asquith 'I am bound to stand by the people's opinion; the referendum takes the people's opinion, and does not enable the House of Lords to disturb the Administration.'

I cannot but believe Scotland would be largely influenced by such a proposal, but Bonar Law, to whom I appealed, did not support me in this view.

Meantime, everybody is going to the country for a holiday, which they mostly require very much, and no attempt will be made on any of the doubtful seats till the whole business is past praying for.

Well, when the crisis comes, it is a good thing to know you will be here . . . Yours ever

St J.B.

3/114

1. On 15 May 1910 Lord and Lady Selborne arrived in Cape Town at the end of a farewell tour of South Africa. Herbert Gladstone arrived on 17 May, and Lord Selborne sailed on the afternoon of 18 May, arriving back in England on 4 June.
2. Asquith's statement on 15 April 1910 that 'in no case will we recommend a dissolution except under such conditions as will secure that in the new Parliament the judgement of the people as expressed at the elections will be carried into law' which amounted to a request that the King would create enough Peers to ensure the passage of Liberal House of Lords reform through the upper House.
3. The Liberals' bid to modify the House of Lords' power of veto, which in the first instance was embodied in a set of resolutions, dealing with the veto of the Lords in finance, ordinary legislation, and the life of Parliament, introduced by Asquith on 21 March 1910. These resolutions were passed by the Commons on 15 April 1910 and were followed by a first reading of a Parliament Bill 'for restricting the existing powers of the House of Lords'. Parliament rose for a short spring recess on 28 April.
4. Lord Rosebery had chaired a Select Committee on Lords Reform, set up in 1907, but not with much success. On 14 March 1910 he introduced three resolutions for reform, calling for a strong and efficient second chamber, reform of the existing chamber, and an acceptance of the principle that the possession of a peerage should no longer of itself give the right to sit and vote in the House of Lords. These resolutions were passed by the Lords.

16.  To Lady Selborne

Ugbrooke Park
Chudleigh
7 December 1910

My darling,

On Monday I left Top and Grace early and got to Bristol in the middle of the afternoon; miles and miles of country in the Severn Valley and on both sides of the railway was under water. I was met at Bristol by a gentleman who took me in charge and looked after me: that night I spoke at Keynsham in North Somerset[1] and then motored with our candidate, one Beauchamp, to his house. Yesterday I went from Bristol to Plymouth and then motored out to Maristow, Sir H. Lopes. He was at Oxford with me and you probably remember his father well – he motored over to Tavistock where the meeting was and then back to Maristow. Today I came on here to speak at Newton Abbot. The Cliffords live here, you will remember R.C. friends of Alice and Harry, and we used to see her in our old hunting days with the H.H. She was a cousin of the Greenwoods and was always staying at Brookwood. Tomorrow I go over to the Pole Carews at Antony to speak for him at Liskeard and then on Friday to Truro and rest till Monday with J.C. Williams, Caerhays Castle, Gorran R.S.O., Cornwall.

On Monday I speak in Yeovil, and on Tuesday go to Scotland where I speak on 14th and 15 though where I do not know yet and that I trust finishes it. My meetings and experiences at Keynsham and Tavistock were exactly the same as what I have described to you in Lancashire and all through. At the former place a band of some 100 Radicals sat together in the middle of the hall very orderly and attentive. After the meeting they sent one of their number to ask me to go down and talk to them. Of course I did and we sat and smoked. At the end they all said 'We have nothing to say against your policy, it seems to us quite fair and the best plan, but it is quite new to us, why did not you put it before us earlier?'

I verily believe that if Arthur had put this policy forward a year ago, or even six months ago, the whole position would have been altered.

Now how bad it is! The gains we began with have evaporated under losses, many of which should not have occurred, and I do not see how we can now ever win twenty seats, the minimum which could help the King.

Lancashire on the whole is a bright spot again and with Warrington, Wigan, and St. Helens, all won, it really looks as if Top had a chance. But all is in God's hands. He alone is allwise and allmighty, and no other power but His can separate you and me. All we can do is to do our duty to the last millionth of an ounce and to trust in Him. Yours

S

101/221

1.  Following the death of King Edward VII on 6 May 1910, his successor George V sounded the leaders of both main parties to see if they would be willing to arrange a truce and settle their differences in a round table conference. On 16 June 1910 eight politicians (four from each party) met behind closed doors. The conference failed to reach agreement on the main issues dividing the parties, home rule and House of Lords reform, and this failure was followed by negotiations between Asquith and the King, the latter agreeing to fulfil Edward VII's promise to create peers on condition that the House of Lords be given an opportunity for pronouncing on the Parliament Bill. The Lords postponed consideration of the bill on second reading using the time afforded to pass counter proposals. On 18 November 1910 Asquith announced a dissolution, to take place ten days later, and it was in the ensuing election that Lord Selbourne was campaigning.

17.   To A.J. Balfour

Blackmoor
Liss
Hants.
24 December 1910

My dear Arthur,

Forgive me if I state to you as briefly as I can the result of my reflexions on my election experiences[1] and on the position of the party and on the present crisis.

1.   Referendum is a winning policy.[2] If we had had it out immediately after the January election, as I think we might have done, the whole position would have been altered. Our electors cannot assimilate a new idea in four weeks or less.

Reform of the House of Lords is a necessary accompaniment of the Referendum, but the electors take no interest in its details nor in the question what the financial powers of the reformed House are to be.

Therefore, while we should unwearyingly advocate the Referendum and enlarge upon its details, we need only express our intention to reform the House of Lords and should not tie our hands unnecessarily as to details.

I found the formula 'such a reform of the House of Lords as will give fair and adequate representation to Liberal and Radical opinion' universally successful for platform purposes.

The adhesion of the Unionist Free Traders, and the unpopularity of the Budget, brought us no increase of votes of any importance, nor has there been yet any secession from the Liberal Party of any value.

2.   We have a splendid programme: The essential thing is not to vary it. I am afraid it is true that many electors do not believe in our solidarity or consistency. The reputation to aim at, as the greatest possible contrast to the Government, is that of a 'rock of principle'. For that reason I would never change my attitude on the corn tax, colonial free foreign 2/–; of course if Canada came to us and said 'Thank you, but the 2/– tax on foreign corn is of no importance to us, pray do not put it on on our account', that would alter the case, but nothing else I think would.

For the same reason it would be suicidal as well as dishonourable to go back on your declaration about the principles of Tariff Reform being made the subject of a Referendum. If our policy for dealing with the constitutional difficulty prevails, we stand pledged by your declaration. This does not mean of course that, if our policy does not prevail and some other policy does, the principles of Tariff Reform alone are to be the subject of a Referendum.

3.   I am bound to confess that everywhere I heard dissatisfaction expressed with the Central Office, sometimes very strongly expressed.

It is my profound conviction that it has become humanly impossible for one man to manage the party organisation, finances, &c., and to act as Whip in the House of Commons.

St. John has shown me the draft of a letter he has written to you and generally I quite concur with the views expressed in it on this subject.

I want to say a word here about the Carlton Club.[3] I am prepared, and indeed anxious, to join the Carlton to-morrow; but I do not want to put Lansdowne or Austen into a difficult position.

Could not some small change of words be made in its constitution which would enable them both to join. The point is really worth your attention.

4.   If the King appeals to you, you are bound to do your best for him; but I do not think that the King would be wise in appealing to you, unless Asquith makes some outrageous request to him, in which case the whole position would be changed, *providing that* the nature of that outrageous request could be made known to the electors.

For the purpose of these reflexions I should not regard a request to make *x* hundred peers under certain circumstances as an outrageous request, nor even should I so regard a request to make them in order to pass the Parliament Bill without the change of a comma, because it can be said that that Bill has been the subject of a special General Election. I should regard as outrageous a request made in advance to create Peers to pass the Parliament Bill *in any form* in which it may emerge from the House of Commons.

The greatest National and Imperial interest is the preservation of the Monarchy, and the King should be kept out of this now at any cost.

In fact I think that, whatever we do in the House of Lords, the King should act on Asquith's advice, unless that advice is outrageous and *can be exposed* as outrageous. Our action in the House of Lords should be taken on its merits and independently of the King's action. There should be no attempt at an nderstanding between us. Let the King keep the Crown out of the quarrel at all costs and leave it to us or our successors one day to restore stability to the constitution.

For the majority of the House of Lords two courses are open.

A.   To refuse any responsibility for the revolution, direct or indirect, and to see that it is only consummated by the creation of Peers.

B.   To abstain altogether from the House of Lords and to allow the minority of Peers to pass the Parliament Bill through the House.

As at present advised, I am in favour of course A, because I believe the greatest evil which can befall a nation is to have its constitutional stability destroyed by a revolution and not to know it, and because I fear that unless the revolution is underlined by the creation of Peers the nation will not repise what has really happened. I have other reasons too, but the above is the most important. I realise that there are serious arguments in favour of course B, but my position is as above stated.

A third course would be to read the Bill a second time and to amend it; but the majority of the House of Commons will accept no amendment of any importance from the majority of the House of Lords and to make important amendments and not to stick to them would be futile, foolish, and undignified. Of course to make important amendments *and to stick to them* would be simply a variant on course A, and possibly a wise variant. That would necessarily depend on the circumstances of the moment, on the nature of the amendments and on their probable effect on the electorate. Yours affectionately

Selborne

1/139

1. The results of the election were: Liberals, 272 seats; Labour 42; Irish Parliamentary Party 84; Unionists 272.
2. On 29 November Balfour had announced his willingness to submit tariff reform to a national referendum if elected. Neal Blewett discusses the influence of the referendum in the election, concluding that 'only in Lancastria was the movement of opinion sufficient to warrant more detailed attention', and that 'even in Lancastria the referendum pledge had at the most but a marginal effect' (*The peers, the parties and the people: the general elections of 1910* [London, 1972], pp. 410–11.)
3. The Carlton Club was founded shortly after the Great Reform Act of 1832, and was the organisational hub of the Conservative Party until the creation of Central Office.

18.   From F. S. Oliver

8 Hereford Gardens
Marble Arch, W.
24 March 1911

Dear Selborne,

I have read the reports of your three speeches[1] with interest and a great measure of agreement. There certainly seems now to be a certain disposition on the part of mankind to listen to the voice of reason.

At the same time I scout danger in several directions.

If you press the Referendum for constitutional questions, and for constitutional questions *alone*, I think you will unite your party and carry your point ultimately if not immediately.

But if you allow the over zealous to extend the scope of the Referendum into other fields I think you will break your party in two.

I judge of course by my own feelings and those of the 'plain man' whom I meet in my daily round. For myself I would sooner – much sooner – have the Parliament Bill than a promiscuous Referendum upon ordinary legislation. Think especially upon financial legislation; the Referendum means bribery, and what Rosebery would call 'the end of all things'.

But if you keep it close to its work it is a good thing; and I admit frankly that I have changed my mind since last midsummer. Outside strictly constitutional affairs, however, I regard it as an invention of the Devil, and must treat it as such.

You have done a very good service to Unionism by your speeches and I hope you feel satisfied with the reception which has been given to them. Believe me, yours very truly

F.S. Oliver

74/62

1. Made in the middle of March 1911 in which Lord Selborne unfolded in some detail his ideas on House of Lords reform.

19. To F. S. Oliver

6 York Terrace
Regent's Park
N.W.
27 March 1911

My dear Oliver,

I am greatly obliged for your letter of the 24th.

You are in favour of the Referendum for constitutional questions alone. I am willing to exclude financial legislation from the scope of the Referendum. I may say in passing that I do not think the danger of bribery depends on the Referendum; I think you will get your Lloyd Georges and Winston Churchills to offer tremendous bribes without the Referendum, and I am not prepared to accept it as a certain fact that the Referendum would assist them rather than obstruct them in their predatory efforts. I say this by way of caveat that I may not be misunderstood. For the purposes of our exchange of ideas, I am fully prepared to agree that the Referendum should not be extended to financial legislation.

Therefore we start with a large measure of agreement. The question between us is with reference to legislation that is neither constitutional nor financial. I do not quite understand why you are prepared to agree to the Referendum on a constitutional question and not on other questions which are as important as many, and more important than some constitutional questions: for instance, the question of the Disestablishment of the Church; or Conscription; or a very long, vexed question like Religious Education. Why should not those go to a Referendum? I am not sure whether you would call Women's Suffrage a constitutional question. Some people would not, in which case, according to your plan, that would not go to a Referendum either.

I fully understand why you should not desire the Referendum to be used too freely. I do not understand why you would exclude from its scope questions such as those I have named. I should hope that on such points as these, we might arrive at a mutual understanding after discussion, but on one thing I am afraid I could never agree with you. You write: 'I would much sooner have the Parliament Bill than a promiscuous Referendum upon ordinary legislation.' There I profoundly differ from you. I consider the Parliament Bill the absolute worst; to me there is nothing whatever beyond. The Referendum at its lowest is a court of appeal from the tyranny of the caucus. You would rather have the caucus without any appeal. I cannot understand that. Believe me, yours sincerely

Selborne

74/64

20.   From F. S. Oliver

8 Hereford Gardens
Marble Arch
London W.
28 March 1911

Dear Selborne,

I forget exactly the terms of the note I wrote you on Sunday, but the last thing that was in my mind was to raise merely dialectical points and if I should happen to have done so you must treat them as having been raised in a Pickwickian sense. I throw out the following suggestions for what they are worth.

As to your first paragraph, I agree that no democracy can be entirely free from the danger of bribery. I am inclined to think however that the more direct it is the worse it is, and that therefore a Referendum on a Lloyd-George Budget[1] would be worse than a Parliamentary discussion upon the same, even though the latter were to be followed by a General Election. However we need not pursue this seeing that you do not want to apply the Referendum to any financial matter.

Now as regards your second paragraph. The Referendum was suggested as a means of settling certain matters of importance when the two Houses were at disagreement in regard to them. I presume that this still stands – i.e., it is only in case of differences between the two Houses that the Referendum is to be called into operation. It has been assumed further in all discussions that such differences will occur in the future as they have occurred in the past; that is, the House of Commons sending up to the House of Lords measures which the House of Lords is unable to agree to. The contrary case of the House of Lords sending down a measure to the House of Commons, with which the House of Commons cannot agree has never been put in the present discussion and therefore we can ignore it. The initiative in legislation of a contentious character is therefore to proceed in the future, as in the past, from the House of Commons.

This being so one of the instances you name, Conscription, would fall out; because it seems to me inconceivable that, if the House of Commons had passed such a measure, the House of Lords would reject it. The question of Disestablishment of the Church on the other hand would fall directly, as it seems to me, under the heading of bribery. If a Referendum were in operation Disestablishers would take very good care to set out the advantages and reliefs which the purses of the tax-payers would obtain through the dis-endowment of the Church. I cannot conceive it possible to maintain that Women's Suffrage is not a constitutional question and I think it is precisely one on which a Referendum is in the highest degree desirable. With regard to your fourth instance, the Education Bill, I am bound to say that I should very much regret to see it put to the Referendum. I do not even see how it *could* be put to the Referendum. I presume that you are speaking of an English Education Bill, about which no Scotsman cares a rap. Neither does any Scotsman understand the facts. The Scotch part of the Referendum would therefore be useless; and the same would apply in the case of a Scotch Education Bill, in the very improbable event of such a thing ever occurring, supposing there were a Referendum upon it to the electors of the United Kingdom, including England; but whether it be feasible or not to submit such a measure as an English Education Bill to the Referendum (and I daresay you might get an instance which would be free from the particular objection noted above) I should still think the dangers much greater than the advantages that might be anticipated.

You misunderstand me if you think I am enamoured of the Parliament Bill or that I should advise anybody to accept it, unless from dire necessity, but at the same time I do not regard the power of delaying for three sessions as purely fictitious, although I admit it is a very slender protection indeed. I entirely sympathise with the fight which is being put up against it. Only I beg you most earnestly not to prejudice the Referendum in the eyes of what I believe to be a very large number of your friends by seeking to extend it beyond purely constitutional matters. Let other things be settled by joint sessions, it you please; or not at all, as I should vastly prefer, although I doubt if this non-solution would be feasible.

Personally I go further than you with regard to the Referendum as applied to constitutional matters. I should like to submit all constitutional changes even when both Houses are agreed – even that would be a great deal less security for permanence than the Yankees enjoy.

I have written a good deal against the Parliament Bill and in favour of what I conceived to have been the intention of Lord Lansdowne's Resolutions,[2] but I daresay it will never be published. There is no possibility of course of completing it until things are further advanced than they are at present. The line I have taken as regards the Referendum is to accept it heartily and commend it for constitutional purposes and to damn it for all others.

I am afraid this is rather a confused letter, but I dictate it in the interval between a Board Meeting about South Africa and sundry other sordid details of my daily round. Yours very truly

F.S. Oliver

1.  Lloyd George's controversial budget of April 1909 included a land tax and was bitterly opposed by the Unionists.
2.  Resolutions moved by Lord Lansdowne on 23 November 1910 restating the case which the Unionists had made in the Constitutional Conference. They called for a 'reduced and reconstituted' House of Lords, and stated that provided a joint committee of both Houses with the Speaker exercising only a casting vote, determined what was and what was not a money bill, the House of Lords would abandon its right of rejection in this field; that where a difference between the two houses on other bills arose and persisted for a year it should be settled by a joint sitting; unless the bill related to 'a matter of great gravity and had not been adequately submitted to the judgement of the people', in which case it should be put to a referendum. These resolutions were carried.


21.   To F.S. Oliver

6 York Terrace
Regent's Park
N.W.
30 March 1911

My dear Oliver,

Many thanks for your letter of the 28th. I am sure we need not excuse ourselves to each other as having any intention of raising merely dialectical points. We both want only to get to the bottom of a big thing.

When I wrote to you, I was not writing from the point of view only of what may be called at present the Unionist position in respect of the Referendum; I was writing from the point of view of my own mind, and therefore I was not considering the Referendum only as a means of settling certain matters of importance when the two Houses are in disagreement. I *was* considering it from that point of view, but also from the same point of view which induced Balfour to promise to send Tariff Reform to a Referendum, even when both Houses were agreed. It was in that connection that I mentioned Conscription, and not on the hypothesis that the House of Lords might reject a proposal for Conscription which had been passed by the House of Commons.

Just as I think that Balfour was right, and that Tariff Reform would not really be fixed as the permanent financial policy of the country unless endorsed by a Referendum, so I think that Conscription should be taken upon their shoulders by the people themselves, and not only by their representatives. Otherwise I should fear the danger of a reaction.

As regards the case of Disestablishment and Disendowment, I quite definitely disagree with you. As a very keen Churchman, I would far rather take my chance with the electors themselves – let the disestablishers frame their bill as they choose, with the object of bribing those electors – than I would from a Radical House of Commons.

The case of the Education Bill I feel much less strongly, but personally, I should settle the question through the Referendum. I am referring of course, as you say, to an English Education Bill. The question has lasted for years, and even the most ignorant voter in England knows roughly what the points at issue are in respect of the controversy over religious teaching, which of course you understand is the point I want settled by a Referendum. After exactly the same controversy as has existed here in England for so many years, this very point was definitely settled both in Queensland and Victoria by a Referendum. The objection which you raise is the only one which I think serious, namely, that the question is an English question, and that under the Referendum the Scotch and Irish voters would have to vote. Well, I would just as soon trust the Scotch and Irish voters on such a question as I would their representatives in the House of Commons. I do not think there is any greater disadvantage in having that question settled partly by the votes of Scotch and Irish electors who are not personally interested than by the votes of Scotch and Irish members who are not personally interested.

The reason why I think the Parliament Bill the very worst possible solution is that it is a veiled revolution which, to my mind, is far more dangerous than a naked revolution. You say that you do not regard the power of delaying for three sessions (surely you ought to say two years) as purely fictitious, but surely it is purely fictitious when you consider that in those two years the House of Lords itself could have been wholly abolished. Personally, I should much prefer that, for the reason I have given. The very nakedness of the revolution would be the commencement of safety. The profound danger of the Parliament Bill lies in the fact that the revolution is veiled. It shows how completely the members of the present Government understand the English people; they have absolutely no imagination, and the majority of them take a thing exactly as it is labelled.

I rejoice that you go further than me with regard to the Referendum as applied to constitutional methods. I am quite open to conviction on this; I think that a great deal could be said for it, and that the answer to the objection that comparatively small and unimportant changes in the constitution would have to go to a Referendum just as momentous changes would, is of no consequence compared to the importance of teaching the electors the difference between what is constitutional and what is not constitutional.

I hope that you will publish what you have written. Don't burn your boats altogether in respect of the application of the Referendum to other than constitutional purposes. We are only at the beginning of Constitution-making, and I do not think any of us should be too dogmatic. Believe me, yours sincerely

Selborne

74/71

22.  Memorandum by A.J. Balfour

11 May 1911

I have promised to write a brief Memorandum on the policy which should be pursued on the Second Reading and Committee stages of the Parliament Bill.

It is generally agreed that the amendments to the Bill should be few and important, and that no attempt should be made by the House of Lords to deal with its minor defects. If this view be correct, which I cannot doubt, I believe the amendments may be reduced to three; two on the first clause and one on the second.

The amendments to the first clause would

(a) provide a definition of a Money Bill so framed as to eliminate as far as possible 'moral' tacking;[1] and
(b) make a joint committee, with the Speaker in the chair, the judge of what *was* a money bill, instead of the Speaker acting alone.

The amendment to the second clause would establish a Referendum in cases where the two Houses of Parliament are disagreed on important issues. I append at the end of this Paper[2] alternative ways of dealing with these three subjects, taken from the order paper of the House of Commons. These may serve at least as a basis for amendments in the House of Lords dealing with the same points.

In spite of what was said at yesterday's meeting, I still feel considerable anxiety with regard to the results that might follow upon the introduction of amendments into Clause 1. As I pointed out, the Government might make this the occasion for declaring war, with the result that the crisis would appear to be provoked by the House of Lords in connection with Money Bills, and not in connection with Home Rule or other great constitutional issues. We should be forced to defend our weakest position instead of our strongest.

I agree of course that this would be a most violent proceeding, that it would justify the Crown in using any constitutional form of resistance, and that to thinking men of moderate opinions it would be very repulsive. I am not sure, however, that these reasons, strong as they are, will necessarily prove a sufficient protection against this mode of attack; or that in certain circumstances an unscrupulous Government might not employ it with success. This would depend very much on the temper of the country at the moment, and on a large number of collateral considerations connected with other legislative projects of the Government, such as the Insurance Bill. It may be admitted that there are at the present moment symptoms that the Government are *not* anxious to have recourse to extreme measures. Nevertheless, the danger is one that should be kept in mind, and every precaution should be taken to make it clear that it is not upon amendments to Clause 1 that the House of Lords will prove intractable.

It has been suggested to me that one method of avoiding the danger would be to postpone the consideration of Clause 1 till after Clause 2 had been disposed of. But it may be worth bearing in mind that it was precisely on a Motion of this kind that Lord Grey's Ministry picked a quarrel with the Lords in '32 and obtained from the King guarantees which proved sufficient to get the Reform Bill through without amendment.

Of course all these fears may be illusory; and indeed I am disposed to think that at the present moment neither the Government nor anybody else can really foresee the probable course of events six weeks hence. The currents and cross currents silently moving below the surface are complex, and defy exact calculation; but so far as the Second Reading debate is concerned, we should proceed I think on the assumption that the Government may, when the Committee stage is reached, regard the most violent procedure as the least dangerous to themselves, and frame our declarations of policy accordingly.

76/147

1. The inclusion in a money bill of matters which, though technically dealing with nothing but finance, had more far-reaching social and political implications.
2. Not attached.

## 23. From George Wyndham

44 Belgrave Square
S.W.
15 July 1911

My dear Willy,

Since writing to you I have seen Scarborough.

We feel that the time is short and that immediate action is needed.

Neither I, nor any other commoner, can help you until the Peers act. We commoners should only hinder you by taking action.

But, if any body of Peers will take action, two results would be possible:–
(i) Lansdowne would know that – so many – Peers meant to act on the resolution carried at your meeting.[1]
(ii) other commoners, and I amongst them, could (a) openly declare on your side and (b) certainly get you 20 or 30 Peers, who tell me that they are sick of 'Politics' and 'compromise', but would *fight* on a straight issue.

Scarborough and I believe that you can lead. I hope you will. Somebody must. Yours ever

George Wyndham

74/100

1. A meeting at Lord Halsbury's house on 12 July where thirty-one peers, including Selborne, resolved to adhere to the line laid down by Lord Willoughby de Broke in a letter to Lord Halsbury of 11 June to 'adhere to such amendments as may be carried in Committee of the House of Lords on the Parliament Bill which would have the effect of securing to the Second Chamber the powers at present exercised by the House of Lords,

notwithstanding the possible creation of Peers, or the dissolution of Parliament'. This was intended as a warning to Lansdowne and those Unionist leaders who, since they had become aware on 7 July of the King's promise to create peers, spoke in terms of 'surrender' as practical politics.


24.   From Lord Willoughby de Broke

Carlton Club
15 July 1911

Dear Selborne,

I think the enclosed very good, and if you think well, I approve of it being sent to a selected list of Peers.

I should however press on you one slight alteration. We want to leave no loophole for that school of thought that considers that 'resistance' means 'resistance till the very last', and then giving way. This is the worst kind of resistance imaginable. Many whom I have canvassed think that honour will be satisfied and the Peerage saved by giving way not at the last minute but at the last second. This will not do.

I therefore suggest that you alter the third paragraph in Page 2 in this manner:– ' . . . would release us from the duty of resistance until we are actually outvoted in the House of Lords by new creations'.

Your own words may be better, so I shall not insist on the alteration, and leave you to use your own judgement.

I think the signatories might be yourself, Lord Halsbury, Lord Salisbury, Northumberland, Bedford, Saltoun, Lovat, Minto, Plymouth, Northcote, Ampthill or any others chosen from the list I sent to Salisbury yesterday,[1] and asked him to shew to you.

If you want a voice from the Backwoods I would sign it myself: but leave this to you.

Our band is increasing daily. I have now got 60 that I think can be depended on. Unless our men who do not want to go to extremes vote with the Rads., the day is ours. If these abstain, as I am told they will, we shall probably have enough to defeat the government. Yours very truly

Willoughby de Broke

74/102


*Enclosure*
HOUSE OF LORDS

We desire to lay before you the reasons which have led us and other Peers to resolve not to acquiesce in the passing of the Parliament Bill without the inclusion of Lord Lansdowne's amendment, and not to facilitate its passage by abstention from voting, supposing the House of Commons to return the Bill to the House of Lords with that amendment struck out.

We believe that the Bill unamended would establish Single Chamber

Government in this country in the most dangerous form possible, because the uncontrolled autocracy of the House of Commons would be partially concealed by the existence of a sham House of Lords. We believe the barren power of two years' delay reserved to the House of Lords to be unworthy of consideration; for indeed the danger to the country would be decreased and not increased if this barren power had not been so reserved, because in that case no Elector could have deluded himself into imagining that the autocracy of the House of Commons was not unchecked. We do not think that we can absolve ourselves from responsibility from the contemplated revolution merely by abstention. We believe that we are supported in our resistance to it by half the nation and that a majority of Englishmen and women deeply resent the violence which is being offered to the Constitution.

We deny altogether the moral authority of the government to force upon the whole people a settlement devised exclusively in the interests of the Radicals and Socialists.

Above all we must be faithful to our trust to the limit of our power, unless we are definitely relieved from it by the nation for whom we are Trustees.

Should a General Election take place, the Electors would for the first time have the opportunity of deciding between the alternative policies of reconstruction and revolution, and of expressing an opinion on the attempt to rob them of their constitutional right to give the final decision on grave national issues. Or on the other hand should Peers be created upon the advice of the Government to drive the Parliament Bill through the House of Lords, we cannot think that such an act, unconstitutional as it would be in its character, would release us from the duty of resistance until it were clear to all men beyond the shadow of a doubt that we had done our utmost.

We do not believe that the credit of the Peerage can be as much injured by the number of new Peers which may be created as it would be degraded by our failure to be faithful to our trust. On the other hand we hold that the creation of Peers to force the Parliament Bill through the House of Lords would "hall-mark" the action of the Government as nothing else could do, and that it would make the electors understand for the first time that full measure of the revolution which is being perpetrated without their consent, whereas surrender to the threat to create Peers would constitute a fatal admission that this method of resolving a difference between the two Houses of Parliament was constitutional and not revolutionary.

| | |
|---|---|
| HALSBURY | LOVAT |
| SELBORNE | WILLOUGHBY DE BROKE |
| SALISBURY | MAYO |

1.  A list of fifty-four peers who 'are prepared to adhere throughout to Lord Lansdowne's amendment, notwithstanding the creation of peers or the dissolution of parliament'. (Copy in MS Selborne 74/98.) Lord Lansdowne's amendment to the Parliament Bill aimed at introducing the referendum for all measures which came under clause 2 of the bill (the clause dealing with general legislation).

25.   From the Earl of Midleton

34 Portland Place
W
16 July 1911

*Private*

My dear Willie,

Supposing your efforts result in a no surrender majority, are you going to stop at the creation of 100 Peers? You I think believe the country will rock; some of us believe the country will golf or bathe throughout August and September and hardly realise how great a shock to all precedent and political morality has been given.

If your object is to impress the public, must you not go a step further?

The moment you admit the new Peers they overwhelm you – Why not adjourn the House and bring Parliament to a deadlock?

This seems to me the only way by which you can make your protest effective.

I say nothing as to the wisdom of your decision, on which I admire your motives without agreeing with the probable results – But in all seriousness I don't think your programme goes far enough to rouse Ulster, much less Great Britain. Yours ever

St. J.B.

3/118

26.   From Lord Willoughby de Broke

Grosvenor House
London, W.
27 July 1911

My dear Selborne,

I have now been through the entire Unionist Peerage and divided it into *Good Bad* and *Indifferent*. *Good* number 109 without the Irish. You know Abercorn has renaged [sic]! *Bad* number 242. (Vide this morning's *Times*) according to Lansdowne's list.

*Indifferent*. I have sent your whip to every one of these.

You were all perfectly splendid at the dinner:[1] and everyone is delighted . . . Yours very truly

W de B

74/149

1.  A 'Halsbury banquet' held on 26 July 1911, called by those peers who refused to follow Lord Lansdowne's advice to abstain from voting against the Parliament Bill. Six hundred guests attended the dinner in the Hotel Cecil, Lord Selborne presiding.

## 27.   To Lady Selborne

20 Arlington Street
S.W.
9 August 1911

My darling,

G.N.C. made a fine speech yesterday,[1] a tremendous indictment of the government, but that only makes his position the more absurd and indefensible. The government put 68 men into the lobby last night, but they will put in 80 or nearly today or tomorrow.

Of the Bishops certainly York, Hereford, Birmingham, Chester, Southwell, Winchester will vote for them possibly more. That combination we can beat. Our danger comes solely from the blackleg Unionist Peers. Really it is a most astounding phenomenon. They include men like Clinton and Fortescue and Longford. If they beat us, then there will be a very serious position in the party. The position already is a queer one. Balcarres, of course with Arthur's approval, is doing all he possibly can to defeat the blacklegs and to get abstainers to leave Lansdowne to help us, but Lansdowne and Curzon won't give him the least assistance.

The Duke of Norfolk is, however, coming out on our side today openly and John has come over and others. So it will be a very near thing. Yours

S

102/23

1.  On 7 August Balfour moved a vote of censure on the government, which was tabled in both Houses, in substantially the same terms. The censure debate in the Lords took place on 8 August.

## 28.   From George Wyndham

St. Fagans Castle
Cardiff
16 August 1911

My dear Willy,

I have waited a few days so as to take a cool view of the situation. I find that with increasing calm there comes increasing certitude that the vote given by the House of Lords for Revolution[1] – owing to Unionist abstentions and acts of treachery – demands prompt and definite action on the part of those who strove to prevent that national disaster.

I cannot pretend that I see, as yet, any clear future for the constitution or the Unionist Party. But of this I am sure. Those who supported you and

Lord Salisbury would themselves be guilty of a great betrayal if they left some millions of honest men, whose hopes they aroused, in doubt and dismay.

I am sure that we ought to take action. I incline to the view that our action ought to be separate from, but not hostile to, the action of Abstainers.

To my thinking, the disaster was primarily due to the fact that our leaders would never decide on a policy and *announce* it. We must not err in the same way.

We are now confronted by a Revolution that is an accomplished fact. We cannot ignore that fact and disperse for two months.

We ought to meet, confer, agree on a policy, announce it, and then never look back until we have won, or the country is ruined because of our failure.

Those are the only alternatives, and no question of political predilections or personal ties should make us shrink from the alternative of deciding and announcing, definitely and promptly, what we consider essential to the safety of the State.

I am available from 1 p.m. on Monday next, 21st August, and believe that the sooner some of us meet the better. Yours ever sincerely

George Wyndham

P.S. The problem before us is difficult, but not insoluble. It can be solved if all who acted together with Lord Halsbury will accept the Referendum for *great* issues, and refrain from insisting on an elected (wholly) 2nd chamber. That would, at present, be a 'sham' policy. It would be advocated as 'democratic' to the crowd, and as 'safe' to the moneyed-interest. Above all no effect could be given to it for some years.

A Revolution demands an *immediate* policy of public safety; not a philosophic debate on alternative constitutions, no one of which could be carried into effect under 3 years.

But the 'Emergency' Policy ought to be sound: i.e. it ought not to traverse any principle of the Constitution we have to restore, or to preclude any solution in consonance with those principles.

For example:– We want *now* a smaller, effective, House of Lords, composed of men who will do their duty; a redistribution Bill – however rough and ready – for the House of Commons; and a Referendum on great issues.

I have read this letter to Plymouth who agrees that action ought not to be delayed.

74/178

1.   On 9 August the Lords received the Commons' amendments to their motion, and there began a bitter debate which ended in defeat for the 'die hards' by 131–114.

29.   From George Wyndham

44 Belgrave Square
19 August 1911

My dear Willy,

I agree that something can be done in public before the beginning of October, with much prospect of success. But I still feel that it would be wise for some of us to exchange views in August.

My reason – of a practical kind – is that I fear ill-advised and discordant outbursts from local politicians. Even some of those who acted together may address meetings.

Willoughby de Broke has written to me asking me as follows 'Will you write to Selborne and ask him to summon a meeting on Tuesday 29th? e.g. Halsbury, Selborne, Salisbury, Willoughby de B, Lovat, Mayo, Milner from Lords: Austen; F. E. Smith, Wyndham, Carson, Robert Cecil and Hugh Cecil'.

I know that Milner will be in London that week as he and I settled we would have a talk.

I am not pressing this and I don't want to be a bore. Indeed I particularly want to shoot Grouse on the 29th with Westminster! This illustrates the impossibility of collecting all with whom we wish to confer.

Let me, therefore, say that *if* you should come to think that an exchange of views was desirable then the 30th of August might be the best day. But, *if*, as I think more probable, you adhere to your present view, then I suggest (a) any one of us with an observation, which he wishes to make *now*, should write it and circulate copies (b) we ought, as you suggest, to meet late in September or early in October.

I could not attend a meeting between 3 p.m. 27th and 30th September inclusive as I must drive Partridges 28th and 29th. There are a good many this year. If you like Partridge driving, have nothing better to do, and do not mind a batchelor party (owing to Death Duties) do come to Clouds and help me to shoot them.

I am, therefore, personally available 25th to middle of 27th September and 2nd to 7th October inclusive.

I am much impressed by your remark about an Elected House of Lords.

That is, precisely, one of the points upon which it is essential that our friends should agree if they can, Otherwise we shall have incompatible views put forward; and derision heaped upon us by the Government and the abstainers.

My own idea – for what it may be worth – is that we ought:

A.   to repudiate the Parliament Act as a possible modus vivendi and

B.   Assert the necessity of an '*Emergency*' Constitution, that would last during the 3 or 4 years necessary to reconstruct a *permanent* constitution.

On that we might all agree if the *Emergency* Constitution, did not traverse our principles, and did not preclude any ultimate form of Constitution in consonance with our principles.

Now that the House of Lords has committed suicide, and that the House of Commons has become the tool of a tipsy tyrant; the country needs 'Constituent' assemblies, that could work out a Constitution and – since we have had a Revolution – these should be established by drastic methods.

For example, as I wrote before – and only for example – we ought to demand the disenfranchisement of Redmond's pocket-boroughs; a reduction in the number of the House of Lords – with say English, Scotch and Irish Peers, elected by their fellows for that *one* Parliament; and a Referendum to sanction fundamental Constitutional proposals made by these two Constituent assemblies.

Some such immediate policy of public safety, would have a chance of rallying all those who acted with us in the crisis; and the rank and file would follow wherever we led. Yours ever

George W

74/184

30.  To George Wyndham

Blackmoor
Liss
Hants
22 August 1911

My dear George,

Many thanks for your letter of the 19th inst.

I do not think we shall get any outbursts even from local politicians in September, therefore I venture to think that if we meet in September and have settled our line of action before October we shall have done what is necessary.

I wrote and told Willoughby de Broke yesterday what I said to you, and I know as a matter of fact that it would have been perfectly impossible to collect either Salisbury or Robert Cecil, and I do not think it would have been any use holding our meeting without them. The first thing to do is to fix a date for the meeting. I should propose Thursday 21st of September. Will that suit you? And to meet again on the 22nd, if necessary. The place I should propose would be 38, Grosvenor Gardens.

It is very good of you to invite me to Clouds from the 27th–30th of September, and I will come with the greatest pleasure.

Now I turn to your suggestion that any of you who have observations to make should write them now, and that brings me to the question on what subject are we going to deliberate when we meet? I would define it thus, let us agree if we can on a common policy in respect to all important matters which now hold the field, and let us speak with one voice on the platform and in the councils of the Party, and thus make our views prevail within the Party.

I know we shall have suggestions made for the formation of a new Party. My reply to that is, and I have had some experience in the formation of a new Party, that the task is impossible to carry out successfully, and that the attempt to do it would constitute a disastrous blunder, therefore I discard that method altogether. On the other hand we can, by united action, I think beyond all doubt, make our views prevail within the Party, which is the same thing as capturing the Party and the Party machine.

Of course it is always difficult for eight or ten men like ourselves to come to an agreement on matters on which we feel strongly, but there our Cabinet training should help us, and I think we ought to be able to come to a common agreement on all subjects except one, and there I do see a great difficulty, that is on Tariff Reform. The Cecils are indispensable to us, but on Tariff Reform there is no concealing the fact that their views are extremely different to those of the rest of us.

The last question is who are to be summoned to our meeting? The suggestion which I have made to Willoughby de Broke is that to our first meeting should only be summoned the front bench men of both sides including therein of course F. E. Smith and Pretyman and the three Peers who acted as our Whips in the Lords; and I even went so far as to question whether we might not meet in the first instance without Lord Halsbury, and I tell you why. I do not think even now he is prepared to consider the reconstitution of the House of Lords, and that is the first thing we shall have to deal with, and if I am correct and that is the attitude which he developed, well then really our whole meeting is thrown away. Yours ever

S

74/190

31.   From George Wyndham

44 Belgrave Square
S.W.
23 August 1911

*Private*

My dear Willy,

Delighted that you will come 27th 30th September to shoot Partridges at Clouds. We ought – with any luck – to have good sport.

Qua business:–

(1) You are right. We cannot meet now.

(2) I hold, as strongly as you do, that we ought *not* to form a Party.

(3) But we ought to agree on a common policy and announce it. We both hold to that.

(4) The preliminary difficulties are – as you say –

(a) Jim Salisbury and Hugh Cecil hate Tariff Reform.

(b) Halsbury and Willoughby de Broke(?) [sic] are opposed to a reconstitution of the House of Lords.

These are the difficulties which we have to surmount.

(5) In my opinion, we can only hope to do so by (i) attacking the Parliament Bill and declaring that it amounts to an abolition of the Constitution (ii) Insisting in an Emergency Policy, to restore a 'temporary constitution' that could construct a permanent constitution. i.e. disfranchise Redmond's rotten boroughs and cut down the House of Lords to, say, 300 to 400 members.

Tariff Reform I cannot give way. Can Hugh Cecil? I think he can; if we concentrate on an 'emergency' constitution.

(6) Date of meeting. Here to my regret I am in a difficulty. My Yeomanry was to attend manoeuvres 9th–23rd September. Manoeuvres are cancelled. But I await orders for training and fear that the training will be for the same period. I am trying to get it ante-dated; and will telegraph when I know my fate. At present Monday 25th or Sunday 24th, or Saturday evening 23rd, seem the earliest moments on which I can count.

(7) I dare to suggest that it would be unwise *not* to ask Lord Halsbury to our first meeting. Please consider the great risk of affronting him and many of the 114. On the other hand, if Halsbury and W de B can agree with those who are prepared to contemplate more drastic measures the game is won.

(8) I ought to tell you that I shall see Milner on 30th and, probably Willoughby de Broke; merely as individuals. But – if I can get them nearer together – the time will not be wasted.

(9) Merely in passing – there are meetings going on now in the country. Mark Sykes M.P. tells me that he has addressed 5 in different parts of the country and that at *all*, the audience waited till he declared himself as a supporter of the 'Forwards' and then cheered to the echo. He tells me that the audience (1) want a constitution; i.e. an effective 2nd Chamber, but (2) are tired of an Hereditary House.

Do not trouble to reply. I write fully as nothing else is of value between men who mean to fight side by side until they win. Yours ever

George W

74/198


32.  To Austen Chamberlain

Blackmoor
Liss
Hants.
4 September 1911

Private

My dear Austen,

. . . I am very sorry to bother you on your holiday, and this letter requires no reply, but I want to tell you why the meeting on October 2 is being summoned. I am responsible for that, and I have summoned it principally, though not exclusively, in order to prevent some of our friends from doing anything foolish. There is a movement towards schism, and some atmosphere of intrigue. Now intrigue I abominate, and schism I will have nothing whatever to do with. You and I know and have had far too much experience to encourage schism, and anything more absurd than to secede from the party, the vast majority of which enthusiastically approve of our recent action, I cannot image. Therefore I have summoned this meeting of those of us who used to meet at 38 Grosvenor Gardens, whether Members of the late Unionist Government or Privy Councillors, in the first place to be sure of stopping this nonsense; but in the second place I do desire that we should have our proper weight in the councils of the party, and our proper influence over the opinion of the party, and I think that this can best be assured if we can agree to speak with one voice on all the important questions of current politics duing the autumn campaign.

I enclose a copy of a little draft memorandum (A) I have been drawing, to show you what is in my mind; and (B) a copy of another one, the object of which is to concentrate attention on the great complexity of the constitutional problem which is opening out before me.

If we can agree on the general lines of the constitutional reform we desire to support, I should not be adverse to establishing an organisation within the party for the promotion of that special object, and for two reasons: in the first place it would be a great instrument for education of the party on the subject, and the party requires education badly, and the Conservative Central Office at all events is extremely loath to take on that work of education; and in the second place it will tend to keep us together who have been working together in this crisis, and so to increase our influence; and remember we may want the strength this bond will give us badly in the near future. I should never be surprised if Arthur Balfour retires, and we have no guarantee yet as to who may endeavour to take his place. Yours ever

Selborne

P.S. I hear that George Curzon is still very busy. I was afraid you might not be able to come on October 2, but you shall know all that passes and we shall certainly have to meet again.

79/71

Enclosure
Memorandum by Lord Selborne

A.

*Confidential*

The great majority of the party approve of our action over the Parliament Bill. We are therefore in a peculiarly favourable position to influence the opinion and so the policy of the party. But to exert this influence it is essential that we should be agreed among ourselves and support each other in our speeches in the autumn campaign: and I have suggested a meeting on October 2 for the purpose of arriving at as complete an understanding as possible on those political questions which are likely to be most discussed in the immediate future.

On Tariff Reform we have almost all of us reached complete agreement, so I need not touch on it here.

On the following additional questions I see no reason why we should not be able to arrive at such an understanding which will enable us to speak with one voice upon them –

1. The Constitution.

| | |
|---|---|
| House of Lords: | Composition and Powers. |
| House of Commons: | Franchise Laws, Distribution of seats, payment of members. |
| Relation of the two Houses. | Referendum. |

2. Home Rule for Ireland.
3. Disestablishment and disendowment of the four Welsh dioceses.
4. The position of Trade Unions as affected by the Osborne Judgement, and the Trades Disputes Act.[1]
5. The settlement of industrial disputes.
6. The Insurance Bill.
7. Poor Law Reform.
8. Land Policy, small owners, etc.

We must also consider how best to consolidate our position inside the party and provide for our mutual support.

If I have omitted a subject which ought to be discussed perhaps one of my colleagues will be good enough to mention it.

B.

*Confidential*

The electors have been very apathetic all through this constitutional crisis. Why? Because they have not understood all that is involved, nor does the British elector understand in the least, as the American elector does, what the constitution of his country means to him. That this is so is not the fault of the elector; it is the natural result of our peculiar history. Of course the Socialists and Radicals will not attempt to teach the elector anything about the constitution, and it is essentially the duty of our party to do so; but the Central Offices have shown a remarkable unwillingness or incapacity to do this, and I believe a special organization which we might call the League of the Constitution, or by some such name, is required for the purpose. The object of this memorandum is not to offer any solution of our constitutional difficulties, but to show how extraordinarily complicated they are going to be, and how necessary the institution of an organization is, the special function of which shall be to try and find the right solution of these difficulties, and to educate the electorate to accept that solution.

If we only had the Parliament Act to consider, the matter would be comparatively simple: we should only have to consider how best to reconstruct the House of Lords, and I think our choice would be confined to two alternatives only. We should discard all fancy franchises, such as County Councils, or Members of Parliament, and if we decided on an elected House would choose our electors from the existing electorate with possibly some limitation of the franchise to voters of 30 years old and upwards. The other alternative would be a House composed partly of Lords of Parliament taken from hereditary peers, and partly of Lords of Parliament appointed by the Crown for a term of years. If there were 150 of the latter chosen in some such way as suggested in Lord Lansdowne's Bill, I think I have a suggestion to make which would meet the objection raised to the election of another hundred by the hereditary peers from their own number that by that process the Unionists would secure an unfair and permanent majority. My suggestion would be that at the beginning of each Parliament the Crown should be empowered on the advice of the Prime Minister to appoint 30 hereditary peers to be Lords of Parliament for that Parliament only.

But our task is going to be nothing like so simple as this. I regard it as quite certain that an Act conferring Home Rule on Ireland is going to pass into law, and the effect of this will be to make the constitutional question very difficult and very interesting, and quite new.

We shall not be able to repeal the Act conferring Home Rule on Ireland.

We cannot possibly allow x number of Irish Members to remain in the British Parliament after Home Rule has been conferred on Ireland and to manage England or Scotch affairs.

We cannot refuse to Ireland a voice on imperial affairs, or on the common affairs of the United Kingdom.

Therefore the inevitable consequence of the establishment of Home Rule in Ireland will be the establishment of Home Rule in England and in Scotland.

This means a federal constitution, and we had better face the facts of the case at once, because it will mean subordinate Parliaments for England, Scotland, Ireland and possibly Wales; and a Parliament for the management of the common affairs of the United Kingdom e.g. the customs tariff, and for the management of the affairs of the Empire, navy, army, foreign and colonial policy, India, etc.

The problem is further complicated by the possibility that some day the Dominions may be prepared to enter into an organic political union with us for the better management of our joint imperial concerns. I shall only note this fact, and touch upon it again presently; I shall not attempt to deal with it exhaustively in this memorandum.

Now consider the second chamber problems which emerge from these considerations.

Shall we want a second chamber or House of Lords at all for the Parliament of England only? I say 'Yes', but surely it could only be an elected chamber.

Shall we want a second chamber or House of Lords for the United Kingdom Parliament? If we were dealing only with the United Kingdom, I would say 'Certainly, Yes', and that for strictly imperial matters and matters common to all parts of the United Kingdom, a second chamber or House of Lords, composed in equal portions of Lords of Parliament appointed from among the hereditary peers and of Lords of Parliament appointed by the Crown for a term of years, would give us exactly what we want for the purpose; but the case would be different if ever the Dominions were prepared to join us in a Parliament which had no concern with the affairs of the United Kingdom, but only with strictly imperial affairs; it is doubtful if we should want a second chamber at all for such a Parliament: certainly I do not think the Dominions would be satisfied with any second chamber that was not elected.

And supposing the Dominions ever do consent to join us for imperial purposes, which is the ideal to which many of us look forward (and which some of us think will be the only possible way not only of maintaining the British Empire, but of preventing the Mother Country and the Dominions alike sinking to a position of comparative unimportance in the world, considering what the size and strength of the United States, of the German Empire and of Russia will be in the future), we shall find ourselves in this position. Four Parliaments, an English, a Scottish, an Irish, a Welsh, concerned only with the local affairs of those parts of the United Kingdom. A fifth Parliament for the United Kindgom concerned only with affairs common to all the parts of the United Kingdom, but which are not imperial affairs. And a sixth Parliament concerned only with imperial affairs common to all parts of the Empire.

What a vista of constitutional change is opening before us! How far it will open we cannot yet say. That it will open to the extent of a federal or semi-federal system for the United Kingdom, if a Home Rule Act passes for Ireland, I feel no doubt. Whether it opens further will depend upon the Dominions, but we must begin to clear our own minds, and settle what line we shall take under these circumstances, and what advice we shall tender to the electors.

S

AC 9/3/58

1.  A judgement in a case brought by the secretary of the Walthamstow branch of the Amalgamated Society of Railway Servants, W. V. Osborne, which held that it was illegal for a trade union to provide for parliamentary representation by means of a compulsory levy. The Trades Disputes Act of 1906 concerned the right to strike and to picket.

33.   From the Marquess of Salisbury

The Camp
Lossiemouth
N.B.
12 September 1911

*Confidential*

My dear Willie,

You have set me a hard task to answer your letter, because not only is the subject rather overwhelming but I recognise the importance and the difficulty of the redemption of the Unionist Party which and no less than which you have good reason to urge.

But first I do not think I was out of the way unfair in associating the views of the *Pall Mall*[1] with extreme Tariff Reform, because the connection is by no means uncommon and is only an extended form of the creed that T.R. is all important and that everything else must be made to give way to it. Not only do many hold this view, but a considerable number not only put T.R. as a whole in this transcendent position but even the food tax by itself. You of course do not go this length, or rather you take much wider ground. You, I understand, contend that we must not choose between political objects (of the first rank) in which we believe and that it would not only be bad principle but bad tactics to drop e.g. the food tax merely because it does not pay. As to principle with submission I do not agree. Sincerity indeed is everything in politics and not only sincerity of the heart but sincerity which will shine before men. But no one will doubt the sincerity of a party who have lost three Elections and many of the capital institutions of their country largely on behalf of this tax. And as to tactics, are you right historically? Even recently the other side have not lost but gained by abandoning – for the time – Home Rule which had twice been rejected by the constituencies. Nor has Home Rule itself lost anything. But I do not desire to press the point at this moment.

I turn to your most interesting memorandum which I have anxiously considered.

I am hardly able to go as far as you do when you say that the passage of a Home Rule Bill is certain. It is, I agree very probable, but there are several considerations on the other side. First the inherent difficulties; e.g. finance, and the position of the Irish members – which you mention in another connection; and next the difficulties on other subjects that beset the Government – in the Insurance Bill and in the tremendous shake that they have probably received through the Strikes.[2] I suspect that this last is so serious that but for the food tax we might almost hope to have them out. But as it is Home Rule I am afraid *is* very probable. Now your memorandum deals with our attitude on that assumption. You suggest the thesis for discussion – not, I understand, as your considered opinion – that the passage of Home Rule for Ireland should make us contemplate as a necessary consequence Home Rule all round; and that Home Rule all round would relieve us of the necessity of contending that any political power should be restored or left to the peerage. There may be much to be said for these views considered in the abstract, but the thesis is of course designed for practical application. Should I be right in going a step further and saying that if it became accepted as our attitude, you suggest we should indicate these conclusions publicly either during the Home Rule discussions or immediately after? Do you think this would be wise?

I look upon Home Rule all round as an evil. Unlike Imperial Federation it is a movement not towards greater consolidation but towards less consolidation – centrifugal not centripetal. But whether you take that view or not, consider the effect of this policy at home. England no doubt would gain by it, but it would surrender Scotland and Wales to the very disasters of violent legislation which it is the whole object of your new movement to prevent; in Wales it would disendow the Church and destroy the Church Schools and in both Wales and Scotland it would hand over the owners of all kinds of property to their bitter enemies. It is true that even as it is we may not be able to ward off these calamities, but what would our friends think of us – our friends in Scotland and in Wales, if we announced it as our policy following on Irish Home Rule to abandon them to their fate? We cannot do it. Moreover there is Ulster. Ulster might resist. The resistance may or may not be futile, but while it lasts we cannot treat Home Rule as definitive. Of course by Home Rule I mean separate Parliaments. Glorified County Council devolution is another matter, and if the units are made small enough such devolution may contain a solution. But that is not what is meant, and if there is to be Home Rule all round it must be done by the Radicals. Very likely that is your view too, but speculation as to necessary consequences, when we do not support those consequences, would be fruitful in misconception. Surely our attitude should be to bring home to the Country the logical and administrative bog into which Irish Home Rule brings them and to convince them that but for the Parliament Act it would never have happened, and as the Government are driven further and further into advocating Home Rule all round, to reinforce with every fresh example the same lesson.

Let me add not a more cogent but a wider consideration; and because it is tactical it does not follow that it is ignoble, for to retain the confidence of our supporters is a trust we are required to fulfil. And our supporters are Conservatives. Anything like sweeping change is in fact repugnant to a large and influential proportion of them. Whatever your own opinion the Conservative Party can only assimilate change gradually. I believe the advocacy of almost any sweeping change will lose you enough votes to put you into a minority. This letter is already portentous and I have not touched on a part of your memo. But I cannot yet pretend that I have sufficiently thought out the situation·if and when we have six parliaments in these islands. I do not however feel at all sure that a second chamber would not be required in the momentous decision which the archi-imperial

Parliament would have to take. Nor should I like to say finally that poor little England who on the whole likes the peers should not when she has a Parliament of her own make use of them. But on these points again I would not anticipate the ultimate outcome. It is agreed that our business is to take the sting out of the Parliament Act. If it is necessary in this process to purpose a scheme of Lords Reform then it should be a Conservative scheme, without reference – I venture to think – to the possibility of Home Rule all round which we need not take account of till it comes.

Beside all this there arises the question of our attitude on the other issues raised in your agenda for October 2nd. You will be relieved to learn that I cannot deal with them in this letter. Broadly speaking we should surely try, while holding on like grim death to our Conservative supporters, to make it easy for those who are horrified at the Strikes to join us. So far as our principles permit, we should leave out from our platform what repels the moderate Liberal, and we should insert what will attract the non-socialist working man – not be opportunists but very moderate when we are going against the current. Yours ever

S

6/116

1. The *Pall Mall Gazette*, Unionist newspaper, at this time edited by J. L. Garvin.
2. From the middle of 1911 serious strikes, often accompanied by violence, broke out, beginning with a seamen's and firemen's strike in June, followed by dock and railway strikes.


34.   To the Marquess of Salisbury

Blackmoor
Liss
Hants.
19 September 1911

My dear Jim,

Now first of all as to food taxes, I think you are quite accurate in associating the views of the *Pall Mall* with extreme Tariff Reform. What I meant was that a man who could so lightly throw over fundamental conservative principles because they did not at the moment happen to pay, would certainly not hesitate to throw over food taxes, if he thought they did not pay. I deplore the fact that the advocates of food taxes have not been as considerate or fair as they should have been to those staunch Members of the party, who could not agree with them; but what I think has never been understood, and perhaps is not even now quite understood by yourself, is that the importance and merit of food taxes is a very deep and genuine conviction with a great many of us.

I do not think your illustration about the Liberals and Home Rule is quite accurate. They have never dropped Home Rule. Their leaders have said 'Home Rule is not the question we put to the front at the present moment', but never has a Liberal leader and practically never has a Liberal candidate said 'I am not in favour of Home Rule'; and surely that is not the attitude you suggest should be adopted. What would be the electoral value of that attitude – we are in favour of food taxes, but we are not going to press them now???

Now I pass on to the Constitutional question. My purpose has begun to be served in turning your mind on to the questions, which I believe are going to force themselves on us. Do not for a moment suppose that it is my intention to meet Home Rule otherwise than with a direct negative, or to fight it otherwise than on a straight issue. I have no idea of putting forward a federal scheme as an alternative to Home Rule. The utmost that I shall say on the platform is that if the Radicals think when they have added Home Rule for Ireland to the Parliament Act, that they have done with the Constitutional question, they are making the biggest mistake of their lives, because that question will then only be beginning. But I do want to try to think ahead a little, and the letter I have elicited from you is a very satisfactory first result. Of course if Home Rule does not pass, then for the moment all this drops. I write on the assumption and belief that it will pass. You are quite right in saying that I am not putting forward any final opinion. I am putting forward these for discussion. If we are forced to a federal system or semi-federal system, I should like to work in the English peerage, I would welcome any way of doing it, but I see great difficulties, though on reflection after your letter I will modify what I wrote. I am disposed to think now that it would not be more difficult to work the English peers into an English Parliament, than to work the United Kingdom peerage into the re-constitution of the United Kingdom Parliament; but that now will be difficult enough.

You go on then to say that, even after Home Rule for Ireland had been forced upon us, the reconstruction of the constitution must be the work of the Radicals and not our work, because 'the Conservative Party can only assimilate change gradually' and 'the advocacy of almost any sweeping change will lose you enough votes to put you in the minority'. That that proposition is generally true, I do not dispute, but I cannot possibly accept it as true of the case which I am considering. I certainly cannot adopt for one moment the position that when the Radical Party have destroyed the constitution, the Constitutional Party is to sit down in despair, and not to attempt to reconstruct it. I for one, under no circumstances, will sit down and allow England to be ruled by fifty or sixty Irish Members, who have a Parliament of their own at Dublin; nor do I for one moment believe that the average Conservative would be other than idignant with us if we did sit down under such circumstances.

Your point about the abandonment of the Scottish and Welsh Conservatives is on the other hand a true one, but if it is admitted to be a true point, it does not follow that the other one is, or that, because we acknowledge our obligation to the Scottish and Welsh Conservatives, therefore we are to submit to the rule of these Irish Members, and to accept whatever constitution the Radicals are pleased to give us. Yours ever

S

6/122

35.   To Austen Chamberlain

Blackmoor
Liss
Hants
7 October 1911

My dear Austen,

Mrs Chamberlain wires me that she has very kindly sent you the draft telegram I was going to send you.

From it you will see how very anxious I am to have you at our meeting at 2.30 p.m. on Thursday October 12 at the rooms of the 1900 Club in Pickering Place off St James's Street, and to see you first either the night before or that morning before noon.

The meeting will be quite private and something under fifty ditchers of both Houses will be present. I hope and believe that I have steered in a way you will approve, to avoid anything like a split in the party and yet to keep the ditchers together as a club within the party which others of the party, who were not ditchers, can join.

The central work of the Club is to be the reconstruction of the constitution after the Government have done destroying it, to do the study and education for this subject for the party which the T.R.L.[1] has done for the tariff, only of course nothing on anything like the same scale will be required.

I think also that the members of the Club will on other matters too fuse themselves to the tip of the party spear. Yours ever

Selborne

Hurrah for Canada![2]

AC 9/3/57

1.   Tariff Reform League.
2.   In September 1911 the Canadian electorate rejected a trade agreement concluded with the United States of America.

36.   Memorandum by Lord Selborne

[November] 1911

*Confidential*

## HALSBURY CLUB[1]

The provisional Committee which was appointed make the following recommendations,

1.   Membership of the Club to be confined to Unionist Peers, Members and ex Members of Parliament, as already decided.

Candidates for admission to the Club to be elected by the Executive Committee.

Each member of the Club to pay an annual subscription of one guinea.

2.   The affairs of the Club to be managed by a President, Chairman of the Executive Committee, Honorary Secretary, and Treasurer (all of which officers have been already elected), and an Executive Committee of twelve members of the Club.

The officers of the Club to be ex officio members of all Committees of the Club, and to be elected annually along with the Executive Committee at a general meeting of the Club.

3.   The objects for which the Club has been founded can be best promoted by the members of the Club meeting as often as possible for mutual consultation and discussion. The Executive Committee should appoint special committees, representatives of all sections of the Club, to work out the problems connected with the great questions for which a solution has to be found, such as the reconstruction of the constitution, national defence, the social problem.

It should be the duty of the Executive Committee to arrange for meetings of the members of the Club, either at wholly informal dinners or at other times, to discuss the various phases of these questions, while the special Committees are considering them, and, when the Committees have reported, special meetings of the Club should be held to consider these reports.

In this way, members of the Club will be able to clear their own minds, systematically thrash questions out, and make a valuable contribution to their solution by the party.

Similarly these informal meetings can be utilised for the exchange of views between Members of both Houses of Parliament as to the immediate, or connected, or consecutive action to be taken in respect of parliamentary opportunities as they arise during the session.

Public meetings can, if necessary, be held from time to time under the auspices of the Club, and the Club will do all in its power to advance the Unionist cause and to strengthen the Unionist party; but the great feature of the Club's work must consist in the constant intercourse of its members for the discussion of public questions before they have reached a critical stage, for the consolidation of their own opinions, and for the initiation of parliamentary and public action according to the opportunities of opposition.

It will be the duty of the Executive Committee to keep in close touch with the leaders of the party, and to keep them informed both by personal communication and through the whips.

Mr. T. Comyn Platt has been appointed to assist Lord Willoughby de Broke as Secretary of the Club, and offices have been engaged at 38 Parliament Street.

It has been decided to hold the inaugural public meeting of the Club at the Caxton Hall at 3 p.m. on Monday November 13.

Selborne: Chairman

75/2

1.    At a meeting of the club on 6 November 1911, L. S. Amery, Waldorf Astor, Sir Edward Carson, Lord Hugh and Lord Robert Cecil, Austen Chamberlain, G. Lloyd, Lord Lovat, Lord Milner, W. Ormsby-Gore, E. G. Pretyman, F. E. Smith, Earl Winterton and George Wyndham were elected to the Executive Committee (75/4). A motion was passed unanimously that 'the members of the Halsbury Club . . . express to their fellow-Unionists in both Houses their desire to co-operate heartily with them in defence of Unionist principles and tender to Mr. Balfour and Lord Lansdowne as leaders of the Party the assurance of their loyal support in the coming struggle' (75/1).

# Chapter 3

## 'Our party is a difficult one to lead': The Unionist Opposition, 1912–1915.

1.  To Robert Palmer

Eastwell Park
Ashford
Kent
10 January 1912

Dearest Bobby,

. . . One month more and the session of 1912 will begin, truly a momentous one and the first under the Parliament Act – any bill read a second time between March and June 1912 will become law between March and June 1914 provided that the House of Commons goes through the form of passing it again twice in the interval. Bills for Irish Home Rule, Welsh disendowment and disestablishment, manhood (and possibly women's) suffrage, the reversal of the Osborne judgement *and others* will be so passed. Many people expect us to defeat the government on one of these bills in the House of Commons. I have no such expectation. We shall knock the Government to pieces in argument and in the country on the English subsidy to an Irish Home Rule Parliament, on the retention of Irish members to vote on British affairs at Westminster, on the miserable meanness and shame of Welsh disendowment; etc. etc.

We shall win by elections, but we shall not defeat them in the House of Commons; these and other measures will all pass into law sometime in 1914; then we shall defeat them, unless they put a similar series of bills into the slot in 1913 which will not emerge from the machine till 1915. For the effect of the Parliament Act will be wholly centripetal on the party in the House of Commons, and the more measures they put into the slot the less centrifugal the influence. With the gag and guillotine as instruments and with supreme audacity in their use it becomes a simple question of arithmetic: 100 days of parliamentary time to spare and four bills = 25 days apiece, or five bills = 20 days, or ten bills = 10 days. You will see that this is not a violently extravagant forecast. There is no more a House of Commons than a House of Lords. There is nothing but the Cabinet, subject to the continuous but slight check of the Crown and the violent but occasional check of the electors.

Meanwhile the industrial outlook is very gloomy. The miners federation is threatening a national strike for a minimum wage,[1] the cotton and wool operatives have both refused to allow the employment of non-union men and have been locked out. Your loving father

S

109/15

1.  In October 1911 the Miners' Federation of Great Britain altered its rules to make it possible to call a general coal strike. They took a ballot on a strike for minimum wage rates and on 18 January 1912 the return showed a majority of over two thirds in favour of a strike. Notices were given to stop work after 29 February, and despite government intervention a strike began on 1 March 1912.

2.   To Robert Palmer

25 March 1912

My dearest Bobby,

The coal strike is still with us and is likely so to be for sometime to come though in a diminishing degree. I mean that the men want to go in and will go in in some places, and the passage of the government bill[1] will probably help those to go in, that is really all that can be said for it. In South Wales they will not go in. There really are only two possible courses. To hold the ring only and to hold it so strongly that every man who wants to work can work and no-one is intimidated. This the government has not done, because, although it has nowhere refused protection, it has carefully refrained from pledging itself to give protection everywhere, and because it has actively interfered.

The other possible course is the establishment of courts of arbitration with power to enforce obedience on masters and men. Of course you cannot put 1000 men into prison but you can put their leaders into prison and you can attack their funds.

The government has not done this either, because, while they have declared for a minimum wage and safeguards, they have been afraid to try and enforce either.

Altogether they have cut a very sorry figure.

I think our people in the House of Commons were right to vote against the second reading of the government bill. It would never have done to make ourselves partly responsible for such a bill. But I am very sure that we should not do so in the House of Lords, because there is no principle involved (for me) the bill is a piffling bill and the occasion of national distress and misery too great to justify our acting for our party advantages, and we cannot vote against it without throwing it out. Such as it is it is a step on the road towards industrial courts with sanctions behind them and, therefore, I approve of it pro tanto.

I hope to be able to speak out all my mind in the debate tomorrow. Your loving father

S

109/41

1.  On 15 March 1912 Asquith announced that the government would bring in a bill to set up a minimum wage machinery on the lines of its proposal of 28 February, i.e that a minimum wage in each district should be fixed by district conferences at which a government representative should be present and should decide, failing agreement. This scheme had been rejected by the owners in Wales and Scotland, and by the Miners' Federation, but the government pressed on with the bill, which was first opposed by the Unionists in the House of Commons. This opposition was withdrawn at the report stage, and the bill also passed through the Lords, whereupon the miners called off their strike.


3.   To Robert Palmer

Brooks's
St James's Street
16 April 1912

Dearest Bobby,

The Home Rule [sic] has been introduced[1] and an impossible attempt it is to compromise between Colonial Home Rule and Federal Home Rule. I do not see how it can possibly work. Even if all the Irish were most reasonable and most loyal and most conciliatory it could not work. It does not give the Nationalists what they want or a system which they could work with any satisfaction to themselves, and it does give them the leverage of 42 members at Westminster to exact amendments.

To Great Britain it offers the impossible fate of subsidising Ireland to the tune of two millions a year with no corresponding influence on its expenditure or on the government or laws of Ireland but with the menace of 42 Irish members able if they choose to interfere actively in all British domestic concerns.

And N.E. Ulster is irreconcileable and cannot be coerced if in earnest. The finance of the bill is still quite obscure, and we cannot begin to analyse and measure it till the bill is printed.

The 'guarantees' socalled are mere flummery. What is the value of guarantees in a case like this which can only be enforced against a recalcitrant Irish government and Parliament by force? It is not true that the scheme is a stepping stone to a federal one. In no federal constitution in the world is the postal service given to the provincial or state government. In this bill it is given to the Irish government. Why? Simply to give it patronage of a petty kind, but invaluable to the Nationalist leaders, in every parish and village of Ireland. Why Asquith has not long before this cut the knot of all his difficulties, Home Rule, disestablishment, education, House of Lords, by going in for one big federal scheme I shall never understand. The nominated Senate of this bill with its small numbers and immediate extinction in case of difference in a joint sitting with the House of Commons is only interesting as showing the kind of second chamber they contemplate at Westminster if and when they do take up that question. This Senate will probably be remodelled or extinguished altogether in Committee. About that the Government are indifferent. But the bill will pass the Commons once twice and thrice although it will be torn to shreds in debate.

The Welsh church bill is to be introduced next week. It is a happy and exact fact, which I did not anticipate, that all Unionist speakers, however personally indifferent to church questions, testify that the interest on this question at all meetings is very great and that the hostility to disendowment is manifested by radicals and noncomformists as well as by Unionists and church people.

The government will let the sleeping dog of the labour problem lie, if it can, and that will be the inclination of our people too. But we must not let them be cowardly.

We must frankly and sympathetically meet the yearning for material betterment, but we cannot allow organised syndicalism to jeopardise the existence of the nation and of our very political and social structure. We cannot allow the existence of two governments in the United Kingdom, one de jure responsible but now partially impotent, the other de facto irresponsible and grasping at mastery. The problem is of enormous difficulty and we must make big blunders. Courage alone can save the nation and the workmen from themselves, and give time to Wisdom to reveal her face. That the government will become weaker and weaker in the country and more discredited, and that we shall have a series of by electoral triumphs I do not doubt.

Nor do the government doubt it. Their plan is to hang on for the necessary two years of the Parliament Act till some date in 1914, or better still from their point of view till some date in 1915, when their unpopular measures will have become law by the effluxion of time, and then to incorporate some new gigantic bribe to the democracy in a budget and couple it with some piece of legislation connected with the tenure of land on which a fresh appeal to class hatred can be based, and then to dissolve. They calculate that the bribe and the passion will obliterate their unpopularity and sweep us into a debacle at the polls. You will think that this is the exaggerated forecast of a too partisan and therefore unfair father.

Nevertheless it is true. But I believe in the political insight and the power of judgement of our people as I am sure of the fundamental justice of their intentions, and I believe the calculations of Lloyd George to be in fact a profound miscalculation. The British democracy is still the least unfit democracy to wield power of which the world has yet furnished example. I am very anxious about the international situation. I can no longer shut my eyes to the proof of the settled determination of Germany to establish a military hegemony over Europe. But more of that when we meet. Your loving father.

S

109/49

1. The third home rule bill was introduced into the House of Commons by Asquith on 11 April 1912.


4.   Memorandum by Lord Selborne

[July] 1912

Radicalism is a dying creed, and the Radical party has ceased to draw inspiration from it. Disestablishment and disendowment are of the essence of the old Radical creed and what is their value as a cry or inspiration in England to-day? Absolutely nothing. Imperialism and Socialism are living creeds and when Radical Ministers seek for ideas which will move the minds of men they have to turn to one or the other of them. To-day Mr. Winston Churchill seeks inspiration from Imperialism and Mr. Lloyd George from Socialism.

When a great party ceases to have a creed of its own and borrows from the creeds of others it sinks into unlovely and unprofitable opportunism and that is precisely what has happened to the Radical party to-day. Little Englanders support a strong navy and a vigorous foreign policy, rigid economists support a recklessly extravagant expenditure, individualists of the Manchester School support measures designed to prepare the way for a collectivist State.

Unionism is a living creed because it includes Imperialism and because Unionists are true to the National ideal. But on the side of domestic politics Unionists, who do not understand the only possible basis of their political faith, are also in danger of lapsing into a lifeless opportunism. The secret of success in politics is to believe something whole-heartedly and to avow it. Men will always follow a steady consistent and fearless lead. A living creed is one which inspires faith and courage.

Unionists believe in the nation and Unionist policy should be always national as opposed to the sectional policy of the Radicals. They oppose disestablishment because it would remove the national recognition of the truth of Christianity, and most of us believe that a national policy not based on the faith of Christ is a political edifice founded on the quicksands. They oppose Home Rule because it would disintegrate the greater nation, which is made up of Irish and British. They have sworn an undying hatred to the Parliament Act because it has deprived the nation of the power to decide national issues and they support the referendum because it would restore that power to the nation. They uphold the right to own private property and the right of a man to work, because they believe that the strength and moral health of the nation is dependent on the liberty of the individuals of which it is composed. They are opposed to unbridled collectivism because it is incompatible with the liberty of the nation, and to uncontrolled individualism because it is incompatible with the happiness of the nation. They know that all men are not equal and that a political system founded on the theory of equality must fail, but they believe that all men and women have a right to the best opportunity which can be afforded them of using their gifts to the best advantage, and therefore they are prepared to use the power of the nation to assist the individual and thus adjust the balance between individualism and collectivism. It is in this faith that the Unionist policy of social reform must be worked out.

In this creed there is immense inherent strength and Unionists will have no difficulty in winning for it the enthusiastic confidence of the nation, provided that they are true to it. The most stupid thing which Unionists can do is to attempt to bid against the Radicals in the opportunist auction mart or to gloss over any part of their political faith which they are told is unpopular. A good illustration of what I mean is to be found in the attitude of certain Unionist candidates to tariff reform. Tariff reform is accepted by the great majority of the Unionist party as an essential part of their policy of social reform, and the repeal of certain taxes on food and the substitution of other taxes on food are part of the policy of tariff reform. A Unionist who is a free trader naturally and rightly does not preach tariff reform, but can anything be more foolish than the attitude of Unionist candidates, who profess tariff reform and do not preach it? Of course free traders vote against them and tariff reformers will not work for them. Courage is far the most valuable quality in politics and the voters will always trust a man who has the courage of his convictions and when he leads they will follow, but they have no respect for insincerity, timidity or evasion.

The Government are going, if they can, to enfranchise more than two million youths without any redistribution of seats. It is not easy to understand on what grounds these youths, from whom no qualification is to be exacted, are considered to be more fitted to exercise the vote than rate-paying women, nor why their somewhat restive natures should be held more capable of contributing to the stability of the nation through the exercise of the franchise than the Mothers of English families, nor how it can be right to remove only electoral anomalies which are unfavourable to the Radical party and tenderly to preserve those which are favourable to it. It is a fresh illustration of that unnational and sectional conception of politics which dominates the Radical party. The attitude of Unionists should be exactly the reverse to stand out for a national settlement of the question such as Mr. Gladstone and Lord Salisbury achieved in 1884.[1]

We are living under a Single Chamber System; under a Single Chamber System there can be no security for liberty, no assurance of national stability; it is a makeshift borrowed from the machinery of revolutions for frankly revolutionary purposes. Some people attach importance to the two years' power of delay left to the House of Lords under the Parliament Act, but the existence of that power of delay does not vitiate the contention that we are living under a Single Chamber System. To recite the fact that the House of Commons, of its sole will by a vote thrice repeated in two years, could abolish that power of delay or the picturesque historical remnant of the House of Lords itself is sufficient proof.

A temporary and discredited majority of the House of Commons are Masters of the fate of the country, and the Electors are powerless to prevent the enactment of constitutional changes on which they have never been consulted and of which they disapprove.

It will be the duty of an Unionist government in the first session of its existence to restore stability to the Constitution. The Referendum must be made part of our Constitutional machinery so that on occasions of sufficient gravity the Electors may be consulted on changes which vitally affect them. In all countries where the Referendum exists it has been used by the Electors to check revolutionary and reactionary legislation equally and it is the only method by which a democratic country can secure itself effectually against usurpations of power by a group of ministers working through the party machine. A Second Chamber must be created permanently representative of the nation, and therefore truly representative of the political parties, classes, and interests, of which the nation is composed, and that Second Chamber must be endowed with those full powers which the experience of the civilised world has found to be necessary for Second Chambers and without which Second Chambers are useless and dangerous shams.

The Unionist Party will naturally be reluctant to break with the historical past in its reconstruction of the Second Chamber, but it must remember that, important as an attachment to historical links is, it is still more important that our Second Chamber should possess the strength which can only be derived from a real representation of the National life and thought. The Second Chamber of the future, no more than the House of Lords in the past, should interfere in the special function of the House of Commons, the supply and appropriation of the money required year by year for the service of the Nation, but it is essential that it should have the power to resist vast social or political changes, disguised as finance, on which the Electors have never been consulted or of which they have not approved.

The fiscal policy of the Unionist Party is Tariff Reform. Through Tariff Reform, more than by any other means, they believe that stability can be given to the National industries, unemployment decreased, the level of wages raised, the increase of small owner cultivators of the soil secured, and the larger share of the trade of the Empire assured to the people of the Empire.

The Unionist Party is resolved to.do its utmost to increase the number of occupying and cultivating owners of the soil in the United Kingdom, because it believes that the greater the number the owners of the soil, the greater the strength of the Nation and the greater stability of the National institutions. The difficulty of the task has been gravely increased by the depreciation of national credit caused by the language and policy of the present Government and the finance of the Scheme will need cautious handling. The rural landowners have made great efforts to provide good cottages for the labourers who work on their land, and the proofs of the success with which they have worked, though at a constant financial loss to themselves, are to be seen spread abroad over every county. But serious gaps in the supply remain, and no task could be more congenial to the National spirit of Unionists than to frame and pass laws which will ensure the filling of those gaps and the completion of the supply of good cottages for the agricultural labourers, a class for which very many of them have an admiration and affection founded on close association from childhood and which they know to be a national asset of incalculable value. The same difficulty has been successfully met in Ireland by special Acts of Parliament and analogous remedies can be applied in England or Scotland or Wales. It should be made a special feature of the Scheme, wherever possible, to attach thirty to forty rods of garden ground to each cottage.

The Unionist policy in respect of agricultural land may be summarised thus, provision of cottages for the labourers, the multiplication of occupying and cultivating owners, the application to England, Scotland and Wales of that splendid scheme of agricultural organisation, privately managed but State assisted, for which Ireland has to thank Sir Horace Plunkett.

The Unionist Party must also grapple with the problem of Urban Housing and Slum destruction and those complicated Social problems which are dealt with in the report of the Poor Law Commission and portions of which have been steadily shirked by the present Government.[2] It will take the National Insurance Act,[3] mismanaged as it has been, as the basis of a really National Scheme. It will not grudge to its authors the praise due to the recognition of the principle of contribution by the beneficiaries nor to the genuine effort to deal with the problem of consumption nor to other excellent features in it, but it should try to remodel its defective parts, the jeopardy of the independence of the great Friendly Societies, the insufficiently considerate treatment of women and the failure of the Act to link up the Nation and organise the help of the weak by the strong. Especially should it consider the wife who bears children and the widow left with young children dependent on her as National Jewels to be guarded and tended as such.

In the matter of Education, we are bound by every consideration of honour and principle to stand by the right of the parent to choose for the child the religious instruction it shall receive. We believe that education without religion brings evil and not good to a nation; we recognise the right of those who think otherwise to withdraw their children from religious instruction altogether, and the right of Nonconformists to secure for their children that particular form of religious instruction which they prefer and which is so oddly termed 'undenominational'. But we uphold with all our strength the equal right of those who cherish the principle of definite religious teaching to secure that teaching for their children.

Outside the field of religious instruction there is a great field open to the Nation for an improvement in its system of Elementary Education. Unionists recognise the splendid and devoted efforts of the Board of Education, of the Inspectors, and of the Teachers, but they feel that there is still something wrong. The Teachers are over-pressed and have insufficient time for thought and improvement. The formation of character has in the children been neglected for the acquisition of knowledge and the knowledge imparted has not always been of the most useful kind . . .

In the pursuit of social reforms the Unionist party must be true to their belief in the principle of Local Government. All who have been brought into contact with the Civil Service at Westminster must unite in admiration of the patriotic devotion, the ability, hard work and administrative purity of the civil servants. Nevertheless one of the evil tendencies of the time is to centralise all government at Westminster, to leave less and less discretion to local bodies and to subject them more and more to the minute inspection, interference, and even dictation of a bureaucracy centralised in the Metropolis. Radicals believe in local Government just as much and as far as they believe in democracy, that is when and only when the majority of a local body or of the electors happen to agree with them. At the present moment the Education Committee of a County Council cannot move a row of hat-pegs from one room to another in an elementary school without obtaining the permission of the Department of Education. Against this tendency the Unionist Party must set its face resolutely. It must give more power to the local bodies, it must free them from the excessive control of the Government Departments, and it must confine these departments to their proper sphere of general superintendence in all matters of local government.

The unrest in the Labour world does not frighten Unionists. They recognise that it arises from the natural and legitimate aspirations of the manual workers to improve their position. Further, it is quite untrue that the Unionist Party is the opponent of the Trades Unions. If the Trades Unions did not exist they would have to be invented. What the country is suffering from is the anarchical condition of the Trades Unions. We see the leaders of Trades Unions bargaining with employers and making an agreement and we see that agreement at once rejected by those workmen whom the leaders represent or repudiated by them a few months later for no apparently adequate reason. We see ballots taken in which the vote of youths of sixteen is allowed the same weight as that of the married man of thirty and we have good reason to believe that those ballots are not really secret. The more workmen in a given trade who belong to the Trades

Union of that trade the better, so long as the ballot is really secret and youths under 21 are not allowed to vote and leaders when once elected are given real power to negotiate and conclude arrangements and those arrangements are honourably observed when once concluded.

It is probably a mistake to try and make arrangements in respect of wages or conditions of work for long periods; probably a two-year arrangement will meet most cases; but when once an agreement has been made it should be a binding legal contract for the period for which it has been made. Organisations, whether of men or masters, who break such agreements, should suffer in heavy penalties and individuals who incite to their breach should be held responsible for their actions and be liable to punishment.

If men and masters cannot trust each other to keep their promises, there is an end to all stability in trade and manufactures and the sufferings of the country will be terrible.

Although the stronger the Union the better, it is the indefeasible right of any individual to refuse to join one. The man may be foolish, or selfish, or he may have an honest distrust of the management of the Union and a dislike of its policy. That is not the question. If he cannot follow his own judgment in the matter, he ceases to be a free man. Or if, having joined a Union, his contributions are taken against his will to support political principles of which he disapproves, he ceases to be a free agent. While supporting Trades Unions as a necessary and beneficial national institution the Unionist Party must stand unflinchingly for the right of the individual workman to hold aloof from them if he chooses, to withhold his money from a political propaganda of which he disapproves if he belongs to them, and to work or strike when he chooses whether he belongs to them or not. It must give protection to all men who want to work always and it must repress intimidation in all forms whether directed against the striker or against the worker.

In old days a strike or lock-out was fought out between employer and employed and the Government confined its function to keeping the peace. Nowadays, no sooner has a trade dispute broken out but the Government is dragged in to try and compose the strife. That this is so is the inevitable consequence of the complexity of modern society and of the fact that important trade disputes now closely and deeply affect the public at large, the nation as well as the disputants. But it may be doubted whether the intervention of the Government has really done good up to now. In most cases its intervention has simply added a third party to the dispute.

Compulsory arbitration is impossible. But when once the Government has been authoritatively invoked to interfere in a dispute it should have the power to refer it for settlement to tribunals established for that purpose and those tribunals should have power to make their decrees effective for a limited period. The organisation of employers is just as necessary as the organisation of the employed, and it is curious and not very creditable to them that employers have found it more difficult to combine than workmen. Such combination is just as necessary for their legitimate self-protection as it is for that of the workmen and without combinations on both sides there can be no effective and binding collective agreements and therefore no stability in industrial conditions. There are certain kinds of strike which no Government could ever allow to become effective. The nation must live and it cannot be sacrificed for either workmen or employers in a trade dispute. The whole nation must not be held up. The nation must under all circumstances be able to eat and work and live, and the Government is bound to intervene decisively in any strike where the existence of the nation is jeopardised. Nor can a Government allow the irresponsible leader of any organisation, however powerful, to usurp the functions of Government and to establish an 'imperium in imperio'. Certainly no Unionist Government would ever allow itself to be so displaced.

Finally the Unionist party should do its best to promote the principle of co-partnership in every form as the antidote to Syndicalism or Socialism and as a surer way than a strike of securing an equitable division of profits.

In the regions of Imperial policy the Unionist position may be simply stated. A Navy definitely and indisputably strong enough for the world-wide service of the Empire, a Regular Army adequate in size for its special duties perfectly trained and equipped, a Territorial Army which shall contain in its ranks the number of officers and men which have been fixed as the necessary establishment and conforming in reality to the standard of training which has been authoritatively declared to be essential; friendly relations with foreign powers on the basis of the equality of all civilised states and the supremacy of none; the loyal support of all servants of the Empire working faithfully for the Empire; the sympathetic but firm administration of India; the pure and unselfish rule of backward races; everywhere the pax Britannica; and always the ideal of a permanent effective organisation for the common purposes of diplomacy and defence of the mother and daughter nations of the Empire.

Nothing has been said about the cost of this policy, and it will cost much, nor about economy, because economy, according to the old meaning of the word, is incompatible with democracy and for modern politicians on either side to promise retrenchment is sheer cant and hypocrisy.

Nevertheless it is a truth from which we cannot escape that financial stability and sound credit are as essential for the life of a nation as the health of the people or the strength of the Navy.

The Unionist programme is therefore an ideal towards which we must work as the means to carry it out become available. Rather let the Unionist party remain excluded from office than involve the nation in expenditure without at the same time seeing clearly whence the money will come to pay for it. To act otherwise is the part only of politicians seeking party ends and not the welfare of the nation.

79/80

1.  In 1884 the House of Lords attempted to delay the Gladstonian government's franchise reform bill by demanding that the government first pass a redistribution bill, reckoning that in the storm of local jealousies raised by the latter both bills would founder. Gladstone denied the right of the second chamber to force a dissolution on this issue, and called an autumn session to re-submit the bill. Meanwhile a fierce agitation against the Lords swept the country and eventually direct negotiations took place between Gladstone and Salisbury. As a result the franchise bill and redistribution bill were passed as agreed measures.
2.  A Poor Law Commission appointed by the Unionist government just before it left office in 1905 which in 1909 produced two reports, a majority report and a minority report, both advocating far-reaching reforms of the Poor Law system. They were fended off by John Burns, the President of the Local Government Board, and were not acted upon until 1929, by a Conservative government.
3.  The National Insurance Act of 1911, which was a contributory scheme to insure the working population against sickness, and certain sections of that population against unemployment, by means of compulsory contributions collected from employers and employees. The Friendly Societies (which had covered much of the less difficult ground on a voluntary basis) were, with the trade unions, brought in as 'approved societies' to administer the money benefits for their members.

5.   To T. Comyn Platt

Blackmoor
Liss
Hants
19 September 1912

My dear Mr. Platt,
I have been greatly interested and touched by your letter of Sunday[1] and I will endeavour to reply to it as indeed it deserves.

My interest in the Irish question arises from two considerations, our obligation of honour to Ulster, and my all absorbing belief in the necessity for the federation of the Empire. If the Empire cannot be federated for the purposes of mutual defence and for Foreign Policy, I do not believe that it can survive, nor do I believe that the United Kingdom can remain permanently without passing under the domination of some foreign power; therefore, whatever remains to me of political life will be mainly devoted to trying to advance the federation of the Empire.

If we succeed it will mean that there will exist a true Imperial Parliament, in which the United Kingdom and the Dominions of the Empire will be represented on some basis of population or wealth, and that it will be concerned exclusively, as well as the Government which will depend upon it, with the Foreign Policy of the Empire, the defence of the Empire, the rule of India and the dependencies of the Empire, and possibly at some future stage with the trade of the Empire, but it will have nothing to do with the domestic affairs of the United Kingdom or with any part of it or with the domestic affairs of the Dominions. The Dominions will each continue to have their National Parliaments as now and their provincial assemblies, and the question we shall have to ask ourselves is how shall then the domestic affairs of the United Kingdom be managed? They will then be as they are now of two classes, first the affairs which are common to every part of the United Kingdom, England, Ireland, Scotland and Wales and secondly matters which are the strictly local concern of the component parts of the United Kingdom. It follows from this that in addition to the real Imperial Parliament in which the Dominions will be represented, there must be a Parliament for the whole of the United Kingdom to manage those affairs which are common to all parts of the United Kingdom as there is a Canadian Parliament which manages those affairs which are common to all the provinces of Canada. In my opinion that Parliament for the United Kingdom might continue to manage the strictly local affairs of England, Ireland, Scotland and Wales as well as the affairs of the United Kingdom. I do not say that there should not be any further devolution say to County Councils, but I do not think there will be any absolute necessity for any other subordinate Parliament in the United Kingdom except the Parliament of the United Kingdom. That is my opinion and my preference, but I know well that there will be another school of thought that will think differently, and which will urge that in addition to the Parliament for the United Kingdom, which will be concerned with the affairs common to the whole of the United Kingdom, there should be a Parliament in England to manage exclusively English affairs, a Parliament in Scotland to manage exclusively Scotch affairs, a Parliament in Wales to manage exclusively Welsh affairs and two Parliaments in Ireland one to manage the strictly local affairs of Ulster, the other those of the rest of Ireland.

Now, although I am not in favour of that solution I should not consider that any great disaster had overcome my country if that solution were to prevail; all that we care for in the principles of the Union would have been maintained and perfected in the Imperial Parliament and in the Parliament of the United Kingdom.

From this point of view let us see what the defects of the Home Rule Bill of the present Government are. In the first place, it endeavours to coerce Ulster into a Parliament for all Ireland. In my opinion this can never be done, if, as I know is the case, the Ulster men are determined it shall not be done. In the second place the Bill is wholly inconsistent with the federal principle in that it gives the Irish Parliament a partial control over customs and complete control over the Post Office, both of which are subjects that under either a unitary or a federal scheme should be preserved to the Parliament of the United Kingdom. But, if Ulster were taken out of the Bill, and if the Customs and the Post Office were reserved for the

Parliament of the United Kingdom, then even this Bill more or less would fit in with a federal scheme for the United Kingdom, if that plan should be preferred to the unitary plan after the federation of the Empire had been secured and a truly imperial Parliament established.

Therefore, while I have just as great a reverence for the principles of the Union as you have, yet I see that the application in the future may be different to what it has been in the past.

I will now approach the subject from another point of view. In every State there must be an ultimate authority. It is the legal existence of that ultimate authority which differentiates a civilised from a barbarious state. Now in the United Kingdom that ultimate authority resides in the partnership of the Crown and the people. The central point of iniquity in the proceedings of the present Government is that in the settlement of the Irish question they are endeavouring to evade that ultimate authority. They are trying to settle it without giving the people through the electors any opportunity of decision. I hold that the attitude of Ulster is morally and constitutionally right under these circumstances, and I am quite sure that the Home Rule Bill will not pass into the irremediable past until the people have had an opportunity of giving their decision.

Now what will that decision be? I am quite certain that it will never under any circumstances be in favour of coercing Ulster to join an Irish Parliament against her will, therefore I put that aside altogether. If the electors decide wholly on our side there is an end of the question; but they may decide that, while Ulster is to have the choice of a separate local Parliament of her own or of remaining as she is now represented at Westminster, the rest of Ireland should have a Parliament of its own. I think that would be a very foolish decision, but under the circumstances I am supposing it would have been the deliberate decision of the people of the United Kingdom and the Crown would under these circumstances undoubtedly give its whole support to that decision. Now am I to take up arms against my King and my fellow country-men because the decision is given against me in a very important matter, but one which I do not think to be irremediable? I should not think it irremediable, because I think that with the establishment of Imperial Federation all dangers could and would be averted.

I have two more observations to make. I will never say that it is always wrong to take up arms. I should myself take up arms without any hesitation for the Monarchy against a republic, and I have already said that I think Ulster is wholly justified in her present attitude. But civil war is the ultima ratio and the last party in the world that ought to turn to arms if it can possibly avoid it or go outside legal and constitutional forms is the Conservative and Unionist Party. If they did so lightly it is likely that it would mean the breaking up of Society and the end of the Nation, for it would remove all restriction on Radicals and Socialists who are blinded to the value of tradition and authority. It would give, in fact, an immense impetus to disruption. Finally it is not really the United Kingdom alone which would be affected by it but the whole Empire, and this brings me to my second observation.

Speaking generally public opinion in the Dominions is against us on the Irish question, it is only natural that it should be. They have known what the value of Home Rule has been to them, and they do not appreciate the fundamental difference between Home Rule 60 miles from England and Home Rule six thousand miles from England, nor have they ever had an Ulster question and they have yet to learn what it means. It is our business to teach them and they can be taught, but I have no hesitation in saying that, if we made a false step, we might put back the federation of the Empire for years, perhaps render it for ever impossible and that is without any comparison the greatest treason of which we could be guilty to England.

You are most welcome to show this letter to Carson or to Willoughby de Broke. Ever yours sincerely

Selborne

77/18

1.  77/14.

6.  To A. Bonar Law

Brooks's
St. James's Street
19 December 1912

My dear Bonar Law,

. . . Our party is a difficult one to lead, at present. I knew it pretty well from 1886 to 1905, and when I returned home in 1910 I saw a great change in it, for the worse.

I saw a want of faith, a vacillation, an opportunism, which disgusted me at least as much from its folly as from the evidence it afforded of shallow convictions and want of moral courage. But my wife knows the party from earlier days. She says to me 'You knew the party only in prosperity from 1886 to 1905. I knew it intimately from 1880 to 1886, *and it was exactly the same as it is now*'. I believe she is quite right, and that the fons et origo mali was the disastrous leadership of the Duke of Wellington and Sir Robert Peel which taught the party to conform to the notions of its opponents and to turn its back on its most cherished convictions; sheer opportunism in fact.

I speak of the bulk of the party, the Tories – I do not for a moment wish to draw any distinctions between them and the old Liberal Unionists, but I do think that the present flabbiness is mainly with the Tories by origin. When leaders lead as you lead, the followers will end by following, and the new style 'to mean what you say and to say what you mean' is really supreme wisdom, because of its simplicity and because of the moral courage which it connotes, and the greatest and rarest and most demonstrably greatest of all the political virtues is moral courage, and yet 'how few these be that find it.' Moreover the English are a simple people and your attitude of mind is one that they will thoroughly comprehend and appreciate. I tell you that because you are not an Englishman and I am a very stupid Saxon. About the Press I can give you no comfort except to say that its influence in England can be very easily exaggerated. It is a will o the whisp (sic) which a leader with convictions must not attempt to follow or it will surely land him in a bog. If he rides straight forward it will come back to his heel like the rest . . . Yours sincerely and faithfully

Selborne

B.L. 28/1/64

7.   From A. Bonar Law

Pembroke Lodge
Edwards Square
Kensington, W.
20 December 1912

Private
My dear Selborne,
Many thanks for your letter.

The position is, as you know, very difficult, and how it will develop I do not know. What I am sure of is that while the great bulk of our Members are agreed in desiring to get rid of the food duties, none of them have any clear idea as to what the policy of the Party would then be. For example, it is Manchester which gives the keynote of opposition to our proposals, but articulate Manchester is not represented either by manufacturers or workmen. The whole cotton trade is done through middlemen, and the men engaged in that trade are opposed to Tariff Reform not at all on account of the food duties, but because many of them deal in foreign goods as well as in English, and I am quite sure that if the Party had agreed to a Referendum on food duties there would immediately have been pressure from Manchester, just as strong as it is now, to submit the whole tariff to a referendum.

For the moment all that we can do is to have patience and see how things develop. Yours very sincerely,

A. Bonar Law

73/75

80.   Memorandum by ?

5 June 1913

*Private and Confidential*

It is provided by Section 2 of the Parliament Act that, when a Bill has been rejected by the House of Lords for the third time, supposing two years have elapsed between the Second Reading of that Bill in the House of Commons on the first occasion of its introduction and the Third Reading in the House of Commons on the third occasion of its introduction, the Bill shall on its third rejection be presented to the King for his assent. It is not quite clear when the House of Lords will reject the Home Rule Bill for the third time within the meaning of this Section. For rejection is defined as not passing; and it would seem that the House of Lords cannot definitely be said not to have passed a Bill until the prorogation which closes the session in which the Bill has been submitted to it. But whatever may be the exact date of the third rejection, it is at least clear that it must be a considerable time after the Third Reading of the Bill in the House of Commons. And the Third Reading in the House of Commons cannot be before the 9th of May, 1914, on which date will be completed the two years from the Second Reading in 1912. There is therefore a year, and probably a little more than a year, before the Home Rule Bill will receive the Royal Assent.

But we must face the fact that unless we are able to stop them, it is probably the intention of the Government, notwithstanding the threatened resistance of Ulster, to pass Home Rule at the time which, under the Parliament Act, it is possible for them to pass it. It seems therefore most important that the leaders of the Unionist Party should be prepared to encounter this Ministerial intention and should know quite definitely what they propose to do to stop the Bill passing or, if it pass, how they will meet the situation that must ensue. The difficulties and disagreements of 1911 arose mainly because the Unionist Party was taken by surprise at the decision of the King to create peers. It is desirable to avoid any such difficulty in the future by a timely review and recognition of probable events and a plan of action well settled beforehand. This Memorandum is humbly intended as a contribution to the discussion of the question: What ought the Unionist Party to do in view of the intention of the Government to pass Home Rule next summer under the Parliament Act?

It is generally agreed that the resistance of Ulster is the main obstacle in the Government's way. And I suggest that if, as we are assured and believe, it is the purpose of Ulstermen to set up a provisional government to carry on the administration of so much of Ulster as adheres to their party, it would be best that that provisional government should be got up immediately on the Royal Assent being given to the Home Rule Bill. If definite action were postponed to a later date, an impression of unreality would be given in England, and every day that passed would give to Home Rule in English opinion, and perhaps also in Irish opinion, the strength of an accomplished fact. But it seems to me that the Unionist Party would incur a grave and even intolerable responsibility, if they did not exhaust every conceivable means of preventing the passage of the Bill and the consequent immediate rebellion of North-Eastern Ulster. It is true that the setting up of a separate government would not necessarily, and perhaps would not actually, lead to violence and the effusion of blood. Theoretically there need be no fighting in the matter, and it is quite possible that fighting might be altogether avoided. But the risk would certainly be very great; especially would it be great in those districts which lie on the borders of Protestant Ulster, where Unionists and Nationalists are mixed in not unequal proportions. Dangerous rioting and violence might easily arise in these districts. Moreover the struggle, if it led to the success of the Unionist Party at a General Election, must result in the repeal of Home Rule; and, though the feeling for Home Rule is much weakened in the South and West of Ireland, it may be doubted whether the people there would quietly submit to its repeal. It seems to me therefore that we are bound to stop Home Rule passing, if by any means we can.

There is a method by which the House of Lords can compel the Government to refer the question of Home Rule to the people. The Army Annual Bill provides that the discipline of the Army is to continue in the United Kingdom until the 1st of May of the following year. Another date is fixed for the rest of the King's Dominions. The House of Lords might next year introduce into the Army Annual Bill an amendment limiting the continuance of the Bill in the United Kingdom to (let us say) six weeks or two months, unless before the expiry of that time, either a Bill had received the Royal Assent referring the Government of Ireland Bill to a poll of the people, or Parliament had been dissolved, and providing that if such a referendum or dissolution had taken place, the Army Annual Bill should in that case continue until the usual date in the following year.[1] This would be a perfectly constitutional proceeding. The Army Annual Bill is passed every year precisely for this very purpose, that Parliament should be able to prevent the Crown using a Standing Army in a manner inconsistent with the liberties of the subject. This Parliamentary control has always belonged to both Houses, and the power of the House of Lords has been in this respect unchanged by the Parliament Act. It is plain that during the year intervening between the 1st of May, 1914, and the 1st of May, 1915, it is not merely possible but exceedingly likely that the armed forces of the Crown might be called upon to suppress the resistance of Ulster. The House of Lords has clearly every right to insist that before the Standing Army is used to establish Home Rule in Ireland against the will of a large section of the Irish population, it should be at least certain that the electorate approve of Home Rule and of such a use of the King's armed forces.

If the House of Lords took this course, what would the Government do? They could not go on and ignore the decision of the House of Lords because the state of the Army would become chaotic on the expiry of the Army Annual Bill and it would be highly unconstitutional, if not positively illegal, to keep soldiers in service at all, so soon as the Army Act had expired. They could not, I think, advise a creation of peers in face of their own precedent of 1911 in which a dissolution was expressly made the condition of the King's consent to such a creation. They might resign, and this would be perhaps technically the constitutional course. But it would certainly be a course advantageous to the Unionist Party rather than otherwise. They might accept a referendum; for Mr Asquith has always maintained that there are very exceptional cases in which a referendum would be legitimate, and this case would plainly be an exceptional one. But I think they are most likely to dissolve, endeavouring to raise again the cry against the House of Lords that was successful in 1910.[2]

The question is whether such a cry would this time be successful. The circumstances are very different. The Budget of 1909 was plausibly and effectively represented to be a measure distasteful to the rich but in the interests of the poor. Nothing of the kind could be said in respect of the Army Annual Act. The Government in fighting the Election would be obliged to deal with the Ulster question and to explain how they proposed to get over the resistance of Ulster; and, discredited by their reluctance to appeal to the people, they would have to attack the House of Lords for having merely insisted that security should be taken against using British soldiers to shoot down Ulstermen before the British people had had an opportunity of expressing their will. The best line that the Government could take, so far as I see, would be to say that Ulster was only a pretence, and that the House of Lords were really anxious to wreck the land programme of Ministers. To avoid this line of attack, I think the Unionist leaders should press rather for a referendum than for a dissolution as the course they would prefer; they could then effectively rejoin to the Government that it was the latter who had chosen to dissolve, the House of Lords and the Unionist Party being perfectly satisfied by the alternative of a referendum, which would not have interfered with the Government's promised land legislation. In general, I may observe, a referendum is a safer thing to ask for than a dissolution, because it is not exposed to the imputation of some indirect motive of party advantage to be gained by a General Election.

I believe that if the Government dissolved they would be beaten; and that the plan of amending the Army Annual Bill would therefore succeed. But if this plan should be adopted, it is most necessary that it should be carefully led up to from this moment onwards. Let me enumerate some of the things that might be done to prepare public opinion for the contemplated action of the House of Lords. A Convention might be held in Belfast at Easter next year, avowedly to organise the provisional government to be set up so soon as the Home Rule Bill received the Royal Assent. Earlier than that an Address should be moved, say in February, in both Houses of Parliament, petitioning the King either to dissolve or to require a reference of Home Rule to the people. A similar Address might be presented by Unionist Privy Councillors. During the winter a Petition to the King should be signed by all Unionists in Ireland imploring him to refuse his assent to Home Rule. This might be presented with some publicity by Unionist Peers and Privy Councillors at the commencement of the session. During the present session something might be done on the same lines. Under the new procedure a Suggestion might be moved to be added to the Home Rule Bill, providing that the Bill should not come into force until it had been referred to the people. If it be objected to this that the Ulstermen could not support it, since Ulster will not undertake to accept Home Rule even after it has been approved by the British people, I should answer that that difference of opinion between English and Irish Unionists is already recognized, and that the effect of it might be completely discounted by openly announcing it in the press beforehand and in the speech of the mover of the Suggestion. But if it be desired to avoid an appearance of disunion in the House of Commons, much the same object might be attained by the House of Lords rejecting the Home Rule Bill on Second Reading with a declaratory resolution insisting that the Bill must be referred to the people. Thereupon on the next day some Unionist peer might move to read the Resolution to which the House had come, and then order a Bill to be brought in referring the Government of Ireland Bill to a special poll of the people. This Referendum Bill would then be carried through all its stages in the House of Lords. But it would not be necessary to have it debated in the House of Commons. It would be quite sufficient for Mr. Bonar Law to ask the Prime Minister whether the Government intended to take up and pass into law the Home Rule Referendum Bill. Of course he would refuse. Thereupon we could say with truth that the House of Lords had made its offer and that the Government had rejected it. If this should be decided upon, it would be necessary to draft a Referendum Bill without delay; but I suppose that could easily be done on the Australian model.

Probably other methods of stimulating public opinion might be hit upon. But what seems to me all important is, first, that the Unionist leaders should make a definite plan how they will deal with the situation that will arise next year; secondly, that they should subordinate everything to carrying out that plan and should systematically prepare the party, the press, and public opinion generally, for what they intend to do. All differences of opinion on other matters must be healed or hidden out of sight, and every resource concentrated on the single object of carrying through a final campaign of resistance to the passing of Home Rule.[3]
1.   Could G of I Bill receive Royal assent in interval?
2.   No they could dissolve and fight on the basis of our unpatriotic actions

77/41

3.   This memorandum suggesting the strategem of amending the Army Act, thus putting all military discipline into suspense and depriving the government of the use of the army everywhere in the United Kingdom for two years, was not composed by Lord Selborne, though it bears a few comments by him in the margin. Possibly it was the work of Lord Willoughby de Broke

who, Lord Blake writes (*The unknown prime minister*, pp. 174–5) was one of those Unionists who 'contemplated action of this sort'. Whosoever its author may have been, it reveals that a plan on these lines had taken definite shape as early as the middle of 1913, some six months prior to the date given by Blake, when a 'correspondent' suggested such a plan to Bonar Law, on 5 December 1913.

## 9. Memorandum probably by Lord Selborne

[September?] 1913

The plan which I sketched to you in conversation yesterday and which you asked me to put upon paper is this: that some sort of pronouncement or manifesto, perhaps most conveniently in the form of a letter to Lord Loreburn,[1] should be made by the Unionist leaders and should be something to the following effect.

The paper would begin by a courteous appreciation of Lord Loreburn's intervention and would go on to assent to, and even to emphasize, his statement of the gravity of the impending crisis in Ireland. It would speak with great respect of his suggestion that there should be a conference with a view to a settlement by consent, and it would recognise the immense social and political advantage of such a settlement as contrasted with the deplorable consequences of even the most righteous appeal to force. It would then proceed in language like the following:

'But we notice that Mr Redmond rejects the idea of a conference unless Unionists first assent to the principle of Home Rule; and the language of members of the Government, though not so uncompromising, appears to be substantially to the same effect. Nor even if Home Rulers were prepared to enter a conference without any limitation, would there seem to be much hope of bringing that conference to a good result unless there were a preliminary understanding as to the main principle on which the contemplated settlement in Ireland should be made. The question follows: Can the Unionist Party in present circumstances assent to the principle of Home Rule? Can they agree, that is to say, to treat Ireland as a distinct nation from Great Britain which, as a distinct nation, must have its own national parliament and government? – for such we conceive to be the principle of Home Rule.

We are very sensible that not only the considerations that recommend a settlement by consent but also the lower counsels of party advantage seem to point to giving an affirmative answer to this question. Plainly, to pass Home Rule would, from a merely party point of view, assist the Unionist Party; for it would involve a great reduction in the Irish representation in Parliament and the detachment of what remained of that representation from its present close alliance with the Liberal Party. The language of part of the press, in imputing to us partisan motives in resisting Home Rule, is therefore extravagantly misapplied. As mere partisans we might well wish for its immediate passing into law. But it is needless to say we cannot so determine our duty. We are soberly convinced that the division of the United Kingdom into two nations would produce calamitous evils, such as have taken place in Scandinavia, in the Austro-Hungarian Empire and elsewhere: nor do we see how, on the one hand, if Ireland be regarded as a nation, anyone can deny the obvious right of Ulstermen to determine whether they will be members of that nation or not; nor, on the other, how a national parliament and government could practically be set up without the approbation of Mr. Redmond and his supporters, who declare that the exclusion of Ulster from Ireland would be inconsistent with Irish nationality. Conscious therefore though we are of the dangers that threaten in Ireland and of the partisan advantage which a surrender of principle would bring with it, we feel that as honest men and patriotic citizens we cannot rightly give consent to Home Rule. If it be answered that there is no lack of honesty and patriotism in bowing to the inevitable and endeavouring to reduce, since we cannot avert, the dangers that we fear, we must rejoin that until it is certain that the people approve Home Rule we cannot trust its passing as inevitable. To come to an understanding behind the backs of the people for enacting a law which would, we believe, be deeply injurious both to Great Britain and Ireland, would clearly be wrong.

Is there then nothing to be done? Must we be content to let our country drift towards the perils which lie so plainly in the future? We think not. It seems to us that the question of principle might easily be determined by the only authority that can determine it, the electorate of this country; and that, when that question was determined, a conference might usefully be held with a view of carrying out the decision of the people peacefully and effectually. That decision might be given at a General Election. By this we do not of course mean to suggest that the Government should forego the advantage of passing Home Rule without the consent of the Lords which they now possess. If there were a dissolution, the new House of Commons would still be able, if it chose, to pass Home Rule under the Parliament Act in spite of the opposition of the House of Lords. The conference might in that case be an assistance to the Government and to Home Rule; it could not possibly be a hindrance. But, if the Government be unwilling to advise a dissolution, we make in precise form an alternative suggestion which we think ought to be acceptable to them. We suggest that Parliament should be immediately convoked and that by general consent a Bill should be passed into law referring to a poll of the people the question: Shall the Government of Ireland Bill be passed? This Referendum might take place before Christmas; and it would be provided that, if it resulted in favour of the Government of Ireland Bill, that Bill should, unless Parliament otherwise directed, receive the Royal Assent on, (let us say), May 1st without further proceedings in either House of Parliament, but that, if the decision of the electors were against the Bill, it should not be passed under the provisions of the Second Section of the Parliament Act. When this Referendum had taken place, whatever its results, a conference might follow between the leaders not only of the two great British parties but also of all sections of opinion in Ireland. Supposing (as we hope and believe would be the case) the decision of the people were against Home Rule, the conference would consider whether any modifications in the present Government of Ireland, any extension of local government, any improvement in legislative machinery, any reform in administration, might be carried consistently with the unity of the United Kingdom: and again, if the electors had pronounced for Home Rule, the conference would revise the details of the Home Rule Bill so as to mitigate if possible the apprehensions of the minority in Ireland and to meet the criticisms which, in Cork and elsewhere, have been made against the Bill's financial provisions. If the conference succeeded, Parliament would be asked to carry out its decisions: but, if it failed, the decision of the people, whether in favour of Home Rule or of the Union, would remain and be operative. In the one case the Home Rule Bill would pass into law on the 1st May: in the other the veto of the House of Lords against Home Rule would become absolute.

This proposal appears to us to deserve the assent of all parties. It does not imperil Home Rule except upon the hypothesis, which we affirm but our opponents deny, that Home Rule is disapproved by a majority of the electors. Supposing Home Rule to be approved by the electorate, it secures to it the best possible chance of a peaceful acceptance. It gives ample room for the exertions of mediators and for counsels of conciliation without requiring of either Unionists or Liberals any sacrifice of principle; it is honourable; it is democratic; it gives hope of peace. Upon these grounds we recommend it.

Contrast our proposal with the plan which apparently finds favour with the Government. They intend, they tell us, to pass the Home Rule Bill into law under the Parliament Act; and they remind us that, if at a subsequent General Election the electorate place a Unionist majority in power, that majority can repeal what has been done. That is to say, they contemplate, first, that a rebellion should be provoked in Ulster and then that all the bitterness and disappointment which would be involved in the repeal of Home Rule should be inflicted upon its supporters in the South and West of Ireland. Such a plan promises not peace but war, not a settlement of the Irish difficulty but its bitter aggravation, is not loyal to the people but perpetrates a fraud upon them, reflects no honour on its authors but shows only a cunning partisanship deeply dishonourable to public men. We trust that even now wisdom and patriotism may be heard in the Cabinet and that Ministers will, for the sake of the country of which we are they are alike citizens, agree to the proposition we have here set forth'.
77/48

1. In a letter published in *The Times* on 11 September 1913 Lord Loreburn, former Liberal Lord Chancellor, drew attention to the possibility that a policy

of 'general devolution' or 'home rule all round', with subordinate legislatures for Scotland, and Wales, as well as Ireland, would perhaps open the way to a solution of the Irish deadlock, and suggested a conference to discuss this possibility.

10.   From A. Bonar Law

Pembroke Lodge
Edwardes Square
Kensington W.
22 December 1913

My dear Selborne,

. . . I think there is a great danger that the Government are simply playing a game with us, but on the other hand, as I said to Bob Cecil, the one impression which I had derived from my interview with A[1] was that he is a funk [sic] about the resistance of Ulster and I am convinced that he will not face that when it comes to the point. In my opinion, at present he is quite at sea and does not in the least know what he can do but *we* certainly must not allow the idea that negotiations can continue indefinitely: and if nothing happens by the time the holidays are well over we must carefully consider what step we ought to take.

Yours very sincerely

A. Bonar Law

77/64

1.   An interview between Law and Asquith took place on 14 October 1913, at Asquith's suggestion. Law's 'notes on conversation with the P.M.' are in Blake, *The unknown prime minister*, pp. 161–3. This was followed by another meeting on 6 November at which the difficulty of excluding 'Ulster' from the home rule bill was discussed (Blake, op. cit., pp. 164–5). At a third meeting, on 9 December, the two leaders discussed the problem again, Law demanding that Ulster's exclusion should be exclusion with an option to join in, after a term of years, and then only if a plebiscite in Ulster so declared. This meeting also proved abortive.

11.   From Viscount Milner

47 Duke Street
S.W.
18 February 1914

My dear Selborne,

I don't think I made my point very well this afternoon. I can always do it more clearly on paper.

This is what Bonar Law has said:

1.   The Unionist Party is pledged, if Government persist in carrying their Bill unmodified without an appeal to the people, to support Ulster in its resistance.

2. That support does not mean merely making speeches but any and every measure that might be effective to prevent the coercion of Ulster.

3. That pledge rests on *the whole body of Unionists* (seeing that they have at meeting after meeting enthusiastically endorsed it), and not merely on the party leader.

I agree with all this, as I think you do, and I ask myself, what can I, with others similarly situated, do to give effect to this pledge?

The suggestion I made today – not my own idea to start with – may not be the best way to begin. I see objections in it, though all the objections would have applied equally to the 'Covenant' which yet has been the starting point and basis of all the practical steps taken by the Ulstermen.[1]

But it is 'up to' those, who don't like the idea of a British pledge, to suggest something better. My object is to bring people sharply to face the situation and to ask themselves what they really mean. They ought to do that now, not to wait till the last moment, and then suddenly awake to the fact that they meant nothing by their promises of support. The object of the pledge is to compel those who take it to cast about in their own minds and think what they can do to give effective aid. And it will at the same time be an indication, who and where the people are, who really desire and mean to do something if they can be shown the way. I want the stalwarts to begin to have some sort of rudimentary organisation, not to leave everything to the last moment, and then see the mischief they wish to avert achieved by a sudden rush of the enemy, as was the case with the Parliament Act. It is quite true, as you say, that many of us, with the best will in the world, may have no chance of doing anything. But it is also true that many chances will be missed, if people are not on the look out for them, and have not realised that it is their duty to try and find some work to do for the cause. Of course a movement of this kind is no good unless it enlists large numbers. That is why I am anxious that it should not be started without a reasonable amount of influential support. If large numbers joined it, the mere fact would be an impressive demonstration of what the revolutionary methods of the Government have brought us to – for when before, in our lifetime, have thousands upon thousands of sober steady-going citizens deliberately contemplated resistance to an Act of Parliament, because they were sincerely convinced that it was devoid of all moral sanction? There are a great many people who still entirely fail to realise, what the strength of our feeling is on this subject. They think it is just an ordinary case of opposition to a political measure, a move in the party-game. And so it may be to a great many Unionists, but there is certainly a large body, who feel that the crisis altogether transcends anything in their previous experience, and calls for action, which is different, *not only in degree, but in kind*, from what is appropriate to ordinary political controversies. How are we to make this evident to the

world and to compel ourselves to live up to this intensity of conviction?
That is the problem. Yours ever

Milner

P.S. Don't trouble to answer. We shall be meeting again very shortly.

12/234

1.  Milner's suggestion, made to the Council of the Union Defence League, was
    that a British 'Covenant' should be drawn up on the lines of 'Ulster's Solemn
    League and Covenant', in which the Ulster Unionists had affirmed their
    determination to resist home rule by 'all means which may be found necessary'.
    The document which Milner prepared appeared in the press on 3 March 1914.
    It declared that the home rule bill was contrary to the spirit of the constitution,
    and bound the signatories to hold themselves 'justified in taking or supporting
    any action that may be effective' to prevent the bill becoming law, and, more
    particularly, 'to prevent the armed forces of the Crown being used to deprive
    the people of Ulster of their rights as citizens of the United Kingdom'. The first
    signatories included Rudyard Kipling, Sir Edward Elgar and A. V. Dicey, and
    by the end of July 1914 it was claimed that nearly two million people had signed
    the British Covenant.

12.   From Sir Edward Grey

33 Eccleston Square
London, S.W.
Thursday 2 April 1914

*Private*

My dear Selborne,

I have not overlooked the point that you raise in your letter that appears in
'The Times' of this morning.[1]

I, amongst others, raised it in private some weeks ago. But high legal
opinion contested my view, on the ground, so far as I can recollect, that, if
the Parliament Act had contemplated the construction that you place upon
it, it would have used the words 'three or more successive Sessions',
instead of 'three successive Sessions' only. Under these circumstances it
was held to be at least possible that the Speaker might hesitate to certify,
under the conditions you suppose, that the provisions of the Parliament
Act had been complied with. It was held that, if this happened, we should
be putting the Speaker in an unfair position by pressing him on the point;
and that he would probably not yield.

So far as I know, the Speaker has not been consulted on the point. But,
some of our best legal opinion being to the effect that I have stated, I
accepted the position that we ought not to press him, or indeed to ask him
whether he would be prepared to do what you suggest he should do.

I write this letter only privately, to show that I have not been so stupid as
to overlook the point. I have not time to discuss it at this moment, nor even
to refer to the wording of the Parliament Act itself and consult our Legal

Advisers about it; but no doubt you can get the point discussed in the House of Lords if you desire. Yours sincerely

E. Grey

77/94

1.  Selborne's letter in *The Times* referred to Sir Edward Grey's statement that the home rule bill must go on the statute book, without a further general election, since an election would mean another two and a half years' delay. Lord Selborne argued that if there were an election in 1914, which the Liberals won, the government would *not* have to wait two and a half years before bringing home rule into operation since the session of 1913 could be taken as the first of the three successive sessions in which section 2 of the Parliament Act required a bill to be passed by the Commons. Therefore the bill could be presented for royal assent at any time between the 25th and 26th month from the date of its second reading in the '*first* of those sessions', i.e. that of 1913.

13.  To Sir Edward Grey

49 Mount Street
W
3 April 1914

*Private*

My dear Grey,

Hereditarily I ought to understand lawyers' arguments, but I often do not; how three sessions can cease to be successive because they are numbered 2, 3, and 4 instead of 1, 2, and 3 passes my comprehension. But why should you not ask the Speaker his view now? or you could ask the Privy Council, and of course the Speaker would be only too pleased to have the guidance of the Privy Council. In Ulster you are up against that most uncompromising historical fact, a community which is ready to suffer any consequences rather than submit to what it believes to be a wrong and an evil of the first magnitude.

Of course you can crush Ulster with the Army and Fleet, but at the cost of thousands of lives, and you can hold Ulster crushed as long as you keep the Army and Fleet there, but not a moment longer. The resistance of Ulster would take all the forms, with which we are familiar in the history of such cases, some heroic and some hideous. Please do not think I am arguing on points where we must agree to differ, I am only stating what I believe on my honour and conscience to be true. On that basis I will proceed.

Are such Russian methods really possible under our system? if they are possible, to what catastrophes in the United Kingdom and in the whole Empire do they not surely lead? above all what possible value to Ireland or to the United Kingdom or to the Empire could Home Rule so achieved be? What would then become of the ideal for which conscientious Home

Rulers have worked all these years? Surely it would be shattered into fragments.

Our country is in danger, I believe in awful danger. That is why I am writing like this on the basis not of our incompatible views of Home Rule and of the causes of the present danger but of our agreement that the country is in danger.

Why do we Unionists insist so strenuously on the necessity of a general election or referendum before the Home Rule Bill is placed on the statute book? In passing let me say that there is really nothing whatever in the experience of the 48 States of the U.S.A. or of Switzerland or of Australia to warrant your fear lest the poll on a referendum should be a small one. I may say this because I have studied almost all the literature which exists on the subject.

Why is it that we are willing to comply with any condition you may impose or to give any assurance or guarantee you like that if you win the general election you shall have your Home Rule in five weeks or five days or five minutes if you want it?

These are the reasons.

If you win, you will have lost absolutely nothing.

If you lose, it seems to us a very grave matter that the King should have assented to a bill, which the electors proceed immediately to repudiate.

If you lose, it seems to us extraordinarily unfair to have saddled us with a bill which the electors proceed immediately to repudiate.

Until there has been a general election no party in this controversy really knows its final strength, or what force of opinion it represents. Till that is ascertained no party will deal decisively as principals in a national settlement. That is true of you and of us, but how much more true of the Ulster people and the Nationalists? Quite certainly you will find the Ulster people more possible to negotiate with when they know what the electors think than you will find them now, and I should imagine that that is also true of the Nationalists.

If the election should turn out stale mate, then both parties must compromise and must join in a national settlement and that settlement must take the form of devolution (I use that word and not federalism, because the process in our case would be one from centralisation to decentralisation and not the converse). Indeed if there is any Home Rule Bill at all we must come to devolution, because the permanent regulation of (e.g.) English affairs by a Parliament containing 40 Irish members after a parliament had been set up in Dublin would constitute an intolerable wrong. There would have to be some form of convention. I do not say that the South African case was the same as the case of the U.K. Obviously the case of the U.K. is more difficult to deal with, but the S.A. case was very difficult indeed for a country so comparatively young in age and small in population.

My experience in S.A. has led me to the opinion that the difficulties of devolution in the U.K. are much less than is commonly supposed and that the whole thing could be settled by a convention far quicker than Balfour supposes. The great crux would undoubtedly be the finance.

But I absolutely despair of the danger to the nation being averted if you insist on putting your Home Rule Bill on the statute book before you have an election or referendum. If you do that, I do not see how your conflict with Ulster can be avoided, and, if that once begins, God in heaven above knows where it will end. Yours sincerely

S

77/96

14.   From Sir Edward Grey

Bridgeton
Orton
Morayshire
12 April 1914

*Private*
Dear Selborne,
. . . I still believe that unless the Ulstermen seize the Customs and Imperial revenue and begin shooting first, there will be a peaceful settlement and no coercion. We have given a pledge that there will be an election before there is any Dublin Executive in existence and that there will be no force used to make Ulstermen submit to Home Rule, till after an Election.

If in face of that Ulster takes upon itself meanwhile and before an Election to displace the Imperial Government and shoot Imperial officers who try to carry on their duties in Ulster and refuse to obey its Provisional Government, we shall use force and, pace Bonar Law, be obliged to do so.

I don't for a moment believe in the coercion of Ulster, even after an Election, as a settlement of the Irish question, but I do believe in the possibility of civil war before an Election if Ulster begins it by attacking the Imperial Government. Yours sincerely

E. Grey

77/104

15.   To Austen Chamberlain

49 Mount Street
W.
1 May 1914

My dear Austen,
I want you to see what I have written to Lansdowne, but, as this is my own copy, please return it.

I of course adhere to all I have said to you about devolution, but whether the party splits or not depends I think entirely on the manner in which we make ourselves a party to any arrangement for the avoidance of civil war. Hence this letter. Yours ever

S

A.C. 11/1/186

*Enclosure*

49 Mount Street

W

1 May 1914

My dear Lansdowne, As we are apparently approaching another critical stage in the Home Rule controversy,[1] may I put down my thoughts as you have so kindly encouraged me to do on similar occasions.

1.   We should not be asked under any circumstances to assent to the second reading of the Government of Ireland Bill, which should pass into a statute only by the operation of the Parliament Act.

2.   If any arrangement about the exclusion of Ulster,[2] &c., &c., be come to, to which we are parties, our consent should be based on the avoidance of civil war pending an appeal to the electors, and the arrangement should be embodied in a separate bill for the amendment of the Government of Ireland Act. That bill we could agree to pass immediately without any infringement of principle and without incurring any responsibility for the Government of Ireland Act.

3.   Of course what we all desire is a general election or referendum on Home Rule before the Government of Ireland Bill becomes a statute under the Parliament Act, but I regard it as almost impossible that the Government should yield on that point. I am quite sure, however, that we can make it a condition that there should be a general election almost immediately after the Government of Ireland Bill and the amending Bill have become law. Grey has practically pledged the Government to this.

4.   If we have not assented at all to the Government of Ireland Bill and if we have assented to the amending Bill solely for the purpose of avoiding civil war pending an appeal to the electors, then we shall be free, and this I think is essential, to declare that, if the electors decide in our favour, we 'shall hold ourselves authorised to deal with the Irish situation as we think best'.

Personally I do not think that we should be strong enough to repeal the whole of the Government of Ireland Bill unless we secured such an overwhelming verdict at the polls in our favour as I for one certainly do not expect. But we could, and we ought to amend the Act, if we thought we could more fully secure the safety of the United Kingdom and the welfare of Ireland by doing so.

You will notice that the two points I have specifically in view are that we should remain true to the two principles for which we have contended throughout, opposition to Home Rule and the constitutional right of the electors to decide the question.

If the party is satisfied that we have given way on neither of these principles and that all that we have done is to save the nation from civil war pending an appeal to the electors, it will approve and support the action taken. But if the party thinks that we have given way on either of these principles I am very much afraid of the consequences.

I should be grateful if you would show this letter to Bonar Law.

Yours &c

Selborne

77/106

1.  The home rule bill passed its final reading in the House of Commons on 26 May, and before that date there were long and anxious discussions among Unionists about the tactics the Lords should adopt when the bill came before them for its second reading.
2.  On 9 March 1914 the government put forward proposals for an amendment to the home rule bill. Any county might by a majority of its parliamentary electors, vote itself out of the operation of the bill for six years. The time limit was thus fixed so that before it expired the electors of the United Kingdom would have been twice consulted (i.e. not later than December 1915 and not later than December 1920), and if they ratified the inclusion of Ulster counties in the bill she should have no cause for grievance.

16.   From Austen Chamberlain

9 Egerton Place<br>S.W.<br>2 May 1914

*Private*

My dear Selborne,

*Parliament Act.* I have not yet had time to look at the draft you have sent me.

As regards the Irish position, I do not think there is much difference between our points of view. I do not want the House of Lords to become responsible for the Home Rule Bill, nor do I want our hands to be tied in any way if it can be avoided. At the same time there is a danger, which must not be overlooked, and seems to me serious. Our reason for entertaining the idea of negotiation or settlement at all is our desire to avoid the awful horrors of civil war and the calamities which it would incidentally bring with it. Some of our friends are inclined to argue that the army has shown that it will not fight,[1] that civil war is therefore impossible, and that we can therefore afford to push the Government to extremes. But I do not take this view. First, because I am not clear that the Army might not be involved in fighting before it knew what it was doing or under circumstances in which large numbers of officers and men at any rate would not hesitate to act. But secondly, & more important, because if the Army is put into a position in which it has to refuse, an injury hardly second to civil war is inflicted both on the Army and on the country. It seems to me that these considerations are so strong that if there is a reasonable method of escape from these dangers we shall be impelled by our own feelings and by the force of public opinion to accept it whatever it is.

Now, if we do nothing to guide events, we may be confronted with the mere exclusion of Ulster without any other alteration in the Bill, and that seems to me almost the worst solution that is possible – certainly the worst solution short of civil war. We are the more likely to be put in this position because those who speak with most authority in our name are not inclined to encourage the idea of what is called a federal solution and do not therefore direct attention to the alterations which are necessary to make a federal solution possible or satisfactory. You and I have both tried to do this at different times and I repeated the attempt at Wolverhampton on Thursday; but unless we show some readiness as a Party to consider such a solution favourably, I am afraid that we shall end by finding ourselves forced to accept a so-called compromise which may indeed preserve peace in Ireland but will be an insuperable barrier to any satisfactory scheme of devolution.

I am very much pressed with work and this letter is dictated rather hurriedly, but I hope it is sufficient to show you the one danger, not as far as I can see present to your mind, against which your suggestions offer no protection. Yours ever

Austen Chamberlain

77/108

1.  A reference to the 'Curragh mutiny' (or 'Curragh incident') of March 1914 when a group of officers led by General Hubert Gough stationed at the Curragh military camp indicated that they would exercise the choice offered to them by General Sir Arthur Paget, Commander-in-Chief in Ireland, and 'accept dismissal' from the army if ordered north against the Ulster Unionists. Gough was summoned to London where he secured from the Secretary of State for War, Colonel John Seely, an assurance that the army would not be used to force home rule on Ulster. This assurance was repudiated by Asquith, but the incident raised the dangerous possibility that the army, or at least a section of it, would refuse to comply with the orders of the government as they affected Ulster.

17.   To Lady Selborne

49 Mount Street<br>W<br>16 June 1914

My darling,

Crewe told us yesterday that he would be willing to introduce the amending bill next week[1] but that if meanwhile negotiations led to general agreement he would introduce a different amending bill later!!

Talk of Nero and Rome and fiddling! We had a meeting of front bench opposition peers in Lansdowne's room afterwards with Milner, and agreed that we should press them again today to introduce the bill, because we much prefer to do our negotiation publicly. On the other hand we agreed that we could not refuse to negotiate privately if asked, but that L or B L, if invited, should write, and get an answer in writing, to ask what the basis of negotiation was to be and what proposals the government had to make, and that, if negotiations were begun, it should be a stipulation that the result should be made public afterwards whatever the result might be.

Afterwards the talk turned to our treatment of the amending bill – It emerged that the majority were in favour of the exclusion of six counties with an adjustment of boundaries so as to exclude as many Protestants of (eg) Monaghan as possible and so as to leave included as many R.C.s of (eg) Fermanagh and Tyrone as possible, indefinitely, i.e. till they willed otherwise. Customs, Post Office etc., would follow. The majority were not in favour of throwing the bill out by insisting on an amendment to make the whole thing contingent on an immediate general election, St. John's plan, or of Linky's plan of rolling the two bills into one.

All this is generally in accordance with my views, so I am satisfied. The chief difficulty is that we can put nothing in, except about the general election, which can satisfy the Unionists of the South and West and Dublin, and they all believe that Asquith will accept the bill so amended. I really believe that too. I do not know how he will square it with Redmond or whether he will press it against Redmond – Even if he did, Redmond has no interest in kicking him out or in letting him be kicked out soon afterwards. Bob and Linky think it impossible that Asquith will accept this against Redmond's wishes, but I do not agree. Up to the last thing last night the government had not made the smallest approach to negotiation with us. I have not been able to see Carson yet. Yours

S

102/126

1.  The amending bill, offering 'county option' for six years with automatic inclusion at the end of this period, was introduced in the House of Lords by Lord Crewe on 23 June 1914.

18.  To Lady Selborne

Brooks's
St. James's Street
17 June 1914

My darling,

I have had a long talk with Carson – I think that he is very sensible. At any rate I agree with him throughout on the points which I will deal with presently.

I proposed the Committee of Irishmen to him to deal with the changes necessitated by the amending bill and including the drawing of the line in Ulster between the excluded and included parts or, alternatively, with the omission of that extracontroversial point. He wouldn't have it; he said that there would be no chance of agreement that way, and that Redmond would never agree to it, and no wonder, for it would be putting him in the most difficult possible position; and I think that Carson thought the same for himself.

You will have seen from the report of yesterday's proceedings in the Lords that there are to be no more conversations, for which heaven be praised, and that the amending bill is to be introduced on Monday or Tuesday. Horace Plunkett told me that it would contain a provision for a recurrent referendum every five years and that customs and post office would be left to the Imperial Parliament. George Murray scouted the idea that the 'details' necessitated by exclusion would be left to a commission to settle; he said it would be done in the bill. I am not so sure.

Horace Plunkett did not know exactly what line the Government would draw in the bill but felt convinced that they would accept an artificial line excluding from the operation of the main bill as many Ulster Protestants as possible and including in it as many Ulster R.C.s as possible; also, that the government would accept (if they did not propose) a provision that the excluded parts should never be included except with their own consent. He said that Redmond would never take the responsibility of accepting such a bill but would refer it to an Irish National Convention and that that Convention would reject it. He said that Asquith would then pass the bill against the Irish Nationalist vote in the Commons by the help of the votes of the Unionists and would then try and stick it out for another year until he had got the plural voting bill – I found that Carson took exactly the same view. Opinions are divided as to whether under these circumstances the Nationalist vote in the Commons would be sufficiently stable and constant to keep the government in power for another year. The government might be beaten by their slackness but I do not think that they will wish to see it turned out.

We are to have a 'shadow' cabinet directly the amending bill is published, but at present the only question on which there seems likely to be a sharp controversy is this. Shall the Lords insert a clause into the amending bill to say that neither it nor the main bill are to come into operation until after a general election, and stick to it? The only one of us, of whom I know at present, who is in favour of this, is St. John, but he is passionately in favour of it. He agrees that Asquith will not accept it, but would let the whole amending bill perish and dissolve on the cry that the Lords had for party purposes insisted on civil war, but he thinks that we should win. His point is that in this way alone can we save the Unionists of the South and West. I fear that we should not win; I quite admit that on the other hand, if Asquith is able to hold out for a year, the Irish question will not then be much of a help to us in the general election and that the government will have the gain of the plural voting bill[1] to set against their general unpopularity, but I am really afraid of a general election fought under the conditions which St. John desires and we certainly should not help the Unionists of the South and West by getting beaten. St. John is afraid of crushing supertaxes on the few remaining landlords.

I had quite a painful interview with St. John today. I am not sure that Jim may not support him, knowing in his heart of hearts that a Unionist victory in July is the only chance of staving off devolution, and not caring much what else happens if devolution is to come. He is quite fanatical against it – so is Bob; but Bob is still more afraid of civil war, so I do not think that Bob will support St. John; mind you I only suspect that Jim may – so far as he has yet spoken he has on the whole taken the other line. Yours

S

102/130

1.  Voters in the counties often had several votes, scattered in each division of a county, if they possessed the requisite qualifications. It has been reckoned that in 1911 there were probably between five and six hundred thousand plural voters, about seven per cent of the electorate (Neal Blewett, 'The Franchise in the United Kingdom, 1885–1918', *Past and Present* no. 36, 1965, pp. 27–56). This system was defended by the Unionists, and Liberal Plural Voting bills (by which electors with a title to vote in several constituencies would have been forbidden to vote in more than one) in 1906, 1913 and 1914 were all turned down by the House of Lords.

19.   To Lady Selborne

49 Mount Street<br>W<br>4 August 1914

My darling,

Jacta alea est.

The government issued an ultimatum to Germany today to respect the neutrality of Belgium, to be answered by midnight. Of course Germany will refuse.

God have mercy upon us. I did not hear Edward Grey's speech yesterday but Jim and Lansdowne and G.N.C. did and they all said that it was a magnificent performance. John Burns has resigned, I respect his courage greatly, and I hear today that John Morley and Simon and Beauchamp have followed suit. The W.O. takes charge of all the railways tomorrow but works them through a committee of the General Managers. A.J.B. is trying to get Asquith to appoint K. Minister of War but he has actually reappointed Haldane for the moment. We had a jolly dinner at No. 20 yesterday with Nigs and Violet and A.J.B. and Top, but there was a shadow over it all . . . .

S

102/150

20.   To Lady Selborne

49 Mount Street
W
6 August 1914

My darling,

There is no more war news today except what I cannot put into a letter. I think that K at the W.O. is the right man in the right place.

I have been to the Admiralty and everything is working as smoothly and unfussily as possible. Preparing mobilisation places for the Admiralty itself was one of the bits of work of my time there. We are still in dire uncertainty and suspense over the fate of the Irish and Welsh bills – but I shall never believe that Asquith is capable of playing such an infamous trick on us as to pass these bills during this truce of God and after what pledges have passed between the two sides about it, until he does it. His press and his wirepullers and his rank and file are pressing him to prorogue, thus automatically bringing the bills forward for the King's assent, instead of adjourning, which reserves the status quo.

But I have found a technical point[1] tonight which I think puts them at our mercy or at least gives Asquith an unanswerable argument for Redmond. I shall not get down till Saturday afternoon. Yours

S

102/156

1.  The 'technical point' was as follows: the clerk of the parliaments could not hand over either the bill for Welsh disestablishment or the home rule bill to the Speaker without the express authority of the House of Lords. If the clerk were asked for either bill he could reply that he must take the Houses' instructions. The question which then arose was whether or not the Speaker could endorse the certificates on the bills to the effect that Section 2 of the Parliament Act had been complied with. The Opposition toyed with the scheme after the government had stated its intention, on 15 September 1914, of placing the home rule bill on the statute book, but decided that no action on these lines should be taken. The Lords duly returned the bills through the Clerk of Parliament, to the Clerk of the House of Commons and the two bills were brought down to the Speaker on 17 September and his certificate endorsed upon them.

21.   To Austen Chamberlain

Blackmoor
Liss
Hants.
12 August 1914

My dear Austen,

Evidently Asquith is going to try once more to get Redmond to agree to complete exclusion of the six counties before August 25th.[1]

Now obviously it would be less impossible for Redmond to agree, if it were admitted on all hands that this arrangement provided no permanent settlement.

If Redmond would agree to the exclusion of the six counties on the pledge of the Government to assemble a conference as soon as possible to ascertain what settlement could be arrived at, which would reunite Ireland etc – your formula in fact – a way out might be found. We would have his act but with six counties excluded, as a temporary arrangement by universal admission though the exclusion of the six counties would be statutorily no more temporary than the act. Cannot you use your special opportunities of talking frankly to the government? Otherwise I despair. But time presses.

I could never follow Bonar Law in accepting the present Government of Ireland Bill with the complete exclusion of the six Ulster counties as a final settlement of the Irish constitutional question, (even if I thought it would work, which I don't), and I cannot conceive it possible that Redmond either should accept it as a final settlement. Yours ever

Selborne

77/184

1. Asquith attempted to reach a compromise on the basis of passing the home rule bill, with its operation postponed for six months, and excluding the six Ulster counties of Antrim, Armagh, Down, Fermanagh, Londonderry and Tyrone for three years, pending a review of the whole exclusion question by the imperial parliament. This was accepted by Law, but proved unpalatable to the Liberal rank and file. Instead Asquith was obliged to place the bill on the statute book, and at the same time to postpone its operation for twelve months, or until the end of the war, whichever was the longer, promising also an amending bill 'during the suspensory period and before the Irish Government Bill can possibly come into operation'.

22.  To Lady Selborne

20 Arlington Street
S.W.1
16 September 1914

My darling,

. . . Never in my political life have I felt so intensely wronged as I feel now about the Welsh Church.[1]

The Archbishop and I both made wholly unprovocative speeches and appealed to our common faith and nationality and to the generosity of the Liberals and Nonconformists.

The government made no attempt to deny that there was not the least chance of our being able to find the money after the War or that the Church would be crippled in her work. They did not utter one word of regret or compassion. Their attitude was one of callous brutality, the Parliament Act must take its course.

By the Welsh Church bill itself all the machinery for disestablishment and disendowment is set up directly the bill passes and commences its ruthless work as soon as it can. This is not changed at all by the amending bill of the government. All that that bill does is this.

By the Welsh Church bill the date of disestablishment is fixed at 6 months after the date of the passing of the bill and may be postponed by order in Council to 12 months after.

By the amending bill the minimum interval is extended to 12 months and the maximum to the end of the war!! Yours

S

102/166

1.   The government placed the bill for disestablishment of the Welsh Church on the statute book, postponing the date also for 12 months or until the end of the war. However, the work of preparing for disestablishment and disendowment was begun immediately because the suspensory bill of 15 September postponed, not the disestablishment bill, but only the date of disestablishment. This meant that clauses which took effect before the date of disestablishment would come into force at once e.g. that no new appointment in the Welsh Church should carry with it a life interest.


23.   To Geoffrey Robinson

Blackmoor
Liss
Hants.
20 October 1914

*Copy Private*

My dear Robinson,

I do not understand how the *Times*, or your Military Correspondent, can take the line it does about the Antwerp blunder.[1] The point is not whether an expedition ought or ought not to have been sent to Antwerp; no one can express a final opinion on that until he knows the facts, and whether Churchill's alleged 'larger combination' had any existence in fact. The point is that, if an expedition had to be sent to Antwerp, it was not the business of the Admiralty or of Churchill to send it; it was the business exclusively of the War Office and of Kitchener; and, if Kitchener had really thought the expedition advisable, he had at least 300,000 troops to draw on, in Special Reserve and Territorials, far better trained and far more effective and better equipped for the purpose than the Naval Brigade sent by Churchill. Why a very large proportion of these officers and men had been recruited since the war, they had no equipment except sea kits, no water bottles, and their bayonets were stuck in their gaiters. No proper casualty list will probably ever be published because there was no proper system of identification nor any actual roll of the men who went over. Great numbers of them had never fired a rifle at all. It is no question of second quality troops, as your Military Correspondent writes, but of tenth quality troops, whereas the War Office had great numbers of really fine second quality troops to send. Yours sincerely

S

92/212

1. In October 1914 Churchill, First Lord of the Admiralty, and Kitchener sent an expeditionary force to help the Belgians in their resistance in Antwerp; Churchill accompanied the expedition, and telegraphed the Cabinet offering to resign from the Admiralty and take personal command of the forces in Antwerp. The amusement occasioned by this was dispelled when Antwerp fell to the Germans with the loss of a Naval Brigade which was obliged to retire into internment in Holland.

24.   To A. Bonar Law

Blackmoor
Liss
Hants
22 November 1914

My dear Bonar Law,

I do not know whether you noticed what Haldane said in the Lords on the first day of the session.[1] In case you didn't I enclose the Hansard. Please return it. Now the real answer is

1.   that the government had neglected to build enough big cruisers.
2.   that the admiralty did not make the best distribution of those they had.

Now I cannot press the first point now or the party issue is raised, and I cannot press the second because the government could not deal with it properly without disclosing what the distribution of the cruisers is, which of course they could not possibly do.

It, therefore, comes to this that the government cannot really now say anything more than Haldane said, and so I am on the whole not in favour of raising the question again. It is quite true as Lieut French writes in the letter quoted in the Sussex paper that it was very probable that 'the ships chased away would return strengthened with their China Squadron', *though of course not certain,* [e.g. they might have tried a coup on the Cape station] and that Haldane simply prevaricates when he says that 'the concentration was a thing which no one could foresee', but he will continue to prevaricate so long as we can't get to grips or with the chivalry for which this government is distinguished put all the blame on Prince Louis! This opinion is of course subject to your further criticism. I may say, I have seen Fisher[2] since the Lords debate and can tell you what he said when we meet. Yours sincerely

Selborne

B.L. 35/3/47

1.　On 11 November 1914 Lord Selborne in the Lords alluded to 'certain naval aspects of the war', including the Antwerp expedition, a recent naval defeat in the Pacific, and the resignation of Prince Louis of Battenburg. Lord Haldane replied, defending the Antwerp episode and its origins, and arguing that the setback in the Pacific was because it was 'impossible to foresee how the German ships would concentrate'. He also reminded Lord Selborne of the difficulties of the time, and expressed his pleasure at the Opposition's sympathetic attitude (*H.L. Deb.*, vol. xviii, cols. 37–51).
2.　Prince Louis was replaced as First Sea Lord by Sir John Fisher on 30 October.

25.　From the Marquess of Crewe

Crewe House
Curzon Street
W.
5 January 1915

*Private*

My dear Selborne,

Many thanks for your note letting me know the questions you propose to ask on Thursday and Friday.[1]

As regards the naval position, we will say as much generally as we can, and I think it may be useful to explain why a good deal of reticence is thought necessary this time. I will ask the Admiralty about the Courts Martial.[2]

If you have not actually put down your motion for the 8th, I wish that you could word it somewhat differently. It is right that we should say all we can about recruiting, but the two subjects, (a) the number of troops which in the course of this year we hope to utilise in Europe, and (b) the possible methods in which they may be employed – are impossible to touch upon. Something quite general may be said about drafts; but I am sure that you will understand that under the *regime* of reticence obtaining in this war, of which we are the victims quite as much as the authors, there cannot be anything specific. Yours sincerely

Crewe

93/13

1.　At a meeting of the House of Lords which had been summoned to hear a statement concerning the war from Lord Kitchener.
2.　Courts martial of captains in respect of ships lost in war.

26. From A. Bonar Law

Pembroke Lodge
Edwardes Square
Kensington, W.
29 January 1915

My dear Selborne,

A memorandum from Long and Curzon is being sent to you[1] and we are to have a meeting at Lansdowne House on Monday evening at 9.30 at which I hope you will be present. In regard to the memorandum, I enclose copy of a letter which I have sent to Curzon and I hope that you will be in general agreement with me on this matter. Yours very sincerely,

A. Bonar Law

93/24

Copy of a letter from Bonar Law to the Marquess of Curzon

Pembroke Lodge
Kensington
29 January 1915

My dear Curzon,

I have been thinking a great deal about the Memorandum sent by Long and yourself, and I see great difficulties in the way of any action such as is in your mind.

I think, of course, it should be made quite plain that we as a Party have no knowledge and no responsibility for what the Government are doing; and this, in my opinion, could best be made by a declaration in similar terms by Lansdowne and myself in the two Houses.

As regards the general question in the Memorandum, this is how it strikes me: I have already asked Talbot to say to their Chief whip that we assume they will take no contentious legislation and we shall see what reply is given to that. If they should attempt to pass the Plural Voting Bill, for instance, in the present conditions, I am not at all sure that we should not openly declare that the truce is at an end, and tell them privately before any action is taken that this is the course which we shall adopt. I do not myself think, however, that they will attempt to pass the Plural Voting Bill.

As regards getting more information, it seems to me that there are only two ways in which this can be done, and they are both open – one to a greater extent than the other – to an objection which seems to me fatal.

One way is to have two or three of our number put on the Special Committee of Defence,[2] which is really as I understand an inner Cabinet for the conduct of the war. If that were done whichever of us were members of such a Committee would be in this position: that if their views were not carried out they would either have to allow things to go on for which they would be regarded as responsible; or, they would have to break away from the arrangement and make it public that they had done so.

If such an arrangement were adopted it would be necessary also that members who represent us should have consultations with our own colleagues; there would be differences of opinion among ourselves, and in my belief, such an arrangement could not work at all.

The other suggestion which has been made to me seems even worse. It is that a small Committee of our Party should be formed which would keep regularly in touch with the inner Cabinet of the Government, and would in that way make our views felt in the conduct of the war. This proposal seems to me to be open to all the objections of the other, and would I think be even more unworkable.

I know how unsatisfactory the present position is, for it means that we are conducting the most difficult war in which we have been engaged probably, in regard to which the nation is united, but half the nation distrusts the men who are carrying it on. That is a very difficult position, and may be found impossible; but in my judgement, much as I dislike the present position, there are I think only two real alternatives open to us: One is to go on as we are doing, without responsibility and with a very limited amount of criticism, such as was made at the meeting of your House; or to face a coalition. The latter proposal I should certainly be against; and on the whole, therefore, I am reluctantly driven to the conclusion that the only proper course for us in the meantime is to continue on the lines on which we have acted since the war began.

I am, yours very sincerely

93/36

Enclosure (2)

*Confidential*

It seems to me that the recent debates in the House of Lords have made an official statement respecting the position of the Opposition most desirable.

At present the whole conduct of affairs is in the hands of the Government. There is little criticism from their supporters in Parliament, in the Press or the Country, and until the debate in the Lords there had been very little from Opposition sources. It has been practically left to the Press who have confined their remarks to the efficiency of public services, and have not dealt with any of the principles which divide Parties. I can best explain the situation by saying that a Unionist could criticise a Unionist Government in the same way without ceasing to be a Unionist. The abandonment of criticism, however, may be carried too far in the interests of the country – and – a secondary consideration – in the interests of the Party.

The present position is, of course, only temporary, and the future already is exercising many minds. I would especially call attention to the letter of Lord Sydenham in the 'Times' of January 12th. He expresses the view which is held also by influential members of Parliament and by the General Public that, at the present time, there ought to be a working arrangement and a complete understanding between all parties in the State, so that the task with which we are confronted may be approached by the ripest wisdom and best brains available.

We are only using half our real power in the direction of affairs, not because the unemployed portion is unwilling or unsympathetic in the prosecution of the work but through adherence in this matter to the Party system.

The position of the Government is unique among the Allies. Take France as an illustration; there the Government is devoting their whole energies to the war. They have abandoned Party politics and have taken into the Government certain representatives of those who were opponents before the war. I mention this for purposes of argument, though I admit the influence of the 'group' system which makes co-operation easier in France.

Here not only has there been no coalition – personally I do not favour it, and I gravely doubt its success – but the Government has persistently pursued those Party aims which occupied them before the War. Last Session it was Welsh Church and Home Rule: this Session it is to be the Plural Voting Bill, and nobody will pretend that the taxation proposals were conceived in a spirit that would recommend them to all Parties. I believe that our interests will suffer severely unless the Country is given a plain exposition of our position. I venture to suggest that it should be stated definitely that the Opposition does not desire – and, I should hope that it might be added, is not prepared to assent to – a Coalition Government. It is prepared to support the Government whole heartedly in a vigorous and unhesitating prosecution of the War, but entire co-operation and confidence is not possible in all matters until the Government agree to drop all Party controversies and devote itself and Parliament entirely to the one great object – the War. If that were done – involving no advantages or disadvantages for any Party – then the Opposition could say that it was ready to support the present Government as cordially as if it were drawn from the Unionist ranks.

That this is the view of many of our countrymen is, I think, clear from the letter of Dr. Arnold Thomas of Bristol, in the 'Times' of January 12th. He is a leading Nonconformist and supporter of Disestablishment and Disendowment, and is prepared to go a very long way in order to secure conciliation and union; see also on this point the Petition of the Free Churches to Prime Minister.

So far this desirable end has been unattainable. I do not wish to say that the Government has actually taken advantage of the weakness of the Opposition in Parliament caused by the War – ninety-eight Unionists are reported to be on active service compared with twenty-nine Liberals – but, at least, it has refused to recognise the new situation in Parliament which the war has produced.

I do not know – indeed, we have no means of telling – whether the number of candidates and electors serving with the Forces is in the same proportion. But the fact is indisputable that in the Country as in Parliament, the War entirely prevents public opinion on matters of domestic controversy presenting itself in its real proportion.

Wails in the House of Commons a division on a question of domestic controversy would produce a result entirely misrepresenting the real opinion of all members, so in the country a campaign against any domestic legislation of the Government would equally show misleading results, quite apart from the disinclination of the country to give its attention to others than the War.

Indeed the Opposition has fully recognised the impossibility and injustice of testing public opinion under existing circumstances by agreeing not to contest by-elections. By so doing it has properly and patriotically deprived itself of the most powerful weapon possessed by an Opposition to influence political controversy and domestic legislation: and it has moreover relinquished this weapon at a moment when its use was bringing about almost entirely favourable results.

Indeed, it is not too much to say that all the advantages of the Party truce remain with the Government: and all its disadvantages with the Opposition. The Opposition has given up contesting by-elections and propaganda work in the country. The Government pursues its course of domestic legislation, retarded and truncated it is true, but nevertheless by no means entirely suspended. It expects from the Opposition entire acquiescence in its war policy, resents criticism of its actions in connection with the war, hints indeed at a joint responsibility when mistakes are pointed out, but takes great care that all praise for successes shall be showered exclusively upon itself.

If the Government maintain their present attitude in the coming session, and the Opposition confines itself to unavailing protests in the House, and also abstains from criticising the Government's mistakes in the conduct of the War, then I submit it will be doing itself incalculable harm in the Country, and will also be injuring national interests by refraining from the first duty of an Opposition.

The Country will accept the view which the Liberal Party present to them, that the Government has made no mistakes, are perfect patriots, cannot be criticised and that the Opposition fully approve and share the responsibility of their policy. Criticism under these conditions from more independent public persons will be treated – as indeed Liberals now treat it – as little less than High Treason, certainly extremely unpatriotic, and the result will be seen at the next General Election whether it comes during the War, or after the conclusion of Peace.

While the Opposition is to have no respite from domestic legislation; (to which it is bitterly opposed but cannot make use of the ordinary weapons) it is clear from Lord Crewe's recent speech in the House of Lords that criticism of blunders is to be met by the Government with the suggestion of joint responsibility for the War policy.

This is a situation which in the highest interests of the Party it seems to me requires immediate attention.

Lord Crewe made definite statements in his answer to Lord Curzon. Mr. Bonar Law and Mr. Austen Chamberlain have replied. My name was mentioned by Lord Crewe. I have not thought it necessary to write to the newspapers, although Mr. Bonar Law's letter only referred to Lord Lansdowne and himself, for I thought that I could fairly consider that the greater included the less and that it was not necessary for me to send a disclaimer also.

Lord Crewe has remained silent, and there has been no withdrawal or even qualification of his statements. Naturally the greatest possible confusion exists in the minds of the people, nobody can by any possibility understand the situation in which the leading men of both parties make statements which are wholly inconsistent one with the other. Surely, this ought to be cleared up in a declaration applying not only to the Leaders of the Party in the two Houses but to the two Front Benches, and our entire absence of responsibility for or previous knowledge of the Government's War policy should be emphatically declared.

It is not of course for me to suggest in what way these objects should be attained. Personally I incline to a statement published in the Press, signed by the two leaders of the Party, and if this statement could include a definite declaration that in order to distribute the burden of Military Service equitably they were prepared to support a system of compulsory service for the period of the War, I believe it would give a healthy and much desired lead to the country, would not only greatly strengthen the position of the Party but also receive support from a very large number of people who would welcome a declaration involving, as it must do, some risk to the Party making it. The statement would of course clearly indicate that all questions of Party policy are subjugated to the great and moment-ous issue of the moment, and also express the opinion that so far as it is consistent with public interests the Country ought to know quite clearly what the Government policy is and, broadly speaking, what steps they are taking to bring it to a successful issue. In this respect I would refer to the article of the Military Correspondent of the 'Times' of January 14th.[3]

I will only very briefly indicate why I think compulsion is necessary now. Under the present system the best men are going. The agricultural districts for instance, are being absolutely denuded of labour, and more men cannot be spared unless agriculture is to come to a standstill. I am informed on excellent authority that the French are so determined that this shall not happen in France that they are temporarily releasing from service, in groups, men connected with the various French agricultural industries in order that the necessary work may be done.

Also a very large proportion – put by some at 60 or 70 per cent – of the men now going to the Colours are married with children dependent upon them. This means an enormous burden to the Country, both to-day and in the future. As an example, a single man – a private – costs, in pay and keep, we will say £1 per week to the country; a married man – a private – with 4 children costs the same, plus provision for his dependants, namely 16s.9d: and more for higher ranks. There are many thousands of unmarried men, especially in the towns, who are not joining the Colours but could well be spared, and who would have to go if some compulsory system were adopted.

I have suggested to the War Office that there should be a return of the population of all recruiting areas and the proportion of men serving with the Colours whether recruited before the 5th August or afterwards. This would show what percentage in each area has gone to the Colours. Compulsion would then follow according to these figures and in such a way as to throw the extra burden upon the districts where the small number had already enlisted.

I learn that at present the War Office declines to give any information on this point on the plea that it would give the case away to the enemy. This, of course, is not to be contemplated but high authorities declare the Germans have full knowledge already.

However, I only throw this out as a suggestion, but I do most earnestly beg that consideration may be given to the general aspect of the case. The country is most desirous that there should be some definite lead given and are most apprehensive as to the present situation. Of this, the book of Mr. Austen Harrison 'The Kaiser's War' and the article by the 'Military Correspondent' of the 'Times', already referred to, give eloquent proof, coming as they do, from the pens of men who have nothing to do in any way with Party politics and who certainly could not be claimed as supporters of the Unionist Party.

W.H.L
27 January 1915

Enclosure (3)

I agree with Mr. Walter Long in thinking that the relations between the Government and the Opposition, if not already intolerable, are quite likely before long to become so. The position appears to me to be this:

We are expected to give a mute and almost unquestioning support to everything done by the Government, to maintain a patriotic silence about the various blunders that have been committed in connection with the War (e.g. *Goeben, Audacious, Hogue, Cressy, Aboukir*, Antwerp, E. Africa, Cradock, *Formidable*, our Submarines at Yarmouth and Hartlepools, etc. etc.),[4] to dismantle our Party machinery, to forgo all possibility of Party advantage, and to allow, without a protest, the most outrageously partizan of measures, such as the Plural Voting Bill, to be carried over our heads, or even with our consent. In other words the Government are to have all the advantages, while we have all the drawbacks of a coalition. They tell us nothing or next to nothing of their plans, and yet they pretend our Leaders share both their knowledge and their responsibility. If we ask perfectly legitimate questions in the House of Lords, we are treated as though we were naughty children, to be snubbed even by Lord Lucas. The Secretary of State for War reads us exiguous Memoranda of platitudes known to everybody, is acclaimed by the Liberal Press as having delivered an almost inspired oration and scored off his impertinent antagonists, he interpolates a curt affirmative or negative to the solitary speech to which he deigns to listen, and he then marches out and leaves the rest of the debate to colleagues who either affect to know nothing or screen their silence behind his authority. The Parliamentary Recruiting Committee[5] was started under the patronage of the leaders and with the aid of the organisation of both Political Parties. But we are not allowed to hear anything about the results. The whole agency of the Unionist Party has been utilised to obtain additions to the Army. But if we ask how the effort has fared, or what is the present situation, we are treated almost as though we were enemies of our Country.

I do not think that this state of affairs can continue indefinitely, both because the temper of our Party will not long stand it, and because in the interests of the Nation, the position is both highly inexpedient and unfair. We are ready enough to give the Government our support, but it can only be if they give us their confidence, and if they refrain from taking advantage of our patriotism. We cannot cease to be an Opposition for our own purposes, and yet remain one for theirs. The question is what steps, if any, should be taken to terminate this situation? Like Mr. Long I am entirely against a Coalition Government, even if, (which I do not at present think in the least likely) it were proposed to us by the other side. A Coalition would tie our hands and close our lips even more effectively than at present. It would make us responsible for many things which we ought to criticise, if not now, at any rate later: and, with politicians so widely severed on almost all questions, save the war, as are the leading members of the two Parties – it might lead to a disastrous breakdown, followed by painful disclosures or injurious recriminations. If the Country were actually and seriously invaded a Coalition Government might become expedient and even necessary. But for the present it does not seem needful to discuss it.

But another remedy is possible, and that is a clear statement of the Leaders of the Opposition of the conditions under which they ought to be asked to give, and are willing to continue to give their unhesitating support to the Government in prosecuting the War. These conditions might include (a) the abandonment of all Party legislation or strife pending the duration of the War; (b) the taking of the Leaders of the Opposition into full confidence about all important matters connected with the conduct of the War, our relations with the Allies, the progress of recruiting, the steps to be taken to supply our armies, in fact the policy and strategy, as well as the incidents of the struggle.

A subsidiary but important feature would be an understanding with regard to the holding or postponement of the next General Election due at the end of this year. If the principle of some such clear understanding were accepted there are several ways by which it might be carried into effect.

Mr. Long favours a public pronouncement made in the newspapers of the two Leaders of our Party.

Another method would be speeches in one or both Houses of Parliament in which the conditions of our support might be explicitly laid down by the Leaders. I should, however, be rather doubtful about this, because, while we could count upon wise speeches from them, others might join in the debate who would be subject to less restraint.

A third idea which I am inclined to favour (if it is decided to move at all) would be a formal communication from the Leaders of our Party to the Prime Minister, inviting either a frank discussion with him of the future conditions of co-operation, and the publication of the decisions arrived at – or, if a Conference is thought for any reason undesirable, then the publication of letters from the Leaders on both sides, indicating the attitude of the two Parties and making clear the degree of responsibility, be it large or small, which we shall henceforward enjoy.

Though I am a National Service man, I should be inclined not to cumber such a correspondence with any pronouncement or invitation about Compulsory Service, not because I doubt the propriety or patriotism of such a declaration, but because I fear that while we shall have universal sympathy in attempting to define both our just obligations and our reasonable demands, we might alienate a portion of this sympathy if we were thought to be utilising the occasion to press forward a particular or in some quarters unpalatable proposal, and might even retard its ultimate adoption by tempting the Government to declare prematurely against it.

C of K

93/26

1. In January 1915 Unionist discontent with the Liberal government's conduct of the war came to a head. Curzon in a debate in the Lords had voiced criticism of the government and Lord Crewe replied that the Unionists had a joint responsibility with the government for war policy. Bonar Law at once wrote to the newspapers disclaiming any such responsibility but this disclaimer was not enough for Curzon and Walter Long who produced memoranda on the difficulties of 'patriotic opposition'.
2. By November 1914 a special committee of the Cabinet, a War Council for 'exploring some of the larger questions of policy' was established on which A. J. Balfour was invited to serve.
3. In which Colonel Charles à Court Repington in an article entitled 'Problems of Defence, 1915 and 1804: Ministers and Mystery' criticised the government for refusing to divulge 'the information which the Opposition speakers in the House of Lords invited them to give on the subject of the war', and warned that 'the British Empire is in no temper to fight behind a veil of mystery'.
4. The *Audacious*, *Hogue*, *Cressy*, *Aboukir*, and *Formidable* were Royal Naval

Vessels sunk by the Germans early in the war. The *Goeben* was a German battleship which gave the slip to her British pursuers in August 1914. Sir Christopher Cradock, a Rear-Admiral, was defeated at Coronel and drowned on 1 November 1914.

5. The Parliamentary Recruiting Committee was an all-party body established in August 1914 with Asquith, Bonar Law and Arthur Henderson as joint presidents to co-ordinate canvassing and propaganda throughout the country.

27.  To Sophia Palmer

49 Mount Street
W.
29 May 1915

Dearest So,

. . . So the war government has become a fait accompli here[1] and I am in it. Do not congratulate me. It is very difficult to sit down and work with the men we have been fighting bitterly for years but we have done it without a reservation. It will be a war cabinet and nothing else. The responsibility is immense, but I do not think that we shall lack courage.

I have got the Board of Agriculture, quite an interesting office to me and with a special war importance of its own, food supply etc . . .

S

114/98

1. On 26 May 1915 a coalition government consisting of twelve Liberals, eight Unionists, one Labour member, and Lord Kitchener, was formed following a major crisis precipitated by the resignation of the First Sea Lord, Sir John Fisher. The fullest account of this crisis is Cameron Hazlehurst, *Politicians at War* (London, 1971), part III, 'A National Government'. See also John O. Stubbs' important unpublished D. Phil. thesis, 'The Conservative party and the politics of War, 1914–16' (Oxford, 1973), ch. 6. The Selborne papers contain no significant references to the crisis of 1915 nor to the negotiations which preceded the construction of the coalition government.

# Chapter 4

## *'Purgatory to almost all of us': A Unionist in Government, 1915–1916*

1.  From Viscount Milner

Sturry Court
Sturry
Kent
6 June 1915

*Confidential*

My dear Selborne,

Not being in the Government myself, I shall make myself an extensive nuisance to my friends who are. *Fortunately there is not the slightest reason to answer* my letters. And it won't take you long to read them.

I think you are the most fortunate of the new ministers because 1) There is more room for doing a big thing in respect of Agriculture than in any other branch, and one *vitally affecting* our power of endurance in the long struggle, 2) You are more likely to be undistracted in making your plans than any of your colleagues. Everybody is now in full cry after 'munitions'. You have the unspeakable advantage of being free to think out your policy in peace and to work out a complete scheme for the emergency without being worried and screamed at all the time by busybodies inside and outside Parliament (*nota bene* I am at present the only such busy body, and when I called attention in August last to the vital necessity of increasing our *home-grown* food supply, Lucas blew me away with a few remarks of amazing superficiality. St. David's – Argentine Railway Man – assured his fellow-Peers that a rise in 'price' of wheat was a bogey – why trouble about growing it, when you could import any amount you wanted? – and nobody else took the slightest interest in the matter. The trifling consideration, that imports have got to be paid for, and that as we *must* import millions upon millions of stuff anyway, not only for ourselves but our allies, it is of the utmost importance we import nothing that we can possibly make or *grow* ourselves, did not then, and does not even now, strike the general mind.

So much the better as long as *you* are alive to it. And I am sure you are, besides having a lot of practical knowledge how to set about it. My own knowledge is only second-hand, though, as far as mere 'mugging-up' the subject goes, I have done more than most people these last 15 years and have formed some very strong opinions. One of these, I fear, is, that the directing minds of the Permanent Department, though I know there are some good men in it, have no conceptions either how big a thing might be done in increasing, and at once – I mean within this very next twelve months – on home production, or how essential it is, or what very drastic measures alone can do it. The delivery of occasional homilies – harmless if not very original – to the farming community won't cut much ice. And the people, who thought even so mild a proposal as guaranteeing 40/- a quarter on wheat last autumn, too revolutionary, are hardly likely to look with favour upon the much stronger measures which alone can do very much good now. I daresay you have under your orders men of considerable knowledge, who will be very valuable as critics. But I am sure *the driving power will have to come from yourself*.

On the other hand, the men do exist – and practical men too – who could, I am sure, help enormously, if they were 'roped in' betimes. There was, I know, at one time a consultative Committee, which contained some of the best of them, but I don't think your predecessor set much store by its recommendations, and it would only be in the nature of things if the officials encouraged him to pooh-pooh them. I don't mean to say that the Committee represented anything like the full strength of available expert opinion, though there were some very good men on it – Strutt, Bathurst, Ailwyn Fellowes, Christopher Turnor. But A.D. Hall was not on it, nor, I think, R. Prothero, and no doubt there are others known to you, whom I could name. My point is that if a bold policy is to be adopted with any chance of success, I think you will have to look outside the Department for your principal helpers.

I know you won't misunderstand me, or think that I want to 'crab' your regular subordinates, which would be quite improper on my part and which your loyal spirit would naturally resent. But we all admit, that this is an exceptional and very critical time and everybody is saying that we must inspan on whole reserves of capacity. Emergency measures, emergency men. I am only an outsider in these matters, but I have followed rather closely for some time the pothering efforts of Government to do something for Agriculture.

Runciman put some life into the business, but there was a sad relapse under Lucas. And now here is the biggest chance that ever was, for, under the pressure of funk you will be able to apply a pressure to the more backward section of the farming community, which would excite fierce resistance and be politically dangerous at ordinary times. 'More power to your elbow'.

Forgive a long screed, which requires no acknowledgement. From, yours ever

Milner

12/246

2. To A. Bonar Law

49 Mount Street
W.
7 July 1915

My dear Bonar Law,

I am never quite comfortable when I disagree with you strongly on a matter of importance. This must be my excuse for writing to you at length about the Dardanelles.[1]

We are in complete agreement about the colossal blundering of our predecessors. I take up the question on the position as we found it when we took office.

Could we have withdrawn, could we withdraw now, from the Gallipoli peninsula?

No.

We might have faced the consequences of the loss of prestige in Persia and in Egypt and the Balkans, involving the certainty that no Balkan state would take up arms in our cause during this war.

We could not face the consequences in India. It would have meant rebellion. It would mean rebellion now. In these respects the consequences of withdrawal would not differ from the consequences of defeat.

In addition the task of withdrawing the army in the face of the Turkish army and of the German submarines is an impossible task. The best naval and military advice we have received is that it would involve an immense catastrophe and Robertson told me at your house that he agreed that that was so.

Therefore withdrawal is impossible.

Could we remain in the Gallipoli peninsula with a passive, or almost passive, defensive?

Our policy would soon have become apparent to everyone, transparent in fact. All chance of obtaining the aid of Bulgaria would have disappeared. The consequences in Egypt, Persia and India must in varying degrees have been very serious due to loss of prestige, the Turks would have resumed their offensive operations against Egypt, against our forces in the Euphrates valley, and against the Russians in the Caucasus. The real relief which in my opinion our action has afforded to the Russians in their time of greatest strain would have disappeared, and we should have had to send more troops to Egypt and to the head of the Persian gulf. By no means all, possibly none, of the troops which we have sent and are sending to reinforce Hamilton, would have been liberated for service in Flanders if we had adopted the policy of a passive defensive. Besides the reinforcements, which, as I suggest, would have had to be sent to Egypt and to the head of the Persian gulf, reliefs for the troops already in the Gallipoli peninsula must certainly have been sent there.

Moreover the naval part of the expeditionary force would have been exposed to exactly the same risks under a policy of passive defence as under our present policy and the effect of the policy on the morale of the heroic army in the Gallipoli peninsula would have been absolutely disastrous. To expose troops to the permanent defensive, to tell them that there is no objective in front of them, that Bulgaria can never come to their assistance, that they will receive no reinforcements, and that mere existence is the best that they can hope for as long as the war lasts, is really to prepare the way for a successful Turkish offensive and for a catastrophe.

Therefore in my judgement the only policy open to us was that which we have adopted, a vigorous, but reasoned as opposed to a headlong, offensive.

Now what are the chances of success for that offensive? There are no certainties in war and war cannot be waged without taking great risks – of course we are taking great risks. Is the risk of a military catastrophe in the Gallipoli peninsula due to the offensive policy we have adopted? In my judgement there is much less risk of such a catastrophe under the policy we have adopted than there would be under a policy of passive defensive. That is of course only an opinion, but it is my opinion.

Is there a fair chance of success? Again that is a matter of opinion, but in my opinion there is.

If the attack from Anzac[2] fails, that will be a fresh serious rebuff but it ought not to involve a catastrophe, and the submarine presence entailing semi starvation of ammunition will still continue and produce its effect.

But if the attack from Anzac succeeds and the Turkish army is hemmed in in the toe of the peninsula, I cannot see how, humanely speaking, it can escape surrender.

I really had no patience with Wilson when he said that it could withdraw to Bulair.[3] Think what that means. The distance across the peninsula where an attack will be made is so short that the Turkish army in the toe has got to make up its mind to retreat before it is clear that our attack is going to succeed at all. Is that really likely? If it waits till we have half succeeded, it will be too late. To attempt to deploy before one army on its flank with another larger army pressing its rear is to make a catastrophe.

But whether the Turkish army in the toe is starved out and surrenders, or whether it safely retreats to Bulair, is it not, humanely speaking, certain that we could take the Khalid Bahr forts.[4] They would be raked with the fire of our big guns on the high ground above them and by the monitors in the Dardanelles. But says Wilson, if you take Khalid Bahr, you will not take Chanak. 'Take', *no*, unless we land troops on the Asiatic side, but 'silence the fire' of the guns so as to enable the mine sweepers to clear the Channel, *yes*. Again this is and can be only an opinion. Let us thrash it out and cross examine the best naval and military experts not K only.

I understand that the best naval opinion says that Chanak and the other defences of the narrows, fixed or mobile could then be dealt with sufficiently to enable the fleet to get up into the Sea of Marmora, to destroy the Russian and Turkish ships, to destroy the arsenals, and possibly to cut the communications of Constantinople by rail and road. If the fleet once gets into the sea of Marmora in my opinion Bulgaria will certainly join us and the trick will have been won. If Bulgaria does not join us, I agree with you that our army will not be strong enough to take and hold Constantinople, but it could easily hold the whole Gallipoli peninsula. That would be a great gain of prestige by itself. The army could rest there securely behind the lines of Bulair, and wait till the Russians were recovered sufficiently to come and help us from the Euxine[5] side or till the Bulgarians or Greeks came in.

But let us suppose that Wilson is right and the sailors are wrong, and that, even if we take the Gallipoli peninsula up to the narrows, we cannot silence Chanak etc and the fleet cannot get through to the sea of Marmora.

That will be a great disappointment, but nevertheless a great improvement of the position.

We ought to be able to take the whole peninsula up to Bulair, and in my judgement Bulgaria would come in, or at the worst we could hold so much of the peninsula as we occupied in security until the Russians were ready or one of the Balkan states came in.

No doubt part of our army would be subjected, as the French are now, to the very trying experience of fire from the Asiatic side, but we could give the Turks just as good as they gave, from the peninsula then, just as now I hope that the French will soon experience substantial relief from the fire of naval guns landed on the peninsula, and from that of our Monitors, when they get out, directed against the Turkish guns on the Asiatic coast which now harass them. Finally I repeat that there can be no certainties in war and that you cannot make war successfully unless you are prepared to take great risks. The one question I have tried to answer to myself is this. Of all possible courses open to us where lies the greatest chance of success and the least proportion of risk? The answer I have formulated is, 'in the policy which we have decided to adopt'.[6] Yours ever

Selborne

B.L. 51/1/10

1.  Lord Selborne was referring to a letter written by Bonar Law on 8 June 1915 in which Law expressed his 'pessimism about the Dardanelles position', and explained his reluctance to support the recommendation of the newly constituted Dardanelles Committee, which met for the first time on 7 June, to send reinforcements to Gallipoli (80/8).

    The ill−fated Dardanelles expedition was planned by Churchill in January 1915, with the original aim of making a naval attack on the Turkish forts on the Gallipoli peninsula, thus providing a diversion to relieve Turkish pressure on the Russian armies in the Caucasus. This was extended to include a landing by troops on the peninsula itself. A naval strike on 18 March was a failure, but the military side of the campaign continued with landings by British and Imperial forces under the command of Sir Ian Hamilton on 25 April 1915. Early optimism was dispelled when the troops were unable to break out of their beachheads, and were forced to dig in under heavy fire from the Turks. Attacks

by the British, Australian and New Zealand troops were pressed with great gallantry, but to no avail. Eventually, in December 1915, the government decided to evacuate the peninsula, which was done by 9 January 1916.
2. Anzac cove was a beach on the Gallipoli peninsula nicknamed after the Australian and New Zealand troops who landed there on 25 April.
3. A fortified town at the neck of the Gallipoli peninsula.
4. Forts on the north east part of the Gallipoli peninsula, separated from Chanak by the narrows of the Dardanelles.
5. i.e. Black Sea.
6. Lord Selborne's opinion about the options facing the government in Gallipoli are also summarised in a Cabinet memorandum 'The Dardanelles', 5 June 1915, copy in 126/24.

3.   From M.P.A. Hankey

13 July 1915

Dear Lord Selborne, I was very much interested to receive your letter this morning describing the practical steps which you have taken towards stimulating an increased production of foodstuffs in this country in 1916.[1] You may be sure of my most cordial assistance in any way possible. In a Memorandum which I sent to the Prime Minister a fortnight ago dealing with the general situation from a military, economic and financial point of view, I urged the great importance of taking the submarine menace seriously, and making preparations beforehand to meet it. I am rather afraid lest the recent successes that the Navy have had against submarines may make the Admiralty over-sanguine as to their power to deal with them. Personally, I believe that the submarines can and will be mastered in time, but it would be quite wrong for us to take any risks in the matter. From this point of view, therefore, it is imperative that we should leave no stone unturned to make our food supplies secure whatever happens, and no means of doing this can be so beneficial as increased productivity.

It is, however, not from this point of view alone that I am anxious to see an increased production of foodstuffs. From the economic point of view it is essential that our imports should be cut down as much as possible, as owing to the inevitable increase to the imports of war material for ourselves and our Allies, for which we have to pay, and owing to the reduced exports, the balance of trade is going badly against us. If we could prduce our own wheat supply, or a considerable portion of it, our imports would *pro tanto* be decreased, and we should have less to pay for abroad.

I will not touch upon the economic importance after the war of a great agricultural development which will give employment to some of the hundreds of thousands of soldiers thrown on the labour market, because it brings me into a controversial subject rather outside my own sphere of activity. From the point of view of the next war, however, whether it comes 10 or 100 years hence, I am absolutely convinced that we must place ourselves beyond dependence on foreign supplies for the necessities of existence, and the steps you propose as an *ad hoc* measure will, I hope, lay the foundations of a great national system which may be a safeguard to us in years to come.

I suppose that your Committee will go into the question of ways and means, and particularly the provision of labour? During my three recent visits to France I have been so much impressed by the amount of work done by old men, women and children. The women seem none the worse for it, and I believe it would be a splendid thing if we could get the women on the land in this country too. Another point of detail which greatly struck me in France was the way corn crops were interspersed with different kinds of root crops, there being no continuous fields of one crop such as one sometimes sees in this country. My thoughts revert to this in connection with a possibility of an aerial attack by incendiary bombs on our crops, which would be limited in scope by the adoption of the system in vogue in France.

I should be very much obliged if you would have a copy of any Report, or interim Report, of your Committee sent to me as soon as it is issued, as I should like to be able to comment on it to the Prime Minister at once.

Please excuse dictated letter, I have two long meetings to-day and a good deal of paper work as well. Yours sincerely

M.P.A. Hankey

80/14

1.  On 17 June 1915 Lord Selborne appointed a departmental committee to consider what steps should be taken to increase the production of food in the country. The committee was chaired by Lord Milner, and included Lord Inchcape, Francis D. Acland, E.G. Strutt, Sir Harry C. W. Verney, Charles W. Fielding, A.D. Hall, Rowland E. Prothero, and J.A. Seddon (copy of minute of appointment, MS Selborne 81 fol. 59).

4.  To H.H. Asquith, A. Bonar Law, Lord Lansdowne, Reginald McKenna, A.J. Balfour, Austen Chamberlain.

15 July 1915

Acland tells me that the Committee which I appointed to inquire whether the amount of food produced in England and Wales next year could be increased is going to send in an Interim Report this week recommending a guarantee to the English and Welsh farmers of a certain minimum price for wheat for three or four years, so that a large additional acreage of land may be put under wheat for the harvest of 1916. And I understand that they are going to make the recommendation on the assumption that the Government consider that it would be prudent to ensure this additional production of wheat during the War as a measure of precaution against the action of the German submarines or otherwise; and that they consider the estimate of the extent of that danger and of the degree of necessity for any precautionary measures to be the responsibility of the Government.

I have not seen the Report in any form at all and I am only reporting the impression which Acland's conversation has given to me, but I should say that this was quite the right attitude for the Committee to assume, and certainly there are no other grounds on which I should recommend to the Cabinet the adoption of any such precaution.

I propose to circulate the Interim Report to the Cabinet the moment I receive it, with a covering memorandum of my own, and hope that it can be considered at an early day, because, if the Cabinet did decide to take any action, legislation would be necessary before Parliament adjourns and I should have to get to work on the draft of the Bill immediately.

81/53

5.  From H.H. Asquith

10 Downing Street
Whitehall S.W.
16 July 1915

My dear Selborne,
By all means circulate the Report.

In my opinion there is not the least fear that any probable or conceivable development of German submarine activity can be a serious menace to our food supply. Yours sincerely

H.H. Asquith

80/23

6.  To H.H. Asquith

Board of Agriculture & Fisheries
4 Whitehall Place S.W.
22 July 1915

My dear Asquith,
I am circulating today the interim report of Milner's Committee[1] with a memorandum of my own.

The details of the proposed guarantee and its conditions must be matter for consideration; but I am recommending the principle to the Cabinet as on the whole the best plan for ensuring a reserve of wheat in the country during the war. I am more anxious about the results of the German submarine warfare during the latter period of the war than you are; but, be that as it may, a reserve of wheat we must have in the country, and there appear to me to be more difficulties and disadvantages in any repetition of the plan adopted by the late Cabinet than there are in the one which I propose. It was quite impossible for me to get these papers circulated earlier, and you propose to terminate the sittings of Parliament next week! If the Cabinet will not accept my plan, cadit qaestor; but, if it accepts the principle, then, as it appears to me, legislation will be necessary. You may be able to suggest a way out, but the difficulty which troubles me is that the farmers must be told next month in order that they may begin ploughing in

September and October, and there will be much organising work to do. And there are very obvious objections to saying anything to the farmers before the approval of the House of Commons has been obtained.

Therefore I hope that the Cabinet may be able to consider the matter early next week, and, perhaps, after you have read the papers you will tell me how the difficulty justify [sic] those possibilities . . . Yours sincerely

Selborne

Enclosure

Printed for the use of the
Cabinet

*Secret*

July 1915

I ENCLOSE herewith a copy of an Interim Report adopted by all members of the Committee which I appointed, with the Prime Minister's approval, to report what steps should be taken for the sole purpose of maintaining, and, if possible, increasing the present production of food in England and Wales on the assumption that the war may be prolonged beyond the harvest of 1916.

The Committee state: 'It has not appeared to us within the terms of our reference to enquire, nor have we as a matter of fact enquired, into the nature and extent of the dangers threatening our imported food supplies. But, if in the opinion of the Government, which is alone competent to judge of this question, an emergency is likely to exist after the harvest of next year, which calls for the adoption of exceptional measures at the present time, there are certain steps, only effective if taken immediately, to which we feel bound to direct attention in the present Interim Report.'

Those steps may be summarised as follows:–

1.   A guarantee of a minimum price of 45s. a quarter for all marketable home-grown wheat for a period of four years, beginning with the harvest of 1916. That is, for the cereal years (September to September) 1916–17, 1917–18, 1918–19, 1919–20.

2.   Any payment to the farmer under the suggested guarantee should be regulated by the difference between 45s. and the 'Gazette' average price of wheat for the year in which the wheat is harvested, the farmer being left free to dispose of his produce in the open market.

3.   No farmer to be able to profit by the guarantee unless he can show either that he has increased his area under arable cultivation by at least one-fifth over the similar area in October 1913, or that at least one-fifth of his total acreage under grass and annual crops is actually under wheat.

The Committee state that as the result of this guarantee agricultural wages ought to rise, and that, in their opinion, they will rise automatically; but that, if they do not so rise, measures should be taken to ensure the necessary rise. They therefore recommend that an enquiry should be instituted at once into agricultural wages and earnings, so that complete information may be available at an early date.

I recommend that the Interim Report of the Committee be adopted by the Cabinet, but with a reservation about the form of the guarantee and with an additional condition to be attached to the guarantee, to which I attach great importance and which I will set forth presently. I hope that I may be authorised to have a Bill embodying the recommendations contained in it drafted and introduced into the House of Commons.

I make this recommendation as a matter of war necessity. We cannot make war without taking risks, but there are some risks which we have no right to take if we can make any provision against them. One of those risks is invasion, and another is shortage of the food of the people. The war may possibly come to an end before the harvest of 1916, but I am afraid that it will not be so. Certainly we cannot be sure that the war will be over by that date, and therefore we must consider the conditions under which we may be waging war subsequently to 1916.

That the closing months of this war will involve a terrible strain in every possible way on the nation no one can doubt, and if that strain should be accompanied by a shortage of bread, however temporary, the effect on the issue of the war might be very grave. It must also be borne in mind that, as there will inevitably be some shortage in the supply of meat, and a large shortage in the supply of fish, the nation will probably consume more bread than usual.

The question is what will be the effect of the submarine warfare carried on by the German Navy on our mercantile marine fifteen or eighteen months hence? I confess frankly that I am very anxious on the subject. The Germans are doubtless building as many submarines as they possibly can, and, therefore, a year hence there will be more submarines operating round the coasts of the United Kingdom than there are at the present moment. I think the way the Navy has met the submarine menace and the way they have kept the losses of our mercantile marine down by ceaseless vigilance is wonderful, but, unless some more certain method of dealing with submarines is discovered, I cannot doubt that much more damage will be done in the closing months of the war than has yet been done; and it is probable that, so far as it is possible for them to make a selection among the ships coming to these shores, the German submarines will endeavour to destroy ships which carry our food. That the German Government would deal us a mortal blow through the submarines if it could, no one can doubt. The following extract from the Daily Graphic of the 14th July seems much to this point:–

Amsterdam, Tuesday
The German Government has circulated through the press an article on 'The Historical Mission of Germany's Submarines.' 'England,' it says, 'must learn by the present war that her world-power is no longer unassailable. This is only to be taught by the submarines. With Russia an

understanding is not impossible, as only a few political questions separate us from the Petrograd Government. France only wanted to fight us over the old quarrel of 1870. The struggle still continues; but as to England, whom we consider our most dangerous and foulest enemy, we must break the principle of "Britons ruling the waves." This is the historical mission of our submarines, which have already partially fulfilled it.'

                                                                    Exchange

   Therefore I think it is a precaution which we should not be justified in omitting to endeavour to increase the amount of wheat produced in England at the harvest of 1916. It is true that we cannot expect, however successful our efforts might be, to get more than 11,400,000[2] quarters grown in England, but that would be raising the proportion from over one-fifth to almost exactly one-third of the total annual consumption; and the additional condition which I should impose in respect of the proposed guarantee is that, while the war lasts, beginning from the harvest of this year, the farmer should not sell a larger proportion of his wheat before the month of May than the Government thought prudent without a licence from the Board of Agriculture. The effect of this condition would be, supposing that three-quarters of the wheat-growing farmers accepted it, and we allowed no home-grown wheat to be sold before May, that we should have an additional reserve of (say) 4,000,000 quarters[3] or six weeks' supply, stored in the country, from September 1915 to May 1916, and of (say) 6,500,000 quarters, or ten weeks' supply, stored in the country, from September 1916 to May 1917, beyond whatever might be in the hands of the corn merchants or millers. This would be a great addition to our security, as the stocks run low from January to September.[4]

   I wish to draw the special attention of the Cabinet to this condition. In my judgment, the fact that we sometimes have not much more than eight weeks' supply of wheat or flour in the United Kingdom at any one time constitutes the danger point from the submarine menace during the latter period of the war. Eight or nine weeks' supply of wheat does not really mean a supply of bread for the nation for that period. There must be a margin for the trade to draw upon, liquid in the country, and long before the period was over there would be a dearth of bread in many parts of the country, while wheat and flour were still to be found in millers' or bakers' or household stocks in other parts of the country, supposing that during these weeks the supply from overseas was suspended or seriously interrupted. But it is certain that the stocks of wheat in the United Kingdom would have fallen considerably below an eight weeks' supply in June and July of this year if it had not been for the large purchases of Indian and other wheat made by the Government. These purchases were said by the merchants to have greatly disturbed the corn market, but is is certain that in some form or other the operation must be repeated as a precaution for 1916, and again for 1917 if the war is prolonged, if we are not to run too great a risk. Some of us believe that it will be impossible for the Government to repeat the operation of last year and buy Indian or other wheat without taking over the whole corn trade of the country, because the merchants will feel that they do not know the conditions of the market, will refuse to take risks, and so the stocks will run down to the danger level. Therefore, if any wheat is bought by us, we may have to take over the whole corn trade of the country for the duration of the war – an operation of immense difficulty and complexity as well as magnitude, and involving an unknown liability certainly greater than that involved in the scheme which I recommend – while possessing none of its subsidiary advantages. This scheme would not disturb the market in the same way. The Government would never enter the market as sellers, and the traders would know all the conditions that they would have to meet. There would be no necessity whatever to take over and manage the corn trade.

In respect of the form of the guarantee, I am not sure that that suggested by the Committee, viz., that 'any payment to the farmer under the suggested guarantee should be regulated by the difference between 45s. and the 'Gazette' average price of wheat for the year' is the best one, or that the provision in respect of the proportion of land to be under the plough or under wheat is adequate for ensuring that the farmer should have really qualified to benefit by the guarantee. These points, and others, would have to be carefully considered by the Board of Agriculture.

I do not pretend that it is possible to make an accurate forecast of the financial liability involved in the adoption of this policy. What will be the duration of the war, or what will be the price of wheat during the war and immediately after the war can only be a matter of opinion. Some may think that the war will not last much longer, and that whenever it ends there will be a sharp fall in the price of wheat. In that case the liability might be large. My opinion, for what it is worth, is that there is little chance of the price of wheat in this country falling below 45s. in the cereal years 1916–17 and 1917–18, even if the war were ended in the year 1916. No one can foresee what the harvests of the world in 1916 and 1917 are going to be, but, even if they are plentiful, there will be a great demand for them during the war and immediately after the war; and the amount of tonnage available for the carrying on of the trade of the world after the war will probably remain short of the demand until new tonnage can be created, and therefore freights will remain high. Many ships will have been destroyed during the war and very little extra tonnage created, and it will be some months after the war before the tonnage which is now being used for military and naval purposes will all be released to carry on the trade of the world. Therefore, so far as I can foresee, the years in which the taxpayer might be called upon to redeem his guarantee to the farmer would be in the cereal years 1918–19 and 1919–20, and I do not think that he would be called upon to pay anything in 1918–19 either if the war is prolonged into the year 1917. In my judgment, based on the best opinions that I can obtain, there is no chance of the price of wheat falling below 40/– a quarter in the years 1918–19 and 1919–20, however soon the war ends.

I have stated that I recommend that Parliament be asked to give this guarantee on the grounds of a war precaution, but I may be permitted to point out that there are other important advantages involved in the adoption of the policy which may be urged in its favour. If the policy was successful in inducing the farmers to grow more wheat, then a large quantity of wheat would be produced in England which otherwise would be bought from abroad. The net result would be a substantial contribution to the equilibrium of the foreign exchange and so to the maintenance of the national credit. Further, a large additional acreage of land in England would have been put under the plough and so would furnish additional employment for the men discharged from the army after the termination of the war.

It has been the wish of all parties to see the rate of wages paid to the agricultural labourer raised, and I agree with the Committee in thinking that that rate would be permanently influenced to his advantage by the guaranteed price of wheat during these years. I agree also with the Committee that, if the rate of his wages did not rise automatically as they believe it would, measures must be taken to ensure that it does.

Finally, I would urge this argument. The submarine menace has come to stay. If the dire calamity of another great war should fall on this country twenty years hence, and if, in the meantime, no sure naval safeguard against the submarine has been evolved, then the overseas trade of the United Kingdom, and with it its overseas supply of food, would indeed be in peril. Meanwhile, and until a sure safeguard has been found, we must take what other measures are open to us to increase our security. One of these measures is the increase of the home production of wheat. What made the farmer hesitate to plough up his poorer grass lands in the agricultural conditions prevailing before the war was the capital cost of the operation and his fear that he might never recover the money he had spent. The effect of a four years' guarantee of a minimum price of 45s. will remove his grounds for hesitation. In my opinion, the effect of the guarantee will be permanent, and the land which has been ploughed up will remain under the plough, and the rate of wages of agriculture will remain raised after the guarantee has come to an end, even should the price of wheat fall once again to what it was before the war, which I do not myself expect.

Since the Committee adopted its report I have received the results of 74 per cent of the agricultural returns for the year, from which it is possible to make a calculation of what the total returns may show. The result of the calculation is that the figures may show an increase of about 390,000 acres of arable and of 483,000 acres of wheat. These figures must be looked at with great caution, as their value depends on the assumption that the remaining 26 per cent of the returns will show the same results as the 74 per cent, and it would not be possible to feel sure of that unless we knew accurately – which I do not – the geographical distribution of the returns already received. If the figures are fairly accurate they would show conclusively that by a guarantee we should obtain an assured reserve of wheat present in the United Kingdom larger than I have suggested, and adequate, so far as we can foresee, to keep us safe against any dearth of bread during the war, however much it may be prolonged or whatever the activity of the enemy's submarines.

A decision is necessary now, because the farmers will begin their operations in connection with the wheat crop of 1916 in the month of September of this year, and because, therefore, any legislation, which is to be effective, must be passed this month, or in August at the latest.

S

21 July 1915

126/50

1. Departmental Committee on the Home Production of Food: interim report, July 1915, copy in the Selborne papers, 126/53.
2. Present production: 7,400,000 quarters, Estimated addition: say, 4,000,000 quarters. From these figures the amount required for seed and wastage must be deducted.
3. The weekly consumption is 660,000 quarters.
4. stocks –

|  |  | Quarters |
|---|---|---|
| October | 1, 1914 | 12,648,000 |
| January | 1, 1915 | 10,107,000 |
| April | 1, 1915 | 6,809,000 |
| July | 1, 1915 | 5,602,000 |

Figures in references 2–4 are Lord Selborne's own estimates.

7.  From H.H. Asquith

10 Downing Street
Whitehall S.W.
26 July 1915

*PRIVATE*

My dear Selborne,

Without entering for the moment into the merits of the questions raised by your Memorandum, I must point out that it is quite impossible for the Government to initiate such legislation as you suggest at present. The subject is a highly contentious one, and both Houses are on the eve of adjournment. Yours sincerely

H.H. Asquith

80/29

8.   To Robert Palmer

49 Mount Street
W.
6 August 1915

My dearest Bobby,

We got your telegram telling us that you were going to join the 4th battalion in Mesopotamia this month so I am writing direct to you there. I am afraid that you will have a very trying experience climatically and that there will be little in your work which is exciting or interesting. I do not think that you can console yourself with any hope of an Arabian Nights entrance into Bagdhad or of an excursion to Ninevah or Babylon. The policy will be a prudent one of beatus possideus. Under such conditions the greatest contribution you can make is to look after the health of your men and your own and to keep their spirits up and that of your brother officers by every means in your power . . .   Milner's committee sent in an interim report recommending a guarantee of a minimum price of wheat of 45/– for four years and I supported this with the attached condition that no farmer should sell his wheat before May without my leave. I knew that 'storage' was the only leverage I had over this Cabinet. But I shall not be able to carry it. In fact no one has supported me except Austen, the unavowed but real reason being fanatical Cobdenism on the one side and the dislike of any interference with landlords and farmers on the other.

We cannot conceal from ourselves the fact that in a life and death struggle such as this intelligently directed autocracy has an immense advantage over democracy.

I shall have to fall back on persuasion and I shall stump the country as soon as the farmers have broken the back of the harvest. I had two technical arguments to meet in my contest with the Cabinet which created great difficulty for me. A.J.B.'s optimism about the German submarine menace, and I *know* that we have not yet experienced its maximum effects. And the result of the figures of the annual agricultural returns to hand since the receipt of Milner's interim report, which show an increase of 23% more land under wheat without any guarantee. As regards storage I shall have to fall back on the inferior device of buying Australian or Canadian wheat and storing it in the U.K.

Warsaw has fallen.

We are very much in the same position as England was in after Austerlitz, except that our test of endurance is not going to be much more than one tenth in time of what our fathers' was and that the allies are not going to desert us. Our P.M. is about as competent for his war task as Pitt's successors were.

That the Everlasting God may keep you guarded in his almighty arms both body and soul is the constant prayer of your devoted father

S

109/61

9.  From A.J. Balfour

Admiralty
Whitehall
1 September 1915

*Dictated*
*private*
My dear Willie,

### Submarines

My view is this:

(1) So far, the losses caused by German submarines have been made up for by building, capture, and purchase; so that our mercantile tonnage is not less than it was at the beginning of the war. On the other hand, we cannot expect this to go on in view of the diminution of shipbuilding produced by the strain on the labour market and other causes.

(2) *If* we are right in our conjectures as to the German shipbuilding, and *if* we are justified in supposing that they will get no more success per submarine in the future than they have in the past, we may hope that, up to the end of next year at all events, the losses in tonnage will not imperil our sea communications.

(3) These, however, partly depend upon the temper of the mercantile marine. I have myself high hopes that our merchant ships will shew as much nerve in the future as in the past. But it has to be observed that neutral shippers already fight shy of the zone of danger. At present the percentage among the crews of sunken vessels who are drowned is not very high. If the submarines were to operate further from land, this would, of course, alter – to our disadvantage.

(4) It is impossible to be satisfied as yet with the success of our patrolling. 23 merchant ships were destroyed in one week in an area where I have established a very energetic Admiral who is devoting his whole time to the subject.[1] And Jellicoe has not, so far, been able to intercept *one* submarine of all those that go north about from Germany, either to the south of Ireland or to the Mediterranean! Now, broadly speaking, this is the course pursued by *all* the big submarines. It is impossible to say that a situation which can be thus described is 'well in hand'!

On the other hand, we are justified in remembering that the Germans themselves are undoubtedly disappointed with the results of their campaign; that their losses have been heavy; and that our own methods of anti-submarine warfare have not yet reached their full development.

Everybody has a right to balance these various considerations according to the best of their judgment, but I hardly think we are any of us justified in saying, or thinking, that the situation is 'well in hand'; though speaking for myself, I am fairly sanguine.

As regards your schemes for wheat supply, my view is shortly this:– There are two objects which we might aim at: one is to increase the total 'world' supply by increasing the home supply: the other is so to arrange that part of the 'world' supply which comes from abroad that we shall never in this country have less than thirteen weeks' available at any time of the year. For various reasons the first has been abandoned but the second I understand is to be carried through. And clearly, from the point of view of the peoples' food, it is the second and not the first, which is the most important. From the point of view of British Agriculture and British Exchanges, the case is otherwise. But these are questions of policy which lead us far away from Submarines and Starvation. Yours affectionately

Arthur James Balfour

1/156

1. Lord Selborne's marginal note: 'we *did* destroy one of the subs which did the damage'.


10.   To Lord Kitchener

49 Mount Street
W.
17 September 1915

My dear Kitchener,

You will remember that I suggested to you to see the Trades Union leaders before the recent Congress. I do not know if you did or not. If you did, your influence was apparent in the loophole of the resolution passed about Compulsory service.[1] If you did not, that loophole shows how great would have been your influence if you had seen them. Some of us in the Cabinet are, as you know, profoundly convinced that the army cannot be kept up to strength through 1916 without compulsory service and that an Act of Parliament on the subject should be passed during the present session of Parliament. But we are as profoundly convinced that we ought to do all in our power to preserve the unity of the nation, if we can do so without conniving at the weakening of the army. Nobody in his senses will take compulsion because Northcliffe presses it upon him.[2] But the Trades Unions and the entire nation will take it from you if you tell them that it is necessary. To carry conviction you must tell them a great deal more than you have yet done. That is your power and opportunity; but there is a great risk for you also. You have immense influence with the officers and rank and file of the army, both at the front and at home, but they are to an enormous majority redhot for compulsion, and, if they think that you delay too long to ask for it, there will be a serious revulsion in their feelings towards you.

Have you considered a plan such as the following? That you should make your case for compulsion now and ask for your Bill to be passsed now, but propose that it should be held in suspense till say Dec. 1. If you had not got your right number of recruits by then, then the Act to be brought into operation by a resolution of the House of Commons and House of Lords. If you had got your right number, and continued to get them, the Act would never come into operation. Meanwhile a summons would be sent in some such form as the following to the men on the National Register[3] of military age and unstarred for exemption, beginning I presume with the younger classes.

### FORM OF SUMMONS

Your service is needed by H.M. The King to help repel and defeat the enemy in arms against your country. You are, therefore, requested to report yourself at                    on                    as fit and willing to serve in the army how and where you may be directed. — — — — — — — — —

This summons would have a tremendous effect if the Act had been passed and was being held in suspense. If it had not been passed, this summons would have very little effect.

Think it over. I should be very ready to come and talk it over with you. You know I hope that I only want to help you in your immense responsibility; but I am feeling my responsibility too very deeply. I shall be away till Tuesday, Yours sincerely

S

80/42

1.  On 7 September 1915 the 47th Trade Union Congress, meeting in Bristol, debated conscription and passed a vaguely worded resolution condemning conscription 'which always proves a burden to the worker, and will divide the nation at a time when absolute unanimity is essential', expressing the belief that the voluntary system properly organised would produce sufficient men, and assuring the government of full T.U.C. support in its effort to secure the men 'necessary to prosecute the war to a successful issue' (*The Times*, 8 September 1915).
2.  In mid August 1915 the Northcliffe press began a major campaign for a scheme of national service.
3.  On 15 July 1915 it was decided that a national register of the total manpower resources of the country of ages fifteen to sixty-five should be compiled. It revealed that over two million single men of military age (eighteen to forty) were not in the armed forces.

11.   From Lord Kitchener

York House
St. James's
17 September [1915]

*Private*

My dear Selborne,

I thought I had made it quite plain that a study of the results of the National Register was in my opinion necessary before any final decision could be profitably come to on the subject of conscription. To act now, as you suggest, would I fear be very unconvincing. I hope shortly to obtain the results of the registration but up to the present we have not had anything to go on.

I daresay notwithstanding the delay the army will trust me to do my best for them whatever that is worth. Yours very truly

Kitchener

80/46

12.   To Robert Palmer

Board of Agriculture & Fisheries
21 September 1915

Dearest Bobby,

I am really writing from rooms in Univ. Coll. where Top and I are staying for a week's session in Oxford of our Church and State Committee.[1]

It is a hardish week for me as I have to carry on my Board of Agriculture etc. work as well and run up to London for Cabinets. Particularly as we are now in a critical time. The question of compulsory service is in danger of splitting the Cabinet and the country, and yet it is a question of fact and not of opinion. It can be shown, as soon as K chooses to show it, that the Army which he has created cannot be maintained all through next year without compulsion. I don't think that there would have been any difficulty if the Harmsworth press had not made a campaign for compulsion and against K and the P.M. simultaneously. The campaign was carried on with complete indifference to genuine Trades Union convictions and suspicions. The *Daily News*, *Daily Chronicle*, and *Star* chipped in with a reckless anti-conscription-at-all-costs campaign. Hence a situation which any foresight on the P.M.'s part might have prevented. It places us who know that compulsion is necessary in a very difficult position. It is our plain duty to strain every nerve to preserve the national unity, but we cannot take the responsibility of conniving at Asquith's 'wait and see' till it will be too late to save the country . . . Your loving father

S

109/79

1.   The Archbishops' Committee on Church and State, established under the chairmanship of Lord Selborne in 1913, which published a report in July 1916. It recommended that the Representative Church Council, composed of bishops, clergy and laity, after certain reforms, should receive statutory recognition, and be given real legislative powers in church matters, subject to parliamentary veto. The report resulted in the Enabling Bill of 1919 which received the royal assent on 23 December 1919.

13.  To H.H. Asquith

Board of Agriculture & Fisheries
4 Whitehall Place
S.W.
23 September 1915

My dear Asquith,

I want to write to you about some matters which are much in my mind.

(1) At Wednesday's Cabinet you decided to appoint a comparatively small committee, with extended powers of action, to meet frequently, and generally to conduct the war for the Cabinet.[1]

I am quite sure that this is right. Some days your meetings might be very brief, but the important thing is that they should be held regularly. I assume that Balfour, Kitchener, Grey and Lloyd George must necessarily be members. There at once you are brought face to face with the difficulty that, if the committee met every day which would be ideal, these Ministers could hardly get through their departmental work. I suggest that you should have Cabinets only on Thursdays and that this committee should meet on Tuesdays and Wednesdays at least. That would leave Mondays free for another meeting of the Committee in case of necessity and Fridays free for a second meeting of the Cabinet if necessary.

I presume that you would add Bonar Law as leader of the late opposition and I for one would feel that the Committee was complete if you added Curzon and Churchill. The great advantage of these two is that they both have ideas, they are both ready critics, and neither of them has an office. I am not sure that it would not be wise to add Henderson.

(2) The next point is the machinery for consultation with our allies. The greatest advantage which Germany has over us in this war is her central position and the elimination of the Austro-Hungarian government for the purposes of the management of the war. Whatever we do we must be badly handicapped in this respect, but we are more handicapped than we need be. I hope that the first thing your war committee will do is to try and devise a machinery for intercommunication and consultation the wheels of which do not creak and groan as do those of the present machine.

(3) Then there is the reorganization of the General Staff. One cannot speak all one's mind in K's presence – 'Do not shout at the man at the wheel, he is doing his best' is a sound maxim. But it is really a public danger of the first magnitude that the effects of a German irruption into the Balkans, which has loomed before us as a possibility for months, has never been studied at the W.O. or any plans devised to meet it, and that all the help we are going to get from the navies or the army is to be the result of a 24 hours consultation between K and Caldwell at the 59th minute of the eleventh hour.

(4) You are going also to constitute a committee of the Cabinet on finance and I am indeed glad of it. May I urge that it should forecast so far as it can what our total power of expenditure may be in the next 18 months.

The war committee could then advise the Cabinet how the means available should be distributed between ourselves and our allies. I wish also to make a suggestion in respect of the next loan. Could not you use the local authorities in each county, county borough, or borough to impress on the wage earners the patriotic duty of living economically and putting their savings into war loan? We have taken care that the burthen of grinding hardship should not fall on them in this war, and the result is that speaking generally they are better off now than they have ever been. But they are spending their money on (to them) luxuries and using it not to increase, but rather to diminish, the financial strength of the country. They are not doing this in conscious selfishness but in ignorance.

(5) Lastly I have been spending the last few days much in the company of A.L. Smith and of some of the best men connected with the Workers Education Association. The men A.L. Smith brought me in contact with belong to the cream of the trades unionists and A.L. Smith himself has been spending his time for many weeks past in talking to the wage earners in the great industrial cities about the war.

They all said to me the same thing and they said it with the most intense earnestness. The government does not take the nation enough into its confidence; the wage earners do not even in the least understand the critical nature of the position or the strain which is going to be put upon the nation; very many of them were never better off in their lives and are well satisfied with the position; they have no conception that the issue of the war is in any doubt; they do not understand the position in France, or in the Dardanelles or in Russia; it has never occurred to them that Germany might win; they do not believe that strikes can affect the fortune of war or that there is any call on them to live carefully or to invest in war loans; many of them say that they do not mind how long the war goes on. One of these men drew a striking picture of the contrast between Bradford, where he lived and where this state of mind largely prevailed, and Sunderland and the Hartlepools which he also knew well. He said that the attitude of mind of the wage earners in those last towns was so different that you would think yourself in a different country, and he attributed the difference entirely to the German raid on those towns.

They all said that the people would rise to any height required of them but that was only on condition that they were spoken to a great more [sic] plainly and oftener than has hitherto been the case. They said that Lloyd George's speech to the Trades Union Congress had done great good, but that that only dealt with a limited aspect of the case. 'Give us more of your confidence', was their cry, 'there are certain men whom we will believe if they speak. The papers are no use to us, they only leave us in hopeless confusion of mind'. Yours sincerely

Selborne

A 28/195

1.  A small committee of the Cabinet known as the War Committee, which did not
    meet until 3 November 1915. At its first properly constituted meeting on 5
    November there were present Asquith, Balfour, Lord Grey, Lloyd George,
    and the First Sea Lord and the C.I.G.S.; but when Asquith announced its
    composition on 11 November he listed as members himself, Balfour, Lloyd
    George, Reginald McKenna, and Bonar Law. Lord Grey always attended as
    did Lord Kitchener after his return from Gallipoli. With the First Sea Lord and
    the C.I.G.S., the total membership of the committee was nine. Later other
    ministers, Curzon (Shipping Control Board) and Austen Chamberlain (India)
    joined.

## 14.  Sir Edward Grey

49 Mount Street
W
8 October 1915

My dear Grey,

As Bob's courage has failed him, I send you his memo

Of course the truth is that we have been pressing K on this very point for
weeks. Why has K failed us? because no human being can do the work
both of S of S for War and Chief of the Staff, and the P.M. has allowed K
to try to do it when he ought to have stopped it long long ago. It is only at
the eleventh hour that he has insisted on Murray's appointment.[1] Alas! he
has no driving force. We really are in the crisis of our fate[2] and we must
thrust all personal considerations aside and try and think clearly and act
promptly. With all this I know you thoroughly agree. But the point is – if
we have a great Eastern expedition, who is to command it? Hamilton will
not do – Should it be K? if so, who should go to W.O.? if not K, who?

The other cause of our danger is insufficient continuous military-political
consultation with the French. This is difficult to devise and the personalities and personal relations of K, French, and Joffre[3] make it most
difficult. But we should try for something better – The *great* advantage the
Germans have had is the central position of unity of control and the driving
and commanding force of the Kaiser. Yours ever

S

## MEMORANDUM 7 October 1915

On September 20th, I ventured to submit a Memorandum in which the
urgency and importance of the military problems in the Balkans were
insisted on. Since then the state of affairs has become much graver.
Germany is definitely threatening an attack on Serbia: Bulgaria has joined
her: Greece is hesitating and Roumania trembling. There was nothing
unexpected in all this. Anyone who has given attention to Balkan affairs
during the past three months must have known that such an outcome was
at least possible. It was, therefore, a great shock to learn from a Cabinet

minister yesterday that as far as he knew no plans existed until yesterday morning at the War Office for dealing with the situation that had arisen. This seems incredible. The military authorities ought surely to have considered in detail the situation which would arise from the present crisis and to have made alternative plans for dealing with it, including full estimates of the troops required and the time which the various operations would take.

May I venture to submit that enquiry should be made on this point, and if it be indeed found true that these obvious and elementary precautions have been neglected, immediate measures should be taken to prevent the recurrence of such a state of things, even if they involve the transfer of the present Secretary of State for War to some other position.

Unless this is done, the Government as a whole will be rightly held responsible for the misdoings of their military colleagues.
80/50

1.  As Chief of Imperial General Staff.
2.  On 7 October 1915 German and Austrian troops attacked Serbia, an attack which had been long anticipated in Parliament and the British press, but for which the government had made no definite contingent plans, despite Sir Edward Grey's assurance in the House on 28 September that Britain would 'give to our friends in the Balkans all the support in our power'. The Allies hoped to secure the support of Greece in aid of Serbia, and to do this it was planned to send a substantial Allied force to Salonika.
3.  Marshal Joseph Joffre (1852–1931). In October Joffre threatened to resign his command of the French armies in the north and north-east if the British refused to support his plan of an expedition to Salonika.


15.  From Lord Robert Cecil

25 Grove End Road
N.W.
12 October 1915

*Confidential*
My dear Willy,
I saw Bonar and later Edward Grey this afternoon. Bonar discoursed to me about the Dardanelles and Salonica. But as he told me he had said it all to you at the War Committee yesterday I will say no more about it – except that personally I should not see my way to differ from the Staff paper[1] which I have read. He then told me something of the Compulsion controversy and L.G. told me more. It seems more a question of numbers and finance with the latter than anything else. He is also greatly enraged at the methods by which the controversy has been carried on. He regards the recent attacks in the Press upon himself as an attempt to utilise our Diplomatic misfortunes in order to get rid of a dangerous opponent of the Compulsionist plans and he regards the whole campaign as unscrupulous

and rather sordid. To some extent I agree with him. But I only mention all this to show the kind of temper he is in. He is disposed to look round for some sufficiently strong reason to justify him in fighting out the quarrel to the bitter end. He talks very bitterly of the threats of resignation – threats which he thinks would never have been seriously made but for our military misfortunes. He talks of advising the Prime Minister to resign, if such resignation should come to pass and leave L.G. to form a Government. And I imagine that is what is intended. It is clearly inevitable if any considerable number of resignations take place.

I confess the prospect appals me. It would mean a Govt. in which L.G., Winston and G.N.C. were the leading spirits – opposed by Asquith, A.J.B. and Grey. Kitchener might remain in the Govt. for a few weeks – it certainly would not be more. I cannot believe that such a Govt. would have the authority to pass Conscription or impose on the country the sacrifices which will be needed if the war goes on for another year. Nor is it at all certain what the effect of such a political convulsion would be on Russia – already in a very uncomfortable condition.

I understand that L.G. contemplates a General Election – though how it is to be fought and who would be the candidates I cannot imagine.

All this seems to me sure madness. I am told that every member of the Cabinet would accept compulsion if it were clearly shown that the number of men necessary to win the war cannot be otherwise obtained. But those who are opposed to compulsion say (1) the number of men asked for is not really necessary or desirable and (2) the number really necessary can be obtained by voluntary recruiting.

As to (1) the question is partly military and partly financial. So far as it is military it surely can be settled beyond legitimate doubt by getting separate signed and reasoned opinions from two or three leading soldiers say, K., A. Murray and W. Robertson. The financial question is more difficult – If it be true that the difference between 50 and 70 divisions[2] would mean a reduction of our subsidies to Russia it might mean a positive loss of men to the Allied forces if we added 20 divisions to our own contingent. On the other hand I am satisfied that Public Opinion would reject the financial argument in the face of strong military pronouncements. And indeed financial prophecies are too uncertain to be relied on. I suggest therefore that the reasoned opinions in writing and separately of the authorities named should be procured and that the whole cabinet should agree to support the result.

As for (2) the matter seems to me perfectly simple. Once you know your requirement you have merely to see what result the present system is bringing in and if it is insufficient the case is complete. But since you have set up Derby and his trade unionists[3] you are bound to give him a trial for a week or two at least. Meanwhile you can be elaborating the machinery necessary to carry out a compulsory system.

Surely on some such lines as these agreement is possible. If not it must be because the Germans are right and we have no longer the grit and fibre necessary to stand the strain of a war like this. Yours ever

Robert Cecil

80/55

1. A paper drawn up by the War Office and Admiralty Staff which recommended a complete concentration of resources on the western front and argued against any diversion of troops to Salonika. It also recommended the continuance of the Gallipoli campaign.
2. On 24 August 1915 Kitchener reported to Lord Crewe's War Policy Committee that the 1,000,000 men he felt he could secure through voluntary enlistment would only maintain an army of fifty divisions in the field. But he had committed himself to the French in terms of a seventy division army, which would require 1,500,000 men.
3. Lord Derby, Director General of Recruiting, was authorised in October 1915 to exploit voluntary recruiting. One of the features of his scheme was a virtual pledge that married men would not be called up until the great majority of single men had enlisted. The Trade Unions were to help canvass for recruiting.

16.  To Robert Palmer

20th October 1915

Dearest Bobby,

I shall be much surprised if about the time you get this letter General Townshend is not endeavouring to tread in the steps of Haroun al Rashid – you ask me if there is any understanding with Russia about the disposal of Mesopotamia. I do not think that there is: I certainly have never heard of it, but I feel pretty confident Russia would agree to our taking just what we like in that region. The present moment is one of extreme anxiety. Indeed, if I did not know that God reigneth, the anxieties of life would be almost insupportable. We have the controversy in the Cabinet about compulsion; if the canvass of the names on the Register, by Derby's organisation and the Trades Unions, fails to produce enough men. The controversy had really reached a point where Squiffy could no longer sit on the fence – He had to come down on the one side or the other. We met in Cabinet expectant of our fate, when we received a message that Squiffy was ill in bed and would not be available for a week.

K said to me 'he is a great man; I thought he had exhausted all possible sources of delay; I never thought of the diarrhoea'.

But that is a small matter comparatively.

It is the German advance on Constantinople which fills my thoughts.

Germany is making a supreme effort to deal the British Empire a mortal blow in the East. The plan is plain, to organise the resources of the Turkish Empire as part of the forces under German control, to annihilate our army on the G.P., and to invade Egypt. With the prestige gained by her start by us the design is to stir up all possible trouble for us in Persia, Afghanistan, and India, as well as Egypt, and German agents, gold, and munitions will be poured out in the venture. Of course the British Army in Mesopotamia (and I hope in occupation of Bagdhad), will be attacked by as large a force as can be collected against it.

To make this plan possible it was necessary to secure Bulgaria and in that diplomatic field E.G. was hopelessly beaten by B.H.[1] – Bulgaria once secured, Germany determined to run great risks in the West and in Russia to create such an army as might crush Serbia with Bulgarian help and overcome Roumania and Greece and open the road to Constantinople. Humanly speaking I do not see how she can be kept from opening a free passage to Constantinople for an uninterrupted supply of Munitions and of as many men as she can spare, and from that moment the position of our army in the G.P. will become increasingly difficult. Do not suppose that all this was not foreseen; but Joffre insisted on his great offensive in France just at this moment and so we are caught without the necessary troops in the East. It is one of the 'prices of alliances', absence of unity of decision and control.[2] We have recalled Hamilton and sent Monro, who rose from the command of a division to the command of the Third Army in France. We shall send a large force to Egypt or elsewhere accordingly as Monro advises us. He will be quite unfettered in his advice how to beat the G.P. embroglio and where to use the troops; but, whatever you read in the papers do not believe that your father will ever make himself responsible for a second 'Dardanelles Enterprise' in the Balkans unless it is recommended on reasoned written arguments by General Monro and by the general Staff at the W.O. as the best use that can possibly be made of these troops. Nothing can be further from their thoughts at present. The French have acted 'on their own'.

With courage and sense we can parry the German blow from our heart, but it will leave its marks on us. We may have to fight in Egypt and in India and in Mesopotamia and Persia before it is clear that the mortal blow *is* parried. If either an army in the G.P. has as a measure of prudence to evacuate with great loss or is forced to do so, the blow to our prestige will be great, very great, in the East, and for that army to maintain its hold on the Peninsula in the face of a ceaseless rain of shell would be a sheer miracle.

But meanwhile Germany is not superhuman and the Eastern effort will be an immense additional drain on her resources, and every month the Russian army in the East will be regaining strength and the allied Army in the West increasing its superiority of numbers over the Germans. Your loving father

S

109/93

---

1. Theobald von Bethmann-Hollveg (1856–1921), German Chancellor, 1909–17.

2.   On 19 October 1915 Lord Selborne circulated a paper in the Cabinet arguing
     for more central direction and control of the war, urging that the conduct of the
     war be entrusted to a 'council of six, sitting in Paris, consisting of one Cabinet
     Minister and one military and one naval officer, selected by the French and
     British governments respectively' (126/231).

## 17.   To Robert Palmer

49 Mount Street
W
27 October 1915

Dearest Bobby,
Your letter of the 16th Sept. opens up a problem of great difficulty and
anxiety, that is, what to do in the case of the time expired men in the 6th
Hants. and other Battalions who want to go home. In my opinion they
cannot possibly be let go home, and yet how keep them justly when
military service is not compulsory? I do not mind a bit the honest
fanacticism against compulsory service, what stirs my wrath is the sheer
hypocrisy on the subject of the great mass of Liberals and Labour people.
They do not mind what pressure is put, or in what revolting form the
pressure is put, on men to enlist so long as the pressure is not legal.

   Before we joined the Government the Government ran through a War
Emergency Bill enabling the Army Council to transfer men, who had
enlisted for the cavalry, artillery or Army Medical Corps, into the infantry,
and it has been done on a large scale. And how does that differ in principle
from compulsion? But worse remains behind. There are now thousands of
men in the army whose time is expiring, that is to say, they have fulfilled
their contract of 12 years' or 21 years' service as the case may be and one
year extra which is a provision of the contract against war, and will now be
claiming their discharge. The Army Council prepared a Bill by which all
these men would have been kept on compulsorily till the end of the war.
There was not a single Liberal member of the Cabinet who objected to that
or who would not have run it through at once; it was we who stopped it. It
struck us as so revolting to compel men who have fulfilled their contract
and have been all through this war while there are still slackers at home
who have not been compelled to serve at all.

   You will want to know from me the explanation of Carson's resignation.[1] I think what operated in his mind mainly was disgust with the way
things are conducted under the Prime Minister, but clearly that is not
playing the game. We have to eliminate our personalities and our own
feelings altogether. The occasion he took was because we would not
undertake to rush blindly into the Balkans to help Serbia against the
unanimous opinion, extremely well argued, of all our military advisers. He
is a splendid fellow and I am devoted to him, but a side of him has been
revealed to me in Cabinet which I did not suspect. He is extremely

emotional and sentimental. He said this in a moment of expansion and without any authority from us whatever. You see at once the difficulties of an alliance. We cannot expose the French folly publicly; at the same time we are not going to risk an army in the Balkans under these circumstances. If we win the war Serbia will be saved: Serbia will not be saved by losing an army in the Balkans.

We are sending troops to Egypt because troops will be wanted in the East when communications are opened with Constantinople. Heaven knows there can be no severer critic of this Government than I am and nobody knows better than I do the source of its weakness, but we shall be most severely criticised for our apparent vacillation and want of purpose in this matter whereas we really have an excellent case.

One of our submarines in the Baltic a day or two ago sunk a German armoured cruiser, the Prince Adelbert, not a battle cruiser but quite one of the best of the armoured cruisers.

We have relieved Ian Hamilton of his command in the Gallipoli Peninsula because it was quite evident that the troops had lost all confidence in him. We have sent out Sir C. Munro who is second only to Haig in the opinion of the army in Flanders. He commanded a Division at the beginning of the war, rose to the command of an Army Corps, and then to the command of the 3rd Army.

The recruiting effort now being made by Lord Derby and the Trades Unions in combination is of a different character to any other previously made because they have the National Register to work on. Every man of military age will be directly canvassed and asked if he will serve or not. If he says Yes he will be enlisted on the spot and sent home till called up. So you see there will be no spurt of recruiting gradually petering out, but before the end of November we shall know the exact maximum that the voluntary system can still give us. If say 1,500,000 men join you will hear very little more of compulsion for a long time to come; if only 250,000 join no honest man can still say that the compulsion system will carry us through the war.

All this is confidential about Greece etc. Your loving father

S

109/99

---

1. Sir Edward Carson, Attorney-General in the Asquith Coalition, angered at Britain's failure to help Serbia and Asquith's ineptitude in government, sent the Prime Minister a formal letter of resignation on 12 October. The letter was made public on 20 October but Carson postponed his resignation speech until 2 November.

18.   To Robert Palmer

49 Mount Street
W
2 November 1915

My dearest Bobby,

. . . Asquith told us in the Cabinet yesterday what he was going to say in the H of C today about compulsion.[1] On that statement I and Austen and Curzon would have resigned, but our views were communicated to him through Lansdowne and I am told that he greatly modified his statement. We must read what he said and then consider where our duty lies. Our path has been made much more difficult by a violent attack which Carson made on the government which he held up to ridicule (which it deserves, but it is not seemly from him) and made some statements which are not accurate, e.g. that we had not sent enough troops to Gallipoli in August, whereas Hamilton asked for three, and we sent five, divisions, suppressed the fact that our military advisers were after Venizelos' resignation[2] unanimous in advising us against an expedition from Salonica, and made some most unjustifiable mad and mischievous statements such as that we ought to coerce Greece. Asquith must be mad to have allowed him to read his letter of resignation in which some of these statements occurred.

On Saturday Joffre came over and persuaded some of our military advisers to concur with the French General Staff in advising a new plan of campaign to help Serbia, involving our sending to Salonica most of the troops which were all going to Egypt. Our military advisers were not unanimous, but about equally divided, but Joffre and the French General Staff were insistent to the last degree that this was the right thing to do from the purely military point of view and this weight of authority convinced the Cabinet.

If I knew that Roumania and Greece were going to be with us, I should agree, but I know nothing of the kind and I am put in a position of great difficulty. My instinct tells me that Joffre is wrong and the plan hazardous and I know that it leaves us with too few troops to fall back upon in case of trouble about Egypt and if the troops on the Gallipoli peninsula want supporting. So you see that your poor father is in the middle of a crisis of great anxiety and perplexity for him. I am very fond of Carson and I cannot imagine how he can have persuaded himself that he was justified in saying what he did. Your loving father

S

109/104

1.   Asquith's speech was enigmatic. He re-affirmed his belief in the Derby scheme and warned that conscription could only be secured by general consent, but at the same time he warned that if a substantial number of unmarried men failed to enlist, then married men who had attested should not be held to their obligation until all the unmarried men had been dealt with, if necessary by compulsion (*H.C.Deb.*, 5s, vol. 75, cols. 519–24).

2. Eleutherios Venizelos (1864–1936), Prime Minister of Greece, 1910–March 1915, August–October 1915, 1917–22, 1928–32, 1933. The Allies had hoped that Greece would intervene on Serbia's side, and Venizelos had favoured this, but on 5 October while an Anglo-French force landed at Salonika, King Constantine overthrew Venizelos and replaced him by a neutralist premier. The allied expeditionary force advanced towards the Bulgarian border, but by mid-December it had been pushed back almost to Salonika.

## 19.   To H.H. Asquith

3 November 1915

Dear Prime Minister,

The terms of your pronouncement on recruiting, which you sketched to the Cabinet on Monday, seemed to us so disappointing that, after full consideration, we had come to the conclusion yesterday that we could not accept responsibility for them. We were jointly members of a Committee appointed by you in August last to consider the future supply of men for the Army. At that Committee we were informed by Lord Kitchener that for the successful prosecution of the war throughout next year he would require not less than 70 Divisions in the field, and that, to provide and maintain this force, he would need a weekly supply throughout the greater part of the year of 30,000 men, or a total of 1,500,000 men. This figure of 30,000 was subsequently repeated by him to the representatives of the Trade Unions, and, at a later meeting of the Cabinet, was expanded by him to 35,000, in order to provide for certain non-combatant services. Further, on October 12th he informed the Cabinet in a printed note that we must have 70 divisions in the field, and that 'without this we should not have done all in our power to avert the disaster that must ensue from an unsuccessful termination of the War'.

Founding ourselves upon these statements of the Secretary for War, we were forced to the conclusion that, if the voluntary system failed to produce the requisite number of men (and the results of the Register have since led us to form the opinion that, after providing for the essential national industries, the desired number is available) there would be no alternative but to resort to some form of compulsion. These views were stated by us to the Cabinet in a printed Memorandum, dated September 7th,[1] in which we adopted Lord Kitchener's figures as the minimum necessary to give us success on a review of the forces then opposed to us. Since that date the enemy's forces have been increased by the addition of the Bulgarian Army. In these circumstances we do not see how it is possible to justify any reduction in Lord Kitchener's original calculations.

The discussion of the matter in Council, for which we repeatedly pressed, was for one reason or another postponed again and again, until on Monday last, within 24 hours of the date at which you were to announce the decision of the Government in the House of Commons, you acquainted us in Cabinet with the formula which you proposed to adopt. In the meantime, without any reference to or consent of the Cabinet, the recruiting scheme of Lord Derby had been launched on its career. To that scheme we sincerely wish triumphant success, and, while it is being carried out, no advocate of compulsion can, in our view, do otherwise than lend to it every assistance in his power. Our doubt arose as to the future attitude of the Government at the time, should it ever arrive, when the efforts of Lord Derby and the Trade Unions might be found not to have produced the required number of men, or to give little or no prospect of continuing to supply them throughout the coming year. We felt that in view of this possibility the Government should make up their mind in advance and should announce to Parliament that they would in such a case be prepared to take the necessary steps to supply Lord Kitchener's requirements by compulsory methods, and that a Bill for that purpose should be at once prepared.

The discussion in Cabinet left us in some doubt as to whether the Army of 70 Divisions was still the basis of our military requirements, whether the failure of the voluntary effort, should it fail, would be followed by compulsion, and whether legislation for that purpose was or was not in contemplation . . .

We decided however to await your declaration in the House of Commons before taking further action.

We hasten to acknowledge that this statement appeared to us more definite and therefore more satisfactory than the forecast of it presented to the Cabinet. In particular, you fixed an early date after December 1st on which the success or failure of Lord Derby's appeal is to be determined.[2] We hope we are justified in understanding this to mean that as soon as the results of Lord Derby's canvass are ascertained, say within ten days or a fortnight of December 1st, the results will be placed before the Cabinet, together with the opinion of the military advisers of the Government as to their sufficiency or the reverse to supply the number of men postulated by Lord Kitchener for the armies in the field, without depleting the necessary garrisons both at home and abroad; so that the Government will be enabled, in the light of this information, to review the entire situation, and if necessary take the new steps that may be required. We think it important to be clear about this point, because your phrase used in the Cabinet and repeated yesterday in the House, that 'if when every just allowance has been made for other necessary work, and the whole of this machinery has been in operation and has achieved what it can, there should still be found a substantial number of men of military age not required for other purposes, and who without excuse hold back from the service of their country, I believe that the very same conditions which make compulsion impossible now, namely, the absence of general consent, would force the country to the view that they must consent to supplement by some form of legal obligation the failure of the voluntary system' – seems to us to hold out infinite possibilities of debate upon what must be largely a matter of opinion, and to foreshadow further and interminable delays.

In this connection we attach great importance to your statement in the House of Commons: 'So far as I am concerned, I should certainly say the obligation of the married man to enlist ought not to be enforced or binding upon him unless and until – I hope by voluntary effort, and if not, by some other means – the unmarried men are dealt with first'.

We understand further from Mr. Bonar Law that, though this was not announced to the House, you will have a Bill for compulsory service prepared at once, so that no time may be lost, if it should be shown to be necessary to bring it into operation. There remains however the question of the 70 Divisions to which, as we have indicated, we attach supreme importance, not merely because it represents the considered opinion of Lord Kitchener, but because it appears to us that, without some such standard in view, we have no definite principle upon which to proceed in recruiting except to catch what we can, and leave the rest to chance.

You were understood by some of our colleagues at Monday's Cabinet to authorise Lord Kitchener to continue to organise the new armies on the 70 Divisions basis. We take this to mean that, whilst preferring not to mention numbers at present, you are prepared to work to that basis unless it is shown, as a result of Lord Derby's canvass, not merely that the men are not forthcoming under the voluntary system, but that they are actually non-existent and could not be obtained by any other means; and we read the words used by you yesterday as signifying that if the men are available but do not volunteer, you will propose the adoption of some form of compulsion to Parliament, and will use your great influence to secure general assent to the proposal. We shall be very glad if you can confirm our understanding of your meaning on this and of the other points to which we have referred, in which case you will have removed our remaining difficulties. We are, yours very truly

Curzon
Austen Chamberlain
Selborne

80/75

1. Memorandum of 7 September 1915 by Curzon, Selborne and Austen Chamberlain, signed also by Churchill, Cab 37/134/7.
2. The Derby scheme was ended on 12 December 1915, and Derby reported to the Cabinet on 15 December that although 1,150,000 single men had attested, 651,160 who were not 'starred' for essential work were unaccounted for. In January, in the face of criticism from Sir John Simon, and of the findings of a committee appointed to examine the results of the scheme, the latter figure was reduced to 316,464.

20.   H.H. Asquith to Austen Chamberlain

*Copy*

10 Downing Street
7 November 1915

My dear Chamberlain, I have read the letter of the 3rd, addressed to me jointly by Curzon, Selborne and yourself. I think you have correctly apprehended the meaning of what I said in the House of Commons on Tuesday.

I have always doubted myself whether the recruitable reservoir, either under a voluntary or a compulsory system, will be found to contain enough men to maintain 70 Divisions: a purely empirical figure.

But I am quite willing (as you justly infer) 'to work to that basis', unless and until the impossibility of reaching it, *quacunque via*, is clearly shown. Yours sincerely

H. H. Asquith

I should be glad if Curzon would give instructions to the draftsman to prepare a Bill (for consideration) on the lines suggested by him.
80/84

21.   Austen Chamberlain to H. H. Asquith

India Office
9 November 1915

*Confidential*

My dear Prime Minister,

Curzon, Selborne and I are much obliged to you for the reply to our letter of the 3rd which you sent to me yesterday.

We are glad to find that our understanding of your declaration in the House of Commons was correct. We quite realise that, if there are not enough men to maintain 70 Divisions, that number cannot be reached, and we are satisfied by your declaration of willingness to work to that basis 'unless and until the impossibility of reaching it *quacunque via* is clearly shown'.

Curzon will at once place himself in communication with the draftsman with a view to the preparation of a Compulsory Service Bill for consideration by the Cabinet.[1] Yours very sincerely

Austen Chamberlain

80/84

1.   The bill eventually drafted was entitled 'Universal Military Service', and was based on a scheme prepared by Curzon and L. S. Amery.

22.   To Robert Palmer

49 Mount Street
W
2 January 1916

Dearest Bobby,

. . . We are absolutely in the middle of the Cabinet crisis.

The Derby canvass disclosed over 600,000 unattested bachelors, which after deducting indispensables and unfits would mean over 300,000 fighting men. By Squiffy's pledge the attested married men could not be called up till these bachelors were taken compulsorily, and without the attested married men we should not be able to supply the drafts after a certain period next year. Actually some of Squiffy's friends in the Cabinet would have liked to contend that 300,000 was a negligible quantity, but old Squiffy wouldn't have that at any price. Of course anyone else, especially anyone with the leadership of men in him, would have seized this moment to pass universal service for the war. But not he; the one thing he cares about is the parliamentary situation of the moment. By saying to Liberals and Labour 'You have never objected to my pledge, how can you object to its fulfilment? I am going to fulfil it but not one hairsbreadth beyond it', he evades the question of principle and reduces his parliamentary difficulties for the moment to a minimum.[1] Simon has resigned – McKenna and Harcourt are hovering on the brink, and Runciman whom I should be very sorry to lose. Henderson is quite staunch. This puts Austen and Curzon and me in a very difficult position. We know that universal military [sic] for the war must come and is already overdue, as the only way to give the army every man that can be spared without unduly depleting essential industries, and yet can we desert Squiffy at such a moment? Your loving father

S

P.S. The German Bulgar attack on Salonica hangs fire, and they have had time to make the defences strong: still I am anxious.
109/133

1.   On 15 December 1915 Asquith appointed a Cabinet Committee under Walter Long to 'consider in consultation with the draftsman what form any amendment in the law in the direction of compulsion should take'. The bill eventually prepared dealt exclusively with Asquith's pledge to the married men, conscripting only men who had been unmarried on 2 November 1915 (the date of Asquith's pledge) and between the ages of eighteen and forty-one on 15 August 1915, the age group canvassed under the Derby scheme. A final draft was printed on 4 January 1916, and the bill introduced on 5 January 1916. It received its final reading on 25 January, becoming law on 27 January, and coming into effect on 1 March 1916.

23.   Memorandum by Lord Selborne, 2 March 1916

(Printed for the use of the Committee of Imperial Defence. March 1916.)
*SECRET*

### FOOD SUPPLY AND PRODUCTION
#### Note by the Earl of Selborne

I SHOULD like to have instructions from the War Committee on the following points:–

If the war is prolonged over this year and through the year 1917, should I take measures to increase the food production of the country next year? It is unfortunately a fact that the food supply from overseas is causing us more and more anxiety. I am not now alluding to the difficulties of foreign exchange which are partly caused by the great volume of food purchases, but to the actual physical difficulty of getting the food across the sea and into the United Kingdom.

There has never been more wheat for sale in the world than there is at the present moment, in Canada, the United States, Argentina, and Australia, and the price of wheat inside those countries is moderate. But the price in Europe is very high and bears no relation to these facts. The reason for this is that the ship tonnage for bringing the wheat to Europe is grievously deficient, and that the demands of France and Italy and of the neutral countries for immediate supplies of wheat are insistent. The result is that there is a clamorous competition for every ton of wheat directly it is brought to a port and put on board ship. Fortunately we have succeeded in eliminating competition between the Allies. All the purchases, whether for the British, French, or Italian armies, or for the civil population of the United Kingdom and of Italy, are now in the hands of agencies controlled by one Committee on which all the Powers are represented. This was not so last year, and if we had not succeeded in making this arrangement this year, I really do not know up to what price wheat might not have been driven.

Last autumn I was authorised to establish a wheat reserve in the United Kingdom against the months of June, July, and August, when experience had shown us our supplies will be at the shortest. I have had altogether unforeseen difficulties in establishing this reserve. I fear that I certainly shall not be able to keep it at the level at which it ought to be kept, and I am full of anxiety in respect of the next six months. We started the cereal year in September with an excellent supply, and we arranged to commence establishing our reserve early in the new year, but our calculations were upset by two unforeseen causes. There was a grievous shortage in the amount of wheat imported into the United Kingdom in November and December, due entirely to the lack of tonnage. The Board of Trade, and then Mr. Whitley's Committee since it has been established, have done and are doing all they can to put more ships into the wheat trade, but their efforts to supply more tonnage for this purpose for the advantage of the

United Kingdom have been largely neutralised by the clamorous demands of the French and Italian Governments for tonnage to take wheat to France and Italy. We had no previous intimation that the shortage of Italian and French supplies would be so great or that it would manifest itself so early.

In the light of this experience I think that we ought to look far ahead. The demands of the Admiralty and War Office and of the Allied Governments on British tonnage show no signs of diminution. The quantity of that tonnage is constantly shrinking owing to the steady toll taken from it by German mines and submarines and by raiders, the number of which may increase. The Admiralty will know whether the chances of a serious interruption of our supplies, extending over several weeks, by the operation of German commerce-raiders are likely to increase or diminish. Further, we cannot foresee what the Canadian and American harvests of 1916 are likely to be. If there was a short crop there might really be a shortage in the wheat supplies in the world.

Therefore, if the War Committee think that we may have to carry the burden of war all through next year, and that I should do all in my power to increase the amount of food produced in England and Wales in 1917, I ought to receive my instructions at once. If I had my instructions soon enough I think I could do a good deal. I have now a complete organisation throughout the country in the War Agricultural Committees of the counties, and with their assistance and the assistance of the various agricultural bodies I think that much could be done to organise an increase of production in the cereal year beginning September 1916 and ending August 1917. But I could not ensure a substantial increase in the amount of wheat produced unless I was authorised to give the farmers some guarantee that, if they plough up grass land, they will receive for the wheat they sell a higher price than that which obtained before the war for a period sufficiently long to ensure them against loss. Such a guarantee could be given in various forms. Probably a guarantee of 40s. a quarter for four years after peace is the form which would be most effective and yet involve the least liability to the national exchequer, but on this point I should see advice from men like Mr. E. Strutt and Mr. A. D. Hall. There would, of course, have to be conditions which the farmer would have to fulfil in order to obtain the benefit of the guarantee, and I should probably have to ask for some men to be returned to the land from the army. I do not think I should have to ask for very many men, but I should certainly have to ask for all those who have been trained to work steam-ploughing tackle.

Of course there is more drastic action which could be taken. I could have power given to me to compel cultivation of land, but in that case I should certainly have to organise a ploughing and reaping corps, and many conditions would have to be adjusted. But if the men were lent me from the army it could be done.

S

24.   Memorandum by Andrew Bonar Law

13 April 1916

In considering what our attitude ought to be in regard to compulsion, I start with the belief which I entertained at the time the present Government was formed, and which I hold now as strongly as ever, that a Coalition Government is best in the national interest. I need not elaborate this. If the attempt to carry on the war by a national Government were abandoned this would have the worst possible effect, in my opinion, on our Allies and on all neutral countries.

If the Unionists leave the Government I think it would be impossible for Mr. Asquith to attempt to continue, and I do not believe he would make the attempt. If he did, it would be impossible for us to act as a benevolent Opposition, for our only justification in breaking up the Coalition would be that the Government refused to take steps which we thought were necessary; and we should, therefore, be driven by ordinary methods of opposition to try to force a change of Government.

Such a change could not be made in the present House of Commons. There would need to be an election, with all the bitterness which that inevitably creates; and even if we got a large majority the war would have to be carried on in the face of a bitter Opposition in the House of Commons which would, I think, encourage every form of Opposition outside. This might mean, and I fear it would mean, that something like martial law would have to be established in many parts of the country; and though it is possible that the war might be carried on successfully under such conditions, it is a risk so great that we should not be justified in facing it unless we were absolutely driven to it.

I had hoped that the figures being prepared by the Co-Ordination Committee[1] would make a case so clear that our duty would be quite plain. This does not appear to be the case. The examination of the figures, as I understand, shows that under the present system we shall obtain the numbers of men recommended in the previous report of this Committee, that the time of securing them will be delayed, and that from the point of view of time nothing will be gained by adopting general compulsion.[2] On the other hand, it is clear that it is necessary to meet our immediate needs that the time expired men should not be allowed to leave the Army; and though this would not add anything to our strength in the immediate future, it is probably right that all those who gradually become 18 should be compelled to serve.

To attempt to carry these measures in the House would raise in an aggravated form the question of the unfairness of the present system and would make our position very difficult. We acquiesced in the previous Compulsion Act although we fully recognised its unfairness on the ground that we preferred a partial measure of that kind, in spite of its military disadvantages, rather than risk the hostility which a general measure of compulsion would have aroused. If, therefore, we insist now upon the adoption of general compulsion it cannot be on the ground which I had myself always regarded as the only ground which would justify us in breaking the Government – that men which were needed and could be spared could not be got under the present system, and could be got if that system were changed. Our case, therefore, now is not nearly so strong as I should have wished as a justification for our leaving the Government.

On the other hand, however, if the Coalition Government is to continue it cannot be continued by sacrifices all on one side; and to my mind the question which we have to decide is whether the difficulties which Mr. Asquith would experience in adopting general compulsion are greater than those which would be experienced by us if we attempted to justify our continuance in the Government without making this change.

At their request I saw the three Labour members of the Government, and they told me in the most emphatic way that if compulsion were extended now it would be impossible for them to carry any considerable section of the Labour movement in favour of it, and not only would it be necessary for them to resign but they felt sure there would be hostility of the most violent kind to the proposal by most of the trade unions of the country. I think they were sincere in expressing these views, but I am not sure that they are in a position to appreciate fully the feeling of the country and I should hope that if an election were to take place and a decisive verdict given in favour of the new policy there would not be so much trouble as they anticipate.

It is the case also that the Prime Minister gave pledges at the time the last Compulsion Bill was introduced which could not be got over by him unless he could show that a completely new situation had arisen, and this would be difficult.

These are the difficulties from the point of view of the Prime Minister: but ours seem to me equally great. Our whole Party has from the first been entirely in favour of compulsion. Those of us who considered that compulsion was the right method in a war like this have refrained from pressing it because of hostility to it in the country. That hostility has, in my opinion, largely disappeared; and in urging that a decision in favour of compulsion ought to be taken now we have the right to point out not merely the unfairness of the present system and the aggravation of that unfairness by attempting to compel the time expired men to serve, but we have the right also to insist that it is quite evident that general compulsion will sooner or later be necessary, and that there is no object in delaying it. I think that if all the Unionist members decided to remain in the Government we should secure for the present the support of the majority of our Party; but I am convinced that the discontent which exists now would become increasingly evident, and that before long our position might be impossible.

The situation is so difficult, and it is so hard to decide in which direction our duty lies that I am not prepared to take a decision today; and whatever

decision is ultimately arrived at I hope it may be possible for all of us to act together. This is necessary if we are to acquiesce in the continuation of the present system, and it is almost equally necessary if we are to attempt to change it, for if any of us find it impossible to insist on compulsion our inability to do so will to that extent diminish our chances of securing a victory if a contest becomes inevitable.
80/157

1.  The Military-Finance Committee appointed in October 1915 to investigate the competing military and economic claims with respect to conscription, which first met on 1 January 1916, and produced two reports dated 4 February and 13 April 1916. Its members were Asquith, Reginald McKenna and Austen Chamberlain.
2.  On 11 April 1916 the Army Council furnished the government with a statement of requirements of men, which could not be met by the voluntary system. Next day the Unionist War Committee in the House of Commons, a pressure group founded in January 1916 to press for a more vigorous prosecution of the war, passed a resolution requesting its chairman Sir Edward Carson to bring forward a motion embodying the policy of universal compulsory military service. Meanwhile the Military Finance Committee reported that no case had been established for the extension of the Military Service Act of 1916 to all men of military age. The government attempted to produce a compromise scheme and announced on 20 April that its decision would be explained in a secret session of the House of Commons which met on 25 April. The opposition of the compulsionists on this occasion obliged the government to adopt new measures and on 30 April Asquith announced the details of a new government bill for the establishment of compulsory military service, which was introduced into the House of Commons on 2 May and made all males between the ages of eighteen and forty-one liable for military service. The bill received the royal assent on 25 May. On 18 April 1918 conscription was extended to all males between the ages of eighteen and fifty-one.


25.  To Lady Selborne

> Board of Agriculture & Fisheries
> Whitehall Place
> S.W.
> 26 April 1916

My darling,
Since this Cabinet was formed last May Birrell has never once mentioned the subject of Ireland and we have had no knowledge whatever of the state of affairs there.[1] As everything seemed calm we assumed that it was calm. Now it appears that Birrell and Mat Nat[2] have had any number of warnings which they neglected on principle. St. John tells me that he is going to read out in the H of L today the warnings which have been sent to them and which they have ignored. An Irish Republic was proclaimed on College Green yesterday, but College Green is now in possession of H.M.'s troops. Mat Nat was shut up in Dublin Castle for 24 hours or more and unable to

get out or to communicate with the outside world. Street fighting, apparently, is still going on, and I daresay there will be outbreaks of a similar kind at Cork or Limerick.

The German wireless to U.S.A. is a gem. Republic proclaimed in Ireland, immense rejoicings all over Ireland, universal flight of English, Plunkett in command of Irish patriots, panic in England, etc. etc.

The real attitude here is that no-one takes the thing as other than the usual Irish tragic comic opera but that everyone thinks that Birrell is a scandal. Yours

S

102/195

1. On Easter Monday, 24 April 1916, elements of various Irish revolutionary bodies, including James Connolly's Citizen Army and the Irish Volunteers, led by Patrick Pearse, occupied the General Post Office in Dublin and declared that a provisional government of the Irish Republic had been established. They surrendered only after a week's hard fighting, and many casualties on both sides.
2. Matthew Nathan, at this time Permanent Under-Secretary for Ireland. He resigned on 3 May 1916.


26.   To A. Bonar Law

8 May 1916

My dear Bonar Law,

I confess that I find it becoming very hard to submit longer to the delay in getting a decision on questions which have been raised but never settled.

It is now ten weeks since I asked the War Committee for instructions about the harvest of 1917. The conduct of the war has been entrusted to the War Committee as I think to the very great advantage of the nation. The question I have asked is essentially one connected with the conduct of the war and it must be decided by the War Committee. Unless the War Committee think that certain precautionary steps are necessary in connection with the harvest of 1917 the Cabinet will certainly not think that any steps are necessary. If, on the other hand, the War Committee think that any steps are necessary the Cabinet are not in the least likely to over-rule them. If the answer to my question is that nothing is to be done then my responsibility will be cleared and I shall be left free to attend to other matters, but if anything is to be done then every week that passes makes it less possible for me to do anything effectual. There is no use in telling me next August to do something. It will then be too late. Therefore, I think I am entitled to an answer, and a speedy answer. It is quite clear to my mind now that the Cabinet were wrong last August in refusing to accept the recommendations of the Milner Committee. If they had accepted these recommendations then there would have been a large increase in the amount of wheat sown at the present moment. That however is nothing but a reflection. What I am asking for now is a definite answer from the War Committee to the question I first put to them on March 2.

Again, it must be six months since Balfour first raised the question of the denunciation of the most favoured nation treaties. It seems to me nothing but a scandal that we have never even discussed this proposition, much less settled it.

Unless therefore you feel sure of a decision on these two questions at a very early date I would beg you to call our Unionist colleagues together that we may discuss what action should be taken. Experience has shown that unless we move unitedly in these matters the influences of obstruction are too strong for us each individually. Yours ever

S

80/161

27.   From M.P.A. Hankey

Committee of Imperial Defence
2 Whitehall Gardens
S.W.
15 May 1916

*Confidential*
Dear Lord Selborne,
Mr Bonar Law tells me that you are pressing him for a decision from the War Committee on the question of the harvest of 1917, and asks me to communicate with you on the subject. I am not clear as to how the question has arisen but understand a proposal has been put forward by Mr Hughes that we should buy up the Australian wheat crop. I should be glad if you could let me have a note on the question to circulate to the War Committee. Yours sincerely

M.P.A. Hankey

80/166

28.   To M.P.A. Hankey

15 May 1916

My dear Hankey,
I said to Bonar Law that it really was not fair to me to leave my request for instructions about the harvest of 1917 unanswered.

I refer to my memorandum of March 2, not to any proposal of Mr Hughes.

The war is being conducted by the War Committee and the question I asked is exclusively one for them to answer – Am I to take any steps to increase the production of food in England and Wales in the harvest of 1917? If the answer is 'no' then my responsibility is cleared and I can free my mind for other work. If the answer is 'yes', then I have to be told which of the two methods I have indicated is to be followed, the greater or compulsory, the lesser or voluntary, involving a guarantee of the price of wheat for a certain number of years.

I have attended two meetings of the War Committee without receiving an answer and I have no wish to attend a third; but I do simply wish to know where I stand. Ten weeks have passed since I asked my question and every day which passes makes it more difficult to do anything effectually supposing the War Committee decided that something ought to be done. There is no use the War Committee coming to me in August and asking me to do something then. Then it will be too late to do anything. I am not sure that it is not too late to carry out the greater or compulsory scheme.

Selborne

80/167

29.   From M.P.A. Hankey

Committee of Imperial Defence<br>2 Whitehall Gardens<br>S.W.<br>16 May 1916

*Secret*

Dear Lord Selborne,

I have looked up the Minutes of the Meeting of the War Committee held on March 23rd when a discussion took place on the question of raising more food stuffs. I find that the Prime Minister and, at any rate, one or two of his colleagues, considered the question being one of future policy was one for the Cabinet rather than for the War Committee. The discussion was adjourned without any decision. I remember that I did consult the Prime Minister subsequently as to whether I should again put it on the Agenda, and he replied 'Not at present'. As soon as he returns from Ireland[1] I will bring your letter to his attention and take his instructions.

Yours sincerely

M.P.A. Hankey

80/168

1.   Where he went on 11 May to examine the post-rebellion situation at first hand. He returned on 19 May.

30.   To M.P.A. Hankey

22 May 1916

My dear Hankey,

1. I am very pressed with work, and I have nothing more to say to the War Committee, only to ask for an answer so pray do not summon me if you can help it for Wednesday and then for the end of the meeting if you must have me.

2. I cannot guarantee that either the hay or the corn harvest will be gathered unless the army help me liberally with military labour; apart from the resulting catastrophe to the nation, the army itself would have no hay. I think that the adjutant general thoroughly understands this; but from the delay which has occurred in making arrangements it is clear to me that he is having serious difficulty somewhere, I expect with Lord French. It would help me greatly if the War Committee would convey a direction both to the Army Council and to Lord French that this is really a matter of vital importance and that the military labour must be provided under such conditions as will in the opinion of the B of A and F enable the harvest to be gathered.

Selborne

80/172

31.   From the Earl of Midleton

Melbury
Dorchester
10 June 1916

*Private*
My dear Willie,
I very much wished to see you before going away for a short holiday to speak to you in the sense of enclosed. I still hope Dillon may be obdurate and realise, as will be the case, that the Home Rule which L.G. offers[1] will inevitably break down and discredit all who are connected with it and that he will refuse it.
    Failing this there is the Cabinet. Surely all of you will realise that
    1.   Redmond cannot enforce martial law or the equivalent.
    2.   The Dublin Resolutions[2] make it clear that martial law will be given up at once. No convictions can be obtained by Jury trial.
    3.   The country is seething with trouble. Every letter shows that the success of the rising by bringing H. Rule at once forward is recruiting the Sinn Feiners.[3]
    4.   Arms have not been given up. L. George informed us the Govt. have warning of fresh landings impending with support from inside.
    5.   Seeing the impetus given to anti British feeling in America by the late rising, the product of Birrell's abdication of rule, could a more fatuous course be taken than to set upon another weak Govt. in the middle of a war?
I say nothing of the 300,000 of the Minority – but if we are to be sacrificed it cannot be till after a war and a General Election. No one knows at present if Redmond would have 30, 50 or 70 supporters in a new Parlt.

L.G. says he cannot carry a single borough in Ireland and I am told he cannot carry 2 seats in Munster.

This is assuming Dillon and Devlin support him. They will go with the extremists in the end. Read the increasing vehemence of the Bishop of Limerick, who protects his priests who were connected with the rebellion.

I hope you will not be a party to this fiasco. We shall fight it to the death.[4] Yours ever

St. J.B.

3/136

ENCLOSURE

## RESOLUTION PASSED AT A MEETING OF MEMBERS OF BOTH HOUSES OF PARLIAMENT

6 June 1916

The Unionist Members of both Houses of Parliament connected with the South and West of Ireland, after conferring with a deputation representing the Commercial interests of the three Southern Provinces, view with the gravest anxiety the proposed establishment of Home Rule, temporarily or otherwise, under present conditions.

They are convinced that the spread of the rebellion and seditious feeling require administrative measures which it is impossible for Mr. Redmond's party to countenance, and that any weakening of Government may result in a second and graver rebellion.

They feel that Mr. Redmond's authority and control is greatly weakened and that the strength of his party will be materially reduced at an Election.

On these and other grounds, they regard the present proposals as highly dangerous from the point of view of the conduct of the War.

SIGNED          FOR THE COMMITTEE
                BARRYMORE
                BERESFORD
                BESSBOROUGH
                DESART
                WALTER GUINNESS
                IVEAGH
                KENMARE
                MIDLETON
                ORANMORE            ) Hon
                J. PRETYMAN NEWMAN  ) Secretaries

3/142

1. On 25 May 1916 Asquith announced in the House of Commons that he had asked Lloyd George to initiate negotiations with leaders of Irish Nationalist and Unionist opinion. Lloyd George soon discovered that Redmond would accept a settlement based on immediate implementation of the 1914 home rule act, with the exclusion for the time being of the six north-eastern counties of Ulster, the whole problem to be reviewed at the end of the war. Carson, acting on behalf of the Ulster Unionists, also accepted this, on the somewhat vague assurances made by Lloyd George on 21 May that 'at the end of the provisional period Ulster must not, whether she wills it or not, merge in the rest of Ireland'. There was more than one draft of the 1916 settlement plan, but the official version ('Headings of a settlement as to the government of Ireland', Cd. 8310 of 1916) does not differ substantially from the other drafts.

2. At a meeting of the Irish Parliamentary Party on 10 June 1916 in Dublin a number of resolutions were passed, including one which read 'That we most earnestly protest against the continuance of martial law in Ireland, for which in view of the present peaceful state of the country no reasonable case can be now established' (*The Times*, 12 June 1916).

3. Sinn Fein ('Ourselves alone'), a political party founded by Arthur Griffith in 1905 which aimed initially at political and economic self-reliance. Griffith hoped for a constitutional settlement of Anglo-Irish relations on the lines of the Austro- Hungarian dual monarchy, and he did not favour complete separation, but the epithet 'Sinn Feiners' came, mistakenly, to be generally applied to all Irish revolutionary bodies.

4. For southern Irish Unionist reaction and opposition to the Lloyd George settlement plan see P. J. Buckland, *Irish Unionism I. The Anglo-Irish and the new Ireland, 1885–1922* (Dublin, 1972), pp. 54–82.


32.   To the Earl of Midleton

Blackmoor
Liss
Hants
14 June 1916

*Private*

My dear St John,

Lloyd George is acting according to his customary methods. He has made no proposal to us and we are wholly uncommitted. I can say nothing more at present. Yours ever

S

3/140

33. Memoranda by Walter Long

15 June 1916

A

*IMMEDIATE*

*SECRET*

*FOR UNIONIST MEMBERS OF THE CABINET ONLY*

*THE IRISH SITUATION*

The situation in regard to Ireland has in my judgment become very grave and I do not see how it is possible for me to remain a member of the Government if Mr Lloyd George's statements are to be accepted as correct. These statements involve for the Unionist Party the following consequences.

1. The acceptance of the view that the Government of the Union in Ireland had broken down and that the present system of Government must be abandoned and Home Rule adopted. (This is stated in effect in Mr Redmond's communication to the Press).[1]

There is in my judgment no justification for such a statement. We all agreed to the abolition of the Lord Lieutenant, but so far as I know we are all agreed also that a strong Chief Secretary without a Lord Lieutenant could and would restore confidence and order in Ireland. So far as my memory serves me it is wholly incorrect to say that the Prime Minister asked the Cabinet to agree that the whole system of 'Castle Government' had broken down and that it was necessary to have resort to Home Rule.

2. The acceptance of the statement made to Sir E. Carson and upon the strength of which alone he advised the Ulster Covenanters to accept Mr Lloyd George's scheme,[2] i.e., that the *Cabinet* including the Unionist Members were *unanimously of opinion that the scheme* as suggested must be adopted by Ulster as an Imperial necessity and in order to avoid American complications, and that if Ulster declined the *Cabinet* had *unanimously decided to force Home Rule upon them.*

So far as I am concerned I have only heard the American difficulty[3] mentioned in connection with Ireland once and not at a Cabinet but at a Cabinet Committee held on June 1st when Mr Lloyd George stated that the difficulty was so serious that he must resign if it was not met. I demurred to this view at the time. I asked the Prime Minister on what ground the drastic change was to be recommended to Irish Unionists in the N. and S. and to the Unionists in Great Britain. I said it would be impossible to refer to the American question in public or indeed outside the Cabinet. The Prime Minister agreed to this emphatically and told me that the ground given would be the necessity of securing peace in Ireland in order that general disarmament might be effected without bloodshed.

3. The breach of the agreement entered into at the commencement of the War and upon which the Ulster Division[4] was invited to enlist,

viz., that no steps should be taken to *set up* a Home Rule Parliament during the War.

4. The acceptance of the statement that the Cabinet as a whole had approved of the *immediate* setting up of a Home Rule Parliament in Dublin.

So far as I know the Cabinet have never had the question before them. The task that Mr Lloyd George was asked to undertake was to secure some basis of agreement among all Irish Unionists which would lead to the acceptance of Home Rule at the *end of the War* without bloodshed and without the delay involved in the passing of an Amending Bill after the War.

In other words the Bill in question was to be passed at once in order that Home Rule in its amended form could come into operation as soon as the War was over. To this the Cabinet undoubtedly assented, but there is all the difference in the world, not merely in form but in principle, between bringing Home Rule into existence after the War and setting up a Home Rule Parliament now whilst all our thoughts are concentrated on the War.

5. The acceptance of the view that a change so drastic as this could be accepted by the Unionists in the Cabinet without any consultation with their followers in the House of Commons.

I have always advocated the view that leaders must lead and followers must follow but when it is suggested that we should adopt a step of this kind involving as it must do the entire destruction of the Unionist Party, I submit with great confidence that no leaders are justified in adopting such a course without taking their followers into their confidence. The *Times* on Monday in speaking of the changes at the War Office made a significant reference to 'Mr Bonar Law and the *Ex*–Unionists'. In my judgment on the information before them they were quite justified in using this term.

6. The acceptance of the view that U.S.A. will break with us and refuse to supply munitions unless we consent to govern Ireland in accordance with the dictates of U.S.A. citizens backed by German Americans and American Irish.

This question has never been discussed by the Cabinet and I personally decline to accept this point of view.

7. That we are to summon an Imperial Conference and ask them to find a constitution for the United Kingdom.

The Cabinet has never been consulted and I strongly object.

I need hardly say that I have no desire or intention to press my personal position but I must claim my right to make my attitude clear in the House of Commons. Mr Lloyd George seems to me to have misunderstood his position from beginning to end, to have committed the Cabinet to wholesale and drastic changes and to definite statements which are not in agreement with the facts.

W.H.L.

B
*SECRET.*
### FOR UNIONIST MEMBERS OF THE CABINET ONLY
### IRISH NEGOTIATIONS

For the convenience of my Colleagues, I append a statement of the sequence of events so far as they are known to me.

1.  The question was considered in the Cabinet after the circulation of the Prime Minister's memorandum. The decision then was to try and bring about a settlement to come into operation *immediately after the War*, automatically and without bloodshed. It was decided that martial law under Sir John Maxwell (with or without a strong Chief Secretary) should be retained until the country was in a satisfactory condition, or until the end of the War, though it was subsequently decided that it would be desirable to have a Chief Secretary for Parliamentary purposes.

This post was offered to Mr Lloyd George, who after consideration declined it on the ground that it would interfere with his war work, but he offered to undertake negotiations and try to find a basis of agreement. The Cabinet decided that if the various Parties in Ireland regarded a scheme as fairly hopeful but were not prepared to accept it voluntarily (the Unionists because of their dislike for Home Rule, the Nationalists because of their dislike for partition) though they would be willing to accept it and try to make it work if it were pressed upon them by the Government, in these circumstances we were to carry the settlement through.

2.  From that time I heard nothing of the negotiations beyond rumours, but on the 29th May I saw Mr George Stewart, Deputy Chairman of the Irish Unionist Association and discussed the general question with him, but at that time neither he nor I knew what the scheme was and we discussed it on the basis of an Amending Bill which should bring Home Rule into force after the War.

3.  I arranged an interview that day between Mr Lloyd George and Mr Stewart, and I afterwards received a request from the former to see him the next morning. I accordingly went to his office at 10.30 a.m. on the 30th when he showed me a rough draft of his scheme which he said had *already been given* to Sir E. Carson and Colonel Craig, to Mr Redmond, Mr Dillon, and Mr Devlin, to Lord Midleton, Lord Desart and Mr Stewart. Lord Midleton had been given permission to show it to Lord Salisbury.

I therefore did not express any definite opinion as the proposals had been sent out without consulting me and I felt I must have time to consider them carefully, and I was of course impressed by the statement that they had been favourably received by all the Unionists, but I did ask him why he proposed to make so drastic a change and bring the Irish Parliament at once into being, and reminded him of the difficulties connected with dual representation. He told me that he thought it would help a solution and that as we intended to continue martial law and the R.I.C., an Irish Government could do no harm. I made no other comment: indeed I had no opportunity of doing so as the interview was interrupted by the arrival of Mr Redmond and his friends. I, however, promised to see Lord Lansdowne and let Mr Lloyd George have our views. I took away some rough notes which I had made of Mr Lloyd George's proposals but I did not myself have a draft of the scheme.

I then saw Lord Lansdowne, and we both, on examination of the proposals came to the conclusion that the experiment was too serious a one to be tried during the War. Lord Lansdowne saw Mr Lloyd George at 6 p.m. that day and conveyed our views to him.

4.   Next day I saw Mr Stewart again. I told him that Mr Lloyd George said that the proposals had been favourably received by himself and his friends. Mr Stewart strongly repudiated this. I therefore asked him to put his views on paper and I forwarded a copy of his statement (which was countersigned by Lord Barrymore), to the Members of the Cabinet Committee.

5.   I also mentioned the outlines of the scheme to one of my colleagues in confidence, and in answer to questions by him I said that Mr Lloyd George meant by bringing the scheme 'immediately into operation' that the Irish Government were to have powers to make the necessary preparations, secure place of meeting, choose a Speaker, Clerks, Officers, etc. and draw up Rules and Regulations and arrange all the details connected with the exclusion of Ulster – matters which would take a very considerable time and would probably mean that the Irish Government would not be in a position to start work so long as the War lasted, or at all events for a very long while.

I had asked Mr Lloyd George whether the exclusion of Ulster would be definite, or open to review at the end of the War. He favoured the latter. On this point there is certainly evidence of divergence of opinion between Sir E. Carson and Mr Redmond.

6.   It is necessary to be quite clear as to what has been told to the various Parties. For instance, has Mr Redmond been informed that martial law, or its proper equivalent, is to be maintained during the necessary period or till the end of the War?

Has he been told that the Imperial Government are to retain the command of the R.I.C.? If so, who is to be the Minister in charge of the R.I.C. and responsible for the maintenance of order in Ireland?

Has he been told that the Irish Government cannot have the Customs owing to the exclusion of Ulster?

None of these points appear in his statement. In my opinion, they would make acceptance of the proposals by the Nationalists impossible but we ought to know the facts.

In a statement which I have received Mr Lloyd George is said to have determined to add 30 nominated members to the Irish Parliament. This was not mentioned by Mr Redmond. Was it communicated to him?

7.   But the most important point of all is this. The decision of the

Cabinet to try and find a solution was based on the Prime Minister's view that there was a general desire in Ireland from N. to S. for a settlement and on the necessity for disarmament. It was clear that the latter step could only be carried out generally and that disarmament in the North could not be enforced so long as Ulster feared inclusion in Home Rule and for this purpose it was necessary to have a settlement. Therefore the first step was to find a basis of agreement and then report to the Cabinet Committee and ultimately to the Cabinet.

8.   At a Cabinet Committee on June 1st Mr Lloyd George referred for the first time to the American difficulty. I have dealt with the point in memorandum A.

9.   I am now informed that Ulster have agreed to accept the proposals solely because they are told that the Cabinet are unanimously of opinion that the scheme must be accepted on account of the American complications and in order to bring the War to a successful issue. I claim that this point has never been submitted to the Cabinet or discussed by them in this relation, nor have they ever to my knowledge seen the scheme proposed by Mr Lloyd George.

10.   I have not had an opportunity to show this statement to Lord Lansdowne but I have to-day received a letter from him which fully confirms all I have said.

W.H.L.

80/185, 189

1.   A report of the meeting of the Irish Parliamentary Party in Dublin on 10 June 1916 was communicated to the press. At this meeting, Redmond referred to Lloyd George's proposed settlement as 'a proposal which we may fairly regard as the proposal of the government'.
2.   Which they did on 12 June 1916.
3.   Lloyd George was at pains to emphasise the damage which hostile American opinion would cause to the British war effort if the Irish question was not settled immediately.
4.   The Ulster Volunteer Force were placed at the government's disposal on the outbreak of war in 1914 and formed the 36th (Ulster) Division


34.   To H.H. Asquith

Board of Agriculture & Fisheries<br>4 Whitehall Place<br>S.W.<br>16 June 1916

My dear Prime Minister,

When you returned from Ireland and told us that all parties there had expressed to you their wish for a prompt settlement of the outstanding dispute between Unionists and Nationalists I concurred with all my colleagues in asking Lloyd George to try and bring the parties together and effect a settlement. But what I understood as a settlement was of a definite and limited kind. I understood that we were to try and get the parties to agree how much of Ulster was to be excluded from the operation of the Government of Ireland Act, that an amending act to effect that exclusion was to be passed during the war, but that neither the principal act nor the amending act would come into operation until the restoration of peace.

Let me remark, parenthetically, that I have had no idea of attempting to procure the repeal of the Government of Ireland Act when once it had been placed upon the Statute Book. I have felt it to be the duty of all of us to give it a fair trial, but of course I believed it also my duty to do all in my power to secure the exclusion of Ulster, or of a part of Ulster, from its operation.

To resume: you will remember that at a meeting of the Cabinet, subsequent to the one at which Lloyd George accepted the Commission to try and bring the Irish parties together and to effect an agreed settlement, he was asked if he had anything to report as to the progress of his negotiations, and that he said he had not. Since that day he has never made any report to the Cabinet or made any proposals whatever to us.

I was, therefore, surprised and alarmed to read the official statement of the Nationalist party published in last Monday's Times. I was in the country and waited, expecting to receive some explanatory Cabinet memorandum or that you would throw light on the situation in your speech at Ladybank.[1]

I came up to London last night and have seen Long today.

He tells me that Lloyd George has given both Carson and Redmond to understand that all the members of the Cabinet are agreed that the Government of Ireland Act, with certain modifications, must be brought into operation during the war and with as little delay as possible, and that he has used arguments to Carson in enforcing this view which I for one utterly repudiate.

I confess never to have been more surprised in all my life.

Not only have I never agreed to any such proposal, but I have never had it made to me, nor have I ever heard it discussed. I never even heard of it, until Long told me of it, from any of my colleagues or friends.

In common honesty I must tell you at once that I hold myself absolutely uncommitted to the acceptance of any such scheme. It is quite impossible indeed that I should accept it, believing as I do that to bring the Government of Ireland Act into operation during the war and in the present state of Ireland would be more perilous to the fortunes of the Empire than any other course open to us.

Unless, therefore, the statement that the Cabinet have agreed to Lloyd George's scheme for bringing the Government of Ireland Act into early operation can be publicly repudiated, I have no alternative but to ask you to accept my resignation. Believe me, yours sincerely

                                                                    Selborne

80/194

1. Made on 14 June 1916, which did not refer in detail to the Lloyd George negotiations but simply wished 'for these negotiations a successful issue'.

35. From Walter Long

Local Government Board
Whitehall, S.W.
22 June 1916

Private

My dear Will,

Lansdowne is with us and I therefore at his request did not send my letter requesting my release.

There has been some odd work.

Look at P.M.'s memo on his visit to Ireland[1] on wh. our policy is founded, 'No H.R. during the war' 'Settlement to be in order to secure peace and disarmament' 'King and Queen to reside in I No Ld. Lt. Single Minister for I'

Why all this suppressed? Whence did Ll. G. derive his authority for H.R. now?

Why does Carson alone refuse to have questions put?

No reference in P.M.'s speech of May 25th to 'Imperial needs' or 'U.S.A.'.

I have seen some of Carson's most trusted advisers in Belfast, and most ardent and devoted supporters. They regard H.R. as 'sheer madness'. Scheme is dead as Queen Anne – but one must have all this unsavoury business cleared up.

Whom can we trust? Yours

W.L.

80/209

1. Asquith's proposals for the future government of Ireland were described in a Cabinet paper 'Ireland. II. The Future', 21 May 1916, Cab 37/148.

36. To Walter Long

49 Mount Street
W.
23 June 1916

My dear Walter,

How stupid of me not to have thought of that memorandum of the P.M. before. Of course that was the basis of my certain confidence that the Cabinet would not do the very thing that they now wish to do. I was certain of the accuracy of my recollection, but till your welcome letter of yesterday reached me I had not my finger on the proof.

My confidence is shattered. There can be no possible justification of the P.M.'s conduct to us. Yours ever

S

P.S. The cause is slackness not dishonesty; but the result is the same.
80/211

37.   From H.H. Asquith

10 Downing Street
Whitehall, S.W.
24 June 1916

*Private*

My dear Selborne,

I shall, of course, be only too grateful if you will continue your work in connexion with the Sub-Committee, and I hope also with other Committees.

In regard to your letter of last Sat. (wh. I enclose) I would venture (after discussing the matter with Bonar Law) to appeal to you not to publish it, but when the time comes to make a short statement in the House of Lords. This is the regular course, and has obvious advantages. If your letter were to be published by itself, without any comment or explanation on Ll. George's part, it might give rise to misconceptions which you are just as anxious as we are to avoid.

I have, at B. Law's request, postponed Monday's Cabinet till Tuesday, and in view of the uncertainties of the position until it has met, I should hope that you might see your way to defer your statement until Tuesday.[1]
Yours sincerely

H.H. Asquith

I thank you very heartily for your kind words about myself.
80/125

1.  Lord Selborne made his explanation on 27 June 1916 (22 *H.L.Deb.*, cols. 387–9).

38.   Memorandum by Lord Selborne

30 June 1916

*Confidential*

MEMORANDUM ON THE CRISIS IN IRISH AFFAIRS WHICH CAUSED MY RESIGNATION FROM THE CABINET JUNE, 1916

When war with Germany broke out in August 1914 the resistance to the principle of Home Rule, which the Unionists had successfully maintained for thirty years, had been broken by the operation of the iniquitous Parliament Act, and the Government of Ireland Act received the King's assent shortly afterwards. On the other hand the Liberal Government had been completely baffled by the refusal of the Unionists of Ulster to be ruled by an Irish government and parliament from Dublin and the 'Ulster problem' was quite unsolved.

The Unionist Party unanimously agreed to accept the accomplished fact about Home Rule and to call a party truce over the Irish question. This was their attitude from August 1914 to May 1915 and it remained their attitude after the 'War Government' of Liberals and Unionists was formed in May 1915. Sir Edward Carson was a member of the Cabinet from May till September 1915, when he resigned because an expedition was not sent to the relief of Serbia (N.B. it was a military impossibility), but neither did he, while he was a member of the Cabinet, nor did the other Unionist members of the Cabinet, at any time seek to interfere with Mr Birrell's administration of Ireland. We all detested his methods of administration but acquiescence in them was an essential condition of the war truce. This would not have absolved us from interference if we had had any knowledge that the condition of Ireland had changed for the worse since the outbreak of war or since the formation of the 'War Government', but we had no such knowledge.

Mr Birrell never at any time even hinted to the Cabinet that the condition of Ireland was not in his opinion satisfactory or that there was any change for the worse; nor did any information to cause us alarm reach us from any external source. This may seem strange to many people, but the fact was that our work was of such an absorbing and exhausting character that we were cut off from the usual social opportunities of acquiring information, and we could only have learnt what was going on in Ireland, if the matter had been raised in the House of Lords or House of Commons, or if it had been reported in the Press, which it was not, or if some private friend had come to tell us or had written to us, which did not as a matter of fact occur. Warnings were addressed both to Mr Asquith and to Mr Birrell but they ignored them and did not communicate them to us. The result was that we knew nothing of the drilling and manoeuvring or generally seditious proceedings of the Sinn Feiners and that the rebellion which broke out in Dublin on Easter Monday 1916 took us completely by surprise.

After the suppression of the rebellion Mr Asquith went to Ireland and on his return circulated to the Cabinet the two papers accompanying this memorandum marked A & B,[1] in the second of which is laid down a fundamental proposition 'that the Home Rule Act however amended cannot come into operation until the end of the war'. Discussions took place in the Cabinet, throughout marked by general concurrence in the attitude adopted by the Prime Minister. We discussed the continuance of martial law. Some members of the Cabinet suggested that martial law was not necessary and that the Defence of the Realm Acts gave us all the powers that were necessary. It was, however, pointed out that if martial law were withdrawn, it would not be easy to justify the suspension of the

'Parmoor Clause' of the Defence of the Realm Act which gives British subjects the right to claim trial by Judge and Jury, and it was felt that Ireland could not be governed if that clause came again into operation. In the end the clear general view of the Cabinet was that martial law must continue. We all agreed that the Lord Lieutenancy should be abolished and we welcomed with acclamation the announcement which the Prime Minister made to us that the King had agreed to make a residence in Ireland and pass there some weeks of every year. The Prime Minister pointed out that when the Government of Ireland Act came into operation after the war the Lord Lieutenant to be created under it was a wholly different person constitutionally to the Lord Lieutenant whose office we had all agreed had ceased to be of any value.

We discussed the appointment of a new Chief Secretary and whether he could for the duration of the war be a soldier like General Sir John Maxwell or whether he must be a parliamentarian.

At the Cabinet Mr Asquith offered the Chief Secretaryship to Mr Lloyd George and pressed it upon him urgently. Mr Lloyd George took some days to think it over and then refused to accept the post. At not one single meeting of the Cabinet did any member of the Cabinet even suggest as a possible course the bringing of the Government of Ireland Act, modified or unmodified, into operation during the duration of the war.

There was complete agreement among us also as to the imperative necessity of effecting a general disarmament in Ireland, of the North as well as of the rest of the country. But we knew that to attempt to disarm the Convenanters in the North so long as they remained subjected by Act of Parliament to the future rule of a Nationalist government in Dublin would provoke their armed resistance, and that was a tragedy impossible even to contemplate. The exclusion of Ulster, or of a part of Ulster, by an Amending Act, from the future operation of the Government of Ireland Act was, therefore, an essential preliminary step to the complete disarmament of Ireland. We could all agree to the disarmament of Sinn Feiners when they could be differentiated from Nationalists, but clearly it was not possible for the Prime Minister to exact disarmament from the Nationalists and not from the Governments.

Consequently when the Prime Minister informed the Cabinet that he had asked Mr Lloyd George to act as mediator between Nationalists and Unionists in Ireland and to ascertain whether any agreed settlement of the outstanding problems between them could be reached, I do not believe that it crossed the mind of one single Unionist Member of the Cabinet that the bringing into existence during the war of Home Rule in any shape or form could possibly form part of such a settlement. I understood, and I believe that my Unionist colleagues understood, that an effort was to be made to get the Ulster Unionists and the Nationalists of Ireland to agree to the exclusion of Ulster or of a part of Ulster from the operation of the Government of Ireland Act, and in addition to see whether there were any safeguards which would induce the Unionists of the South, Centre, and West of Ireland to accept a government and parliament in Dublin for the rest of Ireland. If an agreement on these points could be reached an Act amending the Government of Ireland Act would be passed during the war, but it never entered our heads that anyone contemplated bringing the Government of Ireland Act, amended or unamended, modified or unmodified, into operation during the war. I say this as confidently in respect of Lord Lansdowne, Lord Curzon, Lord Robert Cecil, Mr Austen Chamberlain and Mr Walter Long, as of myself. I believe it to be true also of Sir F.E. Smith, Mr Bonar Law, and Mr Arthur Balfour, but, as they subsequently adopted a somewhat unexpected attitude, I do not state it of them with the same confidence as of the others. In accepting his commission Mr Lloyd George observed that it would probably be impossible to get the Irish Unionists and Nationalists to agree upon a settlement but that they would probably both be very glad if we imposed a settlement on both of them.

Under these circumstances we all concurred in approving the Prime Minister's Commission to Mr Lloyd George. This was where we went wrong. Knowing Mr Asquith and Mr Lloyd George we ought to have insisted on joining some Unionist like Lord Robert Cecil or Mr Austen Chamberlain to Mr Lloyd George in the negotiations.

But believing that the Prime Minister's memorandum of May 21 was the basis and the only basis of negotiation our suspicions were not aroused. Similarly when we heard or read the Prime Minister's speech in the House of Commons of May 25 we interpreted it exclusively in the light of his memorandum and of the subsequent discussions in the Cabinet.

The Cabinet had appointed a small Committee consisting of the Prime Minister, Lord Lansdowne, Mr Walter Long, and Mr Lloyd George to watch the progress of these negotiations. So far as I know this Committee only met once, viz. on June 1. On that day it appears that Mr Lloyd George indicated that the Nationalists would not agree to the exclusion of Ulster or of part of Ulster unless as a quid pro quo Home Rule was brought into operation during the war. It is evident now that Mr Lloyd George had by that time persuaded the Prime Minister to change the basis of the proposed settlement and to accept Home Rule during the war, but I do not gather that either Lord Lansdowne or Mr Walter Long understood the Prime Minister to be thus committed. They both expressed their objections then afterwards to Mr Lloyd George's proposals, but they never reported them to their Unionists colleagues or insisted on a Cabinet being summoned to discuss them. This was their fatal error. For the Cabinet was never informed. I believe that they thought that Mr Lloyd George would make a report to the Cabinet and that meanwhile nothing would be done to commit them. There is no doubt whatever that this is what the Cabinet expected. Mr Lloyd George was not appointed as a plenipotentiary; he was appointed to enquire and report to the Cabinet. But events took quite a different turn.

What I believe had happened was somewhat as follows. Mr Lloyd George had seen the Nationalist leaders and proposed to them the clean cut of the six Ulster Counties. They bluffed him and said 'Yes, but only on condition that we get Home Rule for the rest of Ireland at once, during the war'. He obtained the Prime Minister's concurrence to this new basis of settlement and then saw Sir Edward Carson. What really passed between them I do not think we shall ever know. The two men will always, and inevitably, put a different colour on the attitude which each adopted. What we do know is that some of the members of the Ulster Convention, which took place subsequently, came away believing that the settlement proposed by Mr Lloyd George was the decision of a united Cabinet and that it was urged on Ulster by the Cabinet as essential for victory in the war, because otherwise the Government of the U.S.A. would put obstacles in the way of the delivery to the United Kingdom of the supplies of ammunition. This was the impression which Sir Edward Carson conveyed to some of them at least and those men at any rate only adopted the attitude of the Government. On being questioned by me subsequently at a meeting of the Unionist members of the Cabinet at Lord Curzon's house, at which he also was present. Sir Edward Carson distinctly said that Mr Lloyd George had not told him that this was a decision of the Cabinet but that he had not doubt in his own mind that it was so because of the Prime Minister's speech in the House of Commons on May 25, and because of Mr Lloyd George's attitude. He also said that Mr Lloyd George had impressed upon him the American danger very earnestly.

The proposed settlement had never even been mentioned at the Cabinet nor the argument of the American danger, which was all moonshine. Not only had Mr Lloyd George made no report to the Cabinet but he had been asked at a Cabinet Meeting if he had anything to report and he had said that he had not. The truth seems to be that in his anxiety to effect a settlement Mr Lloyd George had been characteristically sketchy and vague and quite unscrupulous in the arguments he used to Nationalists and Unionists alike, and that Sir Edward Carson was so obsessed by his desire to obtain the clean cut for the six Ulster counties and to have done with the Ulster question that he put far more pressure on his Ulster friends in order to obtain their consent to the proposed settlement than he was justified in doing.

Whether I should have taken alarm or not if I had seen the report of the proceedings of the Ulster Convention I do not know. But I missed seeing that report altogether, I believe because it was published in the papers on one of the days when they were full of the accounts of the battle of Jutland. The first cause of suspicion and alarm to me was the official report of the proceedings of the Nationalist party published in *The Times* of May 12 . . . which I read at Blackmoor where I had gone for the Whitsuntide recess. I waited till May 15. expecting to receive some explanation in some paper which would be circulated to the Cabinet or from the Prime Minister's speech at Ladybank. In both expectations I was disappointed and accordingly went up to London. On May 16. I heard from Mr Walter Long an account of what had happened and on the same day wrote to the Prime Minister placing my resignation in his hands . . . Two meetings of the Unionist members of the Cabinet followed at which Sir E. Carson was present and two meetings of the Cabinet, at all of which I declined to accept any responsibility for the establishment of Home Rule during the war. All the accounts received showed the condition of Ireland to be worse than at any time since 1798 and to establish an Irish government and parliament in Dublin during the war seemed to me to involve a far greater risk to the fortunes of the British Empire in the war than governing Ireland by martial law and the suspension, if necessary, of the Irish Nationalist members from the House of Commons during the continuance of the war.[2]

On June 26. the Prime Minister announced my resignation in the papers and on June 27. I made my explanatory statement in the House of Lords
. . . S

80/226

1. Not attached
2. The Lloyd George negotiations were finally abandoned at the end of July 1916 in an atmosphere of mutual recrimination, and the Cabinet agreed that 'for the immediate future . . . the simplest and least objectionable plan would be to revert for the time being to the old system of a Lord Lieutenant and a Chief Secretary' (Asquith to the King, 27 July 1916, A 8/187–8).

39.   Memorandum by Lord Selborne, 1916

I entered the War Cabinet in May 1915 and left it in June 1916. I will put down my impressions of its members while they are still fresh in my mind, beginning with the P.M. and going round the table at 10 Downing St. from left to right.

**Asquith**. The Unionist party in the country had no confidence whatever in him. The Liberal and Labour parties and, I think, the allied powers believed in him thoroughly. He was always courteous and good natured and pleasant to deal with personally except when one tried to force him to a decision; then his manner became awkward, reserved, and even dour. He was immensely clever and would have made a very great judge. If he chose, he could sum up a case perfectly; and, when driven right up in a corner and forced to give an opinion, it was almost always a wise one. His greatest asset was his imperturbability. Nothing, no difficulty, no disaster, no black cloud, no failure, no worry, nothing flustered him, flurried him or excited him. That was far his greatest asset as a war P.M., and it was a very great asset. For the rest he was quite hopeless as a war P.M. He had no vision, no power or desire of prevision, no ounce of drive in his composition, not a spark of initiative, no power of leadership of any sort or kind. He gave the Cabinet no lead; he never bound our work together; Cabinets were mere wastes of time; he was the worst chairman I ever sat under at any committee, he kept no sort of order at Cabinet councils nor ever attempted to bring us to a decision; he hardly ever expressed any opinion himself. The desire on all occasions to avoid a decision was an absolute disease with him. That the Cabinet was always too late in everything it did, the supply of munitions, the reconstitution of the General Staff, the supply of men, the supply of food, was his fault. In a war Cabinet every member is overworked; he cannot attend to his colleagues' business; and his colleagues can't attend to his. Everything depends on the P.M., and, if his ruling passion is to avoid coming to any decision, he can only be moved by an individual colleague by the threat of resignation, and in a war Cabinet any man, who is not purely selfish, shrinks from that ultima ratio as long as he possibly can. Asquith was intensely patriotic and cared with his whole soul for England's victory, but he never acted except to get out of a grave difficulty into which he ought never to have got.

A much stupider man, but possessed of some vision and with a power of decision, would have made a much better war P.M.

**Kitchener**. A strange mixture of streaks, genius and stupidity, courage and timidity, simplicity and duplicity. His vision of a three years war and the conception of the new army was an immense public service and very great. The nation, the army, and the allied powers all believed in him. The P.M. could not have displaced him, but the two men formed the worst possible combination, neither corrected the faults of the other. K tried to fill three parts, S of S for War, C in C in England, and Chief of the General Staff; an extra plus superman could not have done it, and as a matter of fact K failed in all three parts. He was no organiser, he was incapable of devolving responsibility on other people, it was a grave blunder to divorce the new army from the Territorials, the condition of the W.O. became chaotic, an immense amount of money was wasted, the commands in England became a tangle of responsibility, he who had foreseen that immense numbers of men would be wanted never foresaw that an immense supply of rifles, guns and ammunition would also be wanted. The Unionists in the Cabinet could have forced compulsory service in September or October 1915 and we had the P.M. and the anti-compulsionists beaten. It was K who beat us by publishing his precious Derby Group Scheme. It had never even been mentioned in the Cabinet. The P.M. may have known about it: if he did he welcomed it with open arms because it shelved a decision. No more of the rest of us knew of it, and we could not resign against K! The destruction of the General Staff when the B.E.F. went to France in August 1914 was the cause of all our calamities. Antwerp, Dardanelles, etc. etc. It left the W.O. without a brain – he only began to recover a chance of victory when the P.M. reconstituted the General Staff in the Autumn of 1915. He had been implored by colleague after colleague to do it for months. That the machine worked at all during that first year of war was due to Hankey the

Secretary of the Imperial Defence Committee. The Empire owes him a deep debt of gratitude. K was at his very worst in Cabinet or at the War Committee. He seldom knew his case, his figures were usually wrong, his statements were muddled and confused, and it was impossible to trust them. His conception of truth was distinctly oriental.

He was very fortunate in the manner and time of his death.

**Churchill**. Clever, but quite devoid of judgement; he harangued the Cabinet ceaselessly but never foolishly; his harangues were intolerable because he always repeated his argument three times over; his disease is egotism. He is really patriotic but his conception of England is an England in which everyone talks of Churchill. His great asset is courage; he has that splendid quality in great abundance; I would go out tiger shooting with him anytime, but I could never trust him in the absence of the tiger, because the motive power is always 'self', and I don't think he has any principles. But he has got vision and the power of drive. If he had judgement, principles and less egotism he would be a great man. The P.M.'s ways drove him nearly crazy.

**Long**. One of the straightest, truest, humblest and least selfish men that ever stepped; lots of ability; managed his own department, the L.G.B. a very important one, quite admirably. But the inconstancy of his opinion was such as to make cooperation with him very difficult. There was no faithlessness or want of courage about him; his opinion did vary from day to day quite incomprehensibly and one never knew where he would be. I think his opinion must have depended on what he had for breakfast.

**Carson**. One of the best fellows that ever stepped, clever true and courageous; but very emotional and sentimental; the slaughter of the battles caused him an anguish which disturbed his judgement; he so hated the P.M.'s way of carrying on the Government that he made a somewhat slender occasion for leaving it at the first opportunity.

**Smith**. Succeeded Carson; clever but with a fatal passion for Churchill and his methods.

**Samuel**. Succeeded Simon; a clever efficient and straight little Jew – a Whig in politics I guess.

**Runciman**. Had the Board of Trade, a very hard war department which he ran quite admirably – a very able and efficient and modest, no self-seeking about him and as true as steel. I liked him much the best of all my Liberal colleagues except Edward Grey. An ultra Cobdenite radical – he never spoke in Cabinet except about what he thoroughly understood. Excellent manner.

**McKinnon Wood**. A disagreeable narrow Scotch radical; his one merit was that he never said a word in Cabinet.

**Crewe**. A most perfect gentleman, but perfectly useless as a statesman; a replica of the P.M. with more charm and less ability; the most tedious utterer I ever listened to in Cabinet and in the House of Lords; yet when read it was always good sense though not original – I think he had only one political conviction and that he believed with all his heart, that the party labelled Liberal was necessary to salvation.

**Bonar Law**. A charming personality, so honest so kindly and so unselfish; but no leader; he also lacks vision, initiative and driving power; I am afraid that he also lacks courage; he only once in my time took any strong line in the Cabinet and then he was right and I was wrong. He thought, and I did not think, that the Gallipoli peninsula could be evacuated without disaster to the troops in it or to our position in Egypt and India – generally he gave the impression to the Cabinet that he was an amateur in politics. I certainly think that he led us Unionists very badly. He emasculated our influence from the beginning by starting with and sticking to the theory that Asquith was indispensable as war P.M. and that therefore under no circumstances must the coalition cabinet be allowed to break up, and with the determination that under no circumstances would he consent to form a war Cabinet. I believe all this to have been an utter fallacy. No-one was indispensable. It was the resolution of the British people that was the spring of victory and they would have rallied to any P.M. and Cabinet which showed that it meant to lead and govern, vision and courage, and such a P.M. and Cabinet would quickly have gained the confidence of the allies.

**Lloyd George**. Very clever, with vision, precision, driving power and courage in wonderful combination. His performance at the Ministry of Munitions was a wonderful one, for it was due notwithstanding the fact that his office there was, as always, a perfect welter of disorganisation and intrigue – If George's vision and drive could have been combined with Law's business habits and straightness, the results would have been doubled. But George's services in the matter of Munitions, though done in George's way, were a good war asset to the Empire. I would never wish to go out tiger hunting with him, not because I doubt his courage but because I know that he would leave anyone in the lurch anywhere if he thought it suited his purpose. Self looms almost as large with him as with Churchill, he is a born intriguer and you cannot believe a word he says. I lay stress on his vision, but his judgement is faulty. He had not a real friend among his Liberal colleagues in the Cabinet and most of them evidently hated him.

I cannot imagine a man less fit to be S of S for War; the P.M.'s ways made him mad too, but he revenged himself by bullying the P.M. into giving him what he wanted for himself by threatening resignation.

**Grey**. In Cabinet was a disillusion; he never came to the Cabinet and said 'this is the position, this is what I think ought to be done, do you agree?' He hardly ever took a decision even in comparatively unimportant matters without coming to the Cabinet, and then when he came to the Cabinet he threw the news at its neck and the result was deplorable. He certainly mismanaged the Balkan business badly and the Declaration of London policy during the first 8 months of the war was a dreadful blunder: after that his management of the blockade and neutrals was much wiser than his critics' criticisms. I had the impression at the end of my year in the Cabinet that the allied governments had less confidence in him than they had at the beginning of it. But when I joined the Cabinet his health was greatly impaired by overwork and I fancy that the Grey of 1912 was a different man to the Grey of 1915. His readiness without question or pose to sacrifice his cyesight absolutely pro patria was magnificent. In his personal character he was sans peur et sans reproche, the absolute antithesis in the perfect-Knight sense to Churchill or George. Self did not exist in his conception of things.

**Buckmaster**. Able, nice, equable and sensible, also diffident.

**Balfour**. Did his work at the Admiralty I believe quite admirably, but in Cabinet all the faults which he had shown as P.M. in the 1900 Government were accentuated. He yearned for decisions just as heartily as the P.M. loathed them; yet he never did anything to obtain them. He seldom spoke, (comparatively to his status, second in the Cabinet) and when he did it was critically and destructively and not constructively. He showed the same splendid staying power and absence of nerves as the P.M. He had the vision which the P.M. lacked, but it led to nothing. Philosophy is the worst possible training for politics. Arthur's personal charm was as great as ever; as loveable as ever.

**Curzon**. Quiet ability, courage, driving power and vision: unpopular with the Cabinet, I think quite undeservedly, his manner was not bad as has been alleged. He hated the P.M.'s ways and Bonar Law's attitude as much as I did and he and I worked in partnership with Austen.

**Chamberlain**. I wish for no better company when after tigers; neither of them would ever leave a friend in the lurch. Austen played a very valuable part in the Cabinet and was clearly generally liked. In my opinion he did all that was humanly possible to avoid the blunders of the Mesopotamian campaign.[1] India is governed not by the I.O. but by the Viceroy in Council; how Hardinge came to trust the Indian C in C, Beauchamp Duff, I do not know, but Austen could have done nothing more except remove Hardinge and he was quite right not to remove Hardinge. Austen's is a beautiful nature, as straight as a die, very able and no self in it, but, curiously enough for his father's son, he is inclined to be too conventional. The iron of the Mesopotamian miseries entered into his soul – I love Austen.

**Bob Cecil**. Ought to have come just before Samuel. Everyone knows how I love and admire Bob. He was a tower of strength in the F.O. and Grey came greatly to lean on him. He was too tolerant, however, of the P.M.'s ways.

**Simon**. Very clever, but shifty and at heart an incurable little Englander. He was the author of a bill to compel men who had served 12 or 21 years in the Army to go on serving; he left the Cabinet because we adopted a bill to compel those who had given no service to serve in this war!

**Henderson**. A real good sensible straight efficient Englishman; very valuable in the Cabinet, quite unassuming but with the full courage of definite opinions which he expressed admirably.

**Montagu**. A very clever Jew; a pronounced Liberal but not a narrow one; he will go far; I liked working with him.

**McKenna**. A bigoted Cobdenite radical with a narrow technical mind; with a manner singularly devoid of charm and the appearance of a cock sparrow; he has done his tremendous task pluckily and efficiently and with as small a proportion of blunders as any man could expect; he loathes Lloyd George and always says ditto to what he thinks the P.M. would say if he ever said anything; but he is devoid of vision. I have stated that the Derby Group system was launched without the knowledge of the Cabinet and without one word being said in the Cabinet about it before it was published. I left the Cabinet because Lloyd George and the P.M. were committing the Cabinet to the introduction of Home Rule in Ireland during the war without one word on the subject being whispered to the Cabinet. It is an even more extraordinary fact that the famous resolutions of the Paris Economic Conference were never mentioned or discussed or approved at the Cabinet and that the delegates at that conference had no authority whatever to agree to these resolutions. As we Unionists in the Cabinet all approved of the resolutions we naturally lay low, however much we might regard the method of proceeding as indefensible. But what must have been the feelings of McKenna and Harcourt and two or three more, who beyond question abhorred these resolutions? The fact that they kept a strong silence has made me suspicious ever since of the good faith of the Liberal section of the Cabinet in this matter.

**Harcourt**. A bitter aristocratic Cobdenite Little Englander; said very little in the Cabinet; steadily agreed to decisions which he hated; was constantly intriguing; did his work at the office of works well; always courteous.

**Lansdowne**. The most perfect gentleman in the world, of great experience, ability and good sense; but ridiculously diffident, and a nature too cautious, almost timid; it would be untrue to say that he had no courage, but it is true to say that he lets it loose too seldom; he has some vision, but little initiative, and no driving power. I like him and respect him greatly. I sat between Balfour and Curzon; very good work could have been got out of this Cabinet by a better P.M. As it was we simply stumbled on from day to day, and I think it was purgatory to almost all of us.

80/285

1.  A Royal Commission of Inquiry into the mismanaged Mesopotamian campaign of 1915–16 censured a number of officers in India for the shortcomings of the expedition. Austen Chamberlain felt it his duty to resign from his post as Secretary of State for India in July 1917, though it was widely believed that this was unnecessary.

# Chapter 5

# 'The danger of the situation': The Crisis of Unionism, 1916–1922

1.   To the Editor, the *Morning Post*[1]

5 August 1916

It has been demonstrated by the recent rebellion and by events subsequent to it that a certain number of the Irish people cherish an ideal for Ireland irrealisable within the British Empire or except in hostility to Great Britain.

How large that proportion is we do not know. If once the conviction were forced upon us that it represented half or more of the population, British Home Rulers and Unionists alike would be forced to recast their Irish policy and to base it solely on the military security of the United Kingdom. At present we have not abandoned the hope that the number of our enemies in Ireland, though undoubtedly larger than we believed it to be six months ago, is only a minority of the population. On this hypothesis surely it is time that we all faced the facts of the situation.

Unionists, though deeply convinced that the Act of Union had given to the United Kingdom the solution which combined the greatest measure of national security and welfare with the fewest disadvantages, have always admitted that there were two other possible solutions, autonomy for Ireland on the Canadian or Australian model, and a system of 'devolution' for the whole United Kingdom centring round a United Kingdom Parliament, which should take cognisance only of those matters which are the common concern of all the nations of which the United Kingdom is composed. Home Rulers have believed that a fourth solution was possible, and this belief has found expression in the Government of Ireland Act, 1914, which is now on the Statute Book.

But the history of the last few weeks has thrown fresh light on the problem. Is it not now manifest to us all that on the one hand the great majority of Irish men and women will accept no solution which divides Ireland and on the other hand that the Unionists of Ulster cannot be forced to accept any solution of which they disapprove? Surely the inevitable conclusion is that the Government of Ireland Act, 1914, does not provide a solution of the problem. For the same reason the solution of autonomy on the Canadian and Australian model must be ruled out, because, apart altogether from its rejection by the people of Great Britain as incompatible with their safety, the Unionists of Ulster would refuse to accept it. The Nationalists reject the solution of the Act of Union. Does not the solution of 'devolution' alone remain? It may be that this solution also may be rejected by the Irish Nationalists or by the Ulster Unionists, or by both of them, but it has never been put before them as the only possible alternative to the Act of Union and in my judgment the inexorable logic of facts is rapidly proving it to be so.

Let us see what this solution would involve. It would mean a legislative body and an executive for the whole of Ireland to which would be entrusted the complete control of all matters exclusively Irish, a legislative body and an executive for Scotland to which would be entrusted the complete control of all matters exclusively Scottish, a legislative body and an executive for England to which would be entrusted the complete control of all matters exclusively English, and, unless Wales was prepared to combine with England, a legislative body and an executive for Wales to which would be entrusted the control of all matters exclusively Welsh. In addition it would mean a legislative body and an executive for the United Kingdom which would deal with all matters common to Ireland, Scotland, England and Wales, and which would, in fact, be identical with the present Imperial Parliament.

It would be possible to set up two legislative bodies and two executives in Ireland, one for the six Ulster counties and one for the rest of Ireland, if the six Ulster counties refused to combine with the rest of Ireland, but it is highly improbable that the Nationalists would accept such a solution. If the Ulstermen refused combination and the Nationalists refused division, the Act of Union would continue to hold the field. The cumbersomeness of 'devolution' compared with the simplicity of Union must strike Unionists very forcibly, and the difficulties in framing such an elaborate constitution, and the objections to it when framed, are manifest. But the objections, grave as they are, do not appear to me to be so grave as those inherent in the Government of Ireland Act, 1914, and the difficulties are not insoluble. The constitutional process out of which arose the Dominion of Canada, the Commonwealth of Australia, the Union of South Africa, and the United States of America was one of centralisation, whereas the process in our case would be one of decentralisation, but the difficulties which confront us are analogous to the difficulties which were successfully overcome in those cases and the experience of Canada with its special problem of the Province of Quebec is particularly interesting in this connection.

Although I believe that Mr. Pitt's solution of the Irish problem was the right solution, in my judgment, now that the Government of Ireland Act is on the statute book, it is necessary in the interests of the Empire that after the War 'Home Rule' for Ireland should be given a fair trial. This does not mean that I think that Unionists should acquiesce even temporarily in the treatment meted out to Ulster by the Act or in those of its provisions by which Irish members are given a continuing share of control over matters which are exclusively English or Scottish or Welsh, after British members have ceased to have any corresponding control over matters which are exclusively Irish; but it explains why I ask my fellow Unionists seriously to consider the solution of 'devolution'.

If the political unity of the Empire for common imperial purposes (while each part of the Empire retains complete internal autonomy) is to them as it is to me the greatest and dearest political idea, then they will be careful to carry the public opinion of the Empire with them in their handling of the Irish question.

84/4

1.  This copy is marked by Lord Selborne, 'Sent to *Morning Post* 5.8.16'. It was published on 8 August.


2.  From F.S. Oliver

8 Hereford Gardens
Marble Arch
London, W.
8 August 1916

Dear Selborne,

I read your letter in the 'Morning Post' today with interest and agreement.

I told you in my letter of Sunday why I could not enter the fray; but even if I could, I think it would be more likely to do harm than good, for the reason that crusted Unionists distrust me because I favour Federalism, while crusted Radicals detest me because I have tried to break some of their idols. My name may have some use in political controversy, but not I think in the present connection, where it is more important to remove prejudice than to break heads.

Your letter will provoke answers and comments, and you will no doubt have to write another in a few days' time.[1] I venture to suggest to you that in addition to the reasons for considering 'devolution' which you put forward, there is at least one other very important reason arising out of the war. In pre-war times one of the objections against local parliaments was that having nothing to do they would be sure to get into mischief. We have changed all that! The problem which besets every thinking mind at the present moment is, how are we to find public bodies and individuals, of sufficient ability and in sufficient numbers, to overtake the work which has to be done during the next ten years? There are a heap of questions as regards reconstruction, demobilisation, unemployment, preventing emigration to foreign countries, getting the people on the land, etc., etc., which, although they must proceed upon some set of general principles laid down by a Central parliament, can only be worked out with any hope of success by the energy of local bodies, according to the habits and customs of the countryside.

I don't profess to have penetrated very profoundly into the ways and means; but it seems to me that the future prosperity of the country will, during the next decade, depend more upon (1) *administration* and (2) *bye-laws* than upon anything else. If this is so, there should be plenty of work not only for parliaments in England, Scotland and Ireland, but for some much strengthened County Council Authorities in each of the four provinces of Ireland, the three provinces of Scotland, and I don't presume to say how many provinces in England!

As a matter of fact if we can get these bodies properly started and set to work, their competition one with the other, and their experiments, whether they result in success or failure, will be most valuable to the others.

I am afraid this letter is rather confused, but I have had to dictate it hastily, not having time to write with my own hand.

I am sending you herewith copies of the two Irish pamphlets which I wrote just before the war,[2] not because I want you to read them through – they are very dreary and prolix – but because in the second, at any rate, you will find an analysis of the defects of the Home Rule Bill, and certain suggestions which may conceivably be useful to you. Yours faithfully

F.S. Oliver

84/12

1. F.S. Oliver was right: see the *Morning Post*, 10, 15, 19, 29 and 30 August 1916 for editorial comment and further correspondence on this theme.
2. *The alternatives to civil war* (1913) and *What federalism is not* (1914).

3. To the Marquess of Salisbury

Blackmoor
Liss
Hants
25 August 1916

My dear Jim,
. . . Now about franchise.[1]

For the war register common sense and sanity point to no change of franchise but to allow the men of the fleet and army who were already on the register and who were qualifying for the register, when they left their homes to serve, to vote for the constituencies, in which their homes were, by post.

This simple and sensible expedient has been jeopardised by Bonar Law's incapacity and Carson's emotion, but we must continue to try for it.

To give votes to all fighting men because they are fighting raises inevitably the cases of the munition workers and women. This is true of the proposition if it were only to enfranchise adult fighting men.

Personally I think it would be most unjust to women and dangerous to the State to enfranchise the adult fighting men and no women. Dangerous to the State because I firmly believe in the steadying influence of the women voters in essentials in the long run. Unjust to women because I believe that the interests of labour women, and of the women's view of certain social matters, would be ruthlessly sacrificed.

The proposal to enfranchise boys of 18, 19 and 20 only because they are fighting is mischievous sentimentalism of the worst sort. When I said I was prepared for a bold course I referred to the post war or permanent franchise.

On theory I would always enlarge the franchise by stages. But I think that the history of the war has settled the question for us. In my judgement the way that the men of our race have behaved in this war has made adult manhood suffrage inevitable; we shall have to do in one stage what I should have preferred to do in several.

And if the men have the suffrage then I prefer that the women should have it too: that has for some years been my deliberate preference. Do not attach too much importance to numbers.

I do not believe that 23 million voters will act differently to 15 or 12. I think that a Labour government is not likely to do worse now with a large electorate than a radical government was able to do and was likely to do with the present electorate. On the whole I should prefer the Labour government now. Before the war I should have been more afraid of their attitude on imperial questions. I am not afraid of that now. Of course things will be done which I shall vehemently dislike, but those things were already being done before the war; and the war has confirmed the intense belief which I have had now for a good many years in the instincts and intentions of my fellow-countrymen and women. What I would try and do is to fix the age for the franchise for both men and women at 25 instead of 21, and to introduce the referendum into our constitutional machinery. What I would do with the House of Lords depends on whether we have or have not devolution in the U.K. or whether we have or have not an Imperial Parliament for the whole Empire for foreign policy and defence. We must talk this all over in September or October. Yours ever

S

4th Salisbury, S (4)
78/56

1. In 1916 a bill was introduced for registration of voters who had changed their residence because of war work. This led to pressure, particularly from the Unionist War Committee and the Beach Committee (a ginger group in the House of Lords) to extend the franchise to the nation's soldiers and sailors. A conference was set up in 1916 under the chairmanship of Viscount Ullswater, the Speaker of the House of Commons, to try to reach agreement

on electoral reform, on the issues of one man one vote, women's suffrage, redistribution of seats etc. It sat in October, November and December 1916. Lord Salisbury served on the conference but resigned. By January 1917 agreement had been reached on all main resolutions and on 30 January the Conference report was produced in the form of a letter to the Prime Minister. The proposals were embodied in the Representation of the People Bill, which became law in 1918. It conceded manhood suffrage, giving the vote also to women over the age of thirty if either themselves or their husbands were qualified on the local government franchise by owning or occupying land or premises of an annual value of £5. Two million men and six million women were added to the register. In the December 1918 election, which returned the Lloyd George coalition to power, only about half the electorate went to the polls.

### 4.   From the Marquess of Salisbury

Manor House
Cranborne
Salisbury
4 September [1916]

My dear Willie,

Thank you very much for letting me see Lansdowne's letters.[1] I return them. Very odd way of doing things this Government have. But that is a trifle. The important thing is – next of course to the War – What is the future of the Unionist or Conservative or anti Radical Party?

I conceive it to have had two main functions hitherto. To defend certain capital institutions and in everything else to go slow.

Now what institutions is it now proposed to defend? Not the Union – that the leaders have abandoned. Do you think they will fight for the Church in Wales? I doubt it. Do you think they will repair the damage of the Parliament Act? I don't feel at all sure. Indeed so far from being Conservative as regards the constitution, this poor old thing is to be absolutely revolutionised by our friends. Well then, what about going slow? You tell me not to be afraid of a drastic Reform Bill. Well I am not afraid – in the sense that I have great confidence in the ultimate good sense of my countrymen, rich and poor, male and female. But I think and you think like all the anti Radicals who have gone before us that we should do better to go slow. Why not say so? Why not perform the essential function of a Conservative Party? If people want universal adult suffrage the Radicals will do it for them. Do please think of the question from this point of view. Our job is to maintain in its efficiency that great instrument the Conservative Party – call it what you will. Without it we can neither defend what we wish to defend nor guide the Country where we wish it to go. Perhaps you do not quite agree with me in everything. But the spirit which I have tried to indicate is the spirit of the backbone of the Party. If proper respect is not paid to it it will not play. These people up and down the Country – steady cautious easygoing folk will henceforth mind their own business and let politics go to the devil and you will be left with the labour party and a few journalists and lawyer politicians. Don't be afraid about your women. If the women must have the vote you and your friends on that question have lots of strength to force at any rate a contingent of women into the electorate as a compromise and that is much sounder than giving them all the vote straight off.

As to the Government it is easy to see what is happening. Partly from fatigue and partly from patriotic intoxication our friends in the Cabinet have lost their moorings. The idea seems to be a round table conference about everything. It is suggested that all the old issues ought to be settled. Why? Do they imagine that there is finality in all these things? Or that if any of them should be settled there are not a hundred more successively to rise in their place? They will not get peace, but they *will* paralyse the Conservative forces of the Country.

I have written all this to explain why I do not think I will write to the Speaker. I do not say I would not take part in a Conference if I were asked, but I don't *want* to take part – except with a view of disintegrating it. I would rather – so far as my own conduct is of the slightest importance – keep my hands free so that I can criticise these foolish rushes and gushes and at any rate make an effort for the preservation or it may be the rehabilitation of the Conservative Party hereafter. That will be required in order to direct the growth of Imperial consolidation with infinite caution and circumspection and to promote social reform without injuring security. I agree that our leaders in the Government have no right to abandon Conservative principles without consulting us. I hope that the decisions of the Conference will only be ad referendum and if they are unsatisfactory I hope thereupon the Party will reject them as it did in effect in the case of Ireland. Forgive this tiresome letter. Yours ever

S

6/179

1.  Presumably relating to the Speaker's Conference referred to in No. 3, above


5.  To the Marquess of Salisbury

Blackmoor
Liss
Hants
12 September 1916

My dear Jim,

I fully share your anxiety about the future of our party, not because I feel doubtful as to the line it should take, but because I have little confidence in those who are at present its leaders; so much so that for the present I shall be careful not to associate myself again with them formally.

You define the two main functions of our party thus:– 'To defend certain capital institutions and in everything else to go slow'. You are much more entitled than I am to attempt the definition, but I must say I never should have thought of that as a definition. 'To defend certain capital institutions' of course, but why in everything else to go slow? There is no more inherent merit in going slow than there is in going fast. I should have put it quite differently, somewhat like this:– 'In everything else to see that the changes which are made are made in conformity with the traditions of the past and made in the interests of the nation and not of a section of the nation'. As regards 'the capital institutions' we have been beaten on the Union and on the House of Lords mainly because He failed us on whom we had most right to depend. What therefore should be our task? Not to take the attitude of French legitimists but to reconstruct the constitution. That I should say was essentially the function of our party and one for which the other party was quite unfitted. I do not believe that we can put back the Union or the House of Lords to where it was. Given the circumstances of the British Empire and of the United Kingdom as I see them today I would not recommend the attempt. You know that, rightly or wrongly, for a long time past I have thought that the only alternative to Union was devolution, and that is what I am going to work for, and I am going to work for political union with the Dominions for purposes of foreign policy and defence. I mention this, because you will see at once how that affects the question of the Second Chamber. I think this is a great ideal to work for, because the British Empire will replace the United Kingdom so far as international relations and national defence is concerned, we shall have a Power which will be most potent to keep the peace of the world and will not be aggressive, and we shall be able to keep England for the English uncontaminated and unrevolutionised by the Celtic fringes.

As regards the Church in Wales I feel no confidence in our leaders, and that is one of the reasons why I shall hold aloof from them, to leave myself free to take any necessary action, however disagreable to them. I think before the war Bob was prepared to advise that we should acquiesce in disestablishment without disendowment, and I agree with him. That is what, as far as I can judge, the Welsh Bishops and Churchmen themselves are working for.

Now as regards the Reform Bill. Let us look at facts as I see them. Before the war our party, as I understood, were prepared to agree to put all the cost of registration on public funds and the work of it on public officials, and to reduce the term of residential qualification to six months. This by itself would mean a great addition to the electorate. Then comes the war and the splendid patriotism shown by the men of the nation of all classes and the conviction in the mind of every sensible person that after the war there must be compulsory military service for some force corresponding to the territorial force, but with the obligation to serve abroad in some defined national emergency, and the general feeling that the men who have fought for the country, and the men who are going to be compelled to serve hereafter, have the right to the vote. No doubt there is no logic in this, but the feeling appears to me to be very general, and so far from the bulk of the Conservative Party not sharing this view they appear to me to hold this view in a larger proportion than the Liberals. Indeed I notice a very strong desire among the backbone of the Conservative Party – the very people whom you think will be frightened – to secure the votes of the men who have fought as a deliverance from the domination of the Trades Union influence. They will have seen that only two days ago the Trades Union Congress passed an apparently unanimous resolution against compulsory service after the war,[1] and they will be confirmed in the opinion which I have attributed to them that the only men to save them from such folly will be the men who have fought, and I think their instinct is sound. I think those men will be an immense support to us for many years to come against Radical and Liberal insanity in the matter of foreign policy, navy, etc. They also think that these men will have shed to a great extent the class hatred which permeates the Trades Unions. I think this is also true; but if they think that this will lead the men who have fought to separate themselves from the Trades Unionists on questions of what is called 'social reform', then I agree that they will be disillusioned.

But if the qualifying residential period is reduced to six months, and the vote is given to the men who have fought in the past and the men who are going to be forced to serve in the future, then we are really face to face with something that is not easily distinguishable from manhood suffrage. Here I would note that it is an interesting fact that Bismarck stated as his reason for agreeing to manhood suffrage for the Reichstag that it was in his opinion an inevitable corollary of compulsory military service. I said in my previous letter that I should always go slow in such mattters if I had my own way, but I did not mean by that that after the tremendous fact of the war I would go as slow as I would have before or without the war, and of course never before or after the war would I have agreed to an extension of suffrage to men without bringing in the principle of the women's vote. The Conservative Party has had at least two opportunities of bringing in a moderate instalment of women's suffrage, which in my judgement would have been far the most Conservative thing they could have done; but they rejected them both, and now they will have to have a great many more women voters than they otherwise would have had. They might have 'gone slow' in this matter but they would not even start, and you require 'to start' in order to 'go slow', just as much as to go fast.

I do not think that it necessarily follows by any means that because you have something like manhood suffrage that therefore you would have to have something like womanhood suffrage too, but I think you will have to add to the men voters not only the women rate-payers but the wives of householders. Here I agree with you that the bulk of the Conservative Party will be frightened and alarmed. They will in my judgement want the fighting men as voters; they will not want the women, and I am quite conscious that I am out of sympathy with my party on that subject. I can only say that I think they are profoundly mistaken, and that women will prove to be the most stable and conservative element in the constitution. I would certainly contend that it is in conformity with the traditions of the past as interpreted by the Conservative Party to extend the privilege of the franchise to men or women on the grounds of proved patriotism and self-sacrifice for King and country.

There is no form of Government which looks more ludicrous on paper than democracy, and for most nations democracy is a very bad form of Government, but on the whole I believe it to be the best form for our race in the 20th century. I cannot therefore take exactly the attitude you do about it. If I thought that a large increase in the number of male voters and the introduction of women voters was on the whole, and in the long run, going to make for less national stability and worse government, then of course I should try and obstruct, but I do not think that. Although I think that the unenfranchised will, when enfranchised, behave exactly the same as those now enfranchised and show the same trends and cleavages of opinion, yet I also think that the existing franchise gives organised labour a larger share of power than it is entitled to considering its proportion to the whole population, and I think that an enlargement of the franchise, and especially the introduction of women voters, will tend to correct that error. Plural voting should be defended on its merits: the comparatively rich will be taxed more and more, and that is just up to a certain point but may well cease to be wise even before that point is reached: it is therefore both just and wise that the votes of the comparatively rich should not be swamped more than can be avoided in any democratic constitution; but I do not believe for a moment that the existence of a powerful Conservative Party depends upon plural voting. Yours ever

S

6/185

1.  The T.U.C. meeting at Birmingham passed a resolution that it 'views with grave misgiving the introduction of compulsory military service into Great Britain . . . and instructs the Parliamentary Committee to lose no opportunity after the war to press for the repeal of all Acts of Parliament imposing economic, industrial, and military compulsion upon the manhood of the nation . . . ' (*The Times*, 8 September 1916).

6.   From the Marquess of Salisbury

Hatfield House
Hatfield
Herts.
18 September 1916

My dear Willie,

As I said yesterday the National Mission report[1] is probably far more important than any of the issues which you discuss so thoroughly in your other letter. But as regards this last I certainly am not proud of my hasty definition. For one thing it does not cover constructive legislation in defence of our institutions which with you I certainly look forward to. The truth is that definitions are of very little use. May I say that your alternative definition that changes should be made in the interests of the Nation and not a section of the Nation fails in the essential of a definition – that it is what every party would subscribe to. And similarly Maud's definition – to guide reforms into safe channels – would be accepted by every Radical as describing his own position. So we will abandon the task.

As regards the Union I have written a rather didactic letter to the Times[2] and if it is published you will see what I say.

As regards the rest I need not tell you that I agree with you in looking on to closer union of the British Empire so far as international relations and national defence is concerned. How soon do you think that is going to be brought about? Philip Kerr thinks it is a matter of a very few years. He may be right. I certainly would not assert that he is wrong. But my impression is that it will take a very considerable time. That is all right from my rotten stick-in-the-mud point of view. I do not want to hurry. I am sure we shall make a sounder job of it if we go slow. However that is not the point – what I wish or you wish in the matter – but what is going to happen. Supposing I am right, what are you going to do in the meantime? You want to have something like Manhood Suffrage and I agree in thinking that that probably will be the case within a very short delay. You are going to have a large mixture of women though I am very glad that you feel with me that there ought to be a limit here – perhaps not the same limit as I should favour but still a limit. You will admit that probably this new electorate will make any number of mistakes and yet you propose to do nothing to remedy the mischief of the Parliament Act until the new Imperial Constitution, after many years, is in being. Or am I wrong and you would have a Referendum in the meantime? That would be business.

As to the Welsh Church I should not break my heart if we lost the Establishment for good – as distinguished of course from the Endowment. But you will have some difficulty won't you in fitting that on to the new Church Constitution for which we are going to work? But upon that subject you are a twenty times better authority than I am. But let me just put in a word of respectful protest against your attitude about the Celtic fringes. I need not say I sympathise with it. Why should poor dear England be dragged about at the heels of these Scotchmen and Welshmen? And yet I can't think that such an attitude is very gallant. These Welsh Churchmen and these Scotch owners of property have they not some claim upon us? I can assure you I think the situation in Wales might be very serious. Nothing has made a greater impression upon me than my close acquaintance with the Conscientious Objectors. Many of them are Teachers. Not a few of these Teachers are Welsh Teachers and over and over again the Welsh Teacher who came before us was an Agnostic or even an Atheist. Have the children of Wales no claim upon us?

However I won't bore you any more with my reactionary apprehension. We will talk about these matters when we meet.

Will you thank Maud very much from me for her letter and tell her I shall not give way to despair even if we have Womanhood Suffrage. The women will govern pretty well though it won't make anything like the difference in. a Conservative direction which some people think. Ever yours

S

6/194

1. The report of the Archbishops' Committee on Church and State, published in July 1916.
2. Lord Salisbury's letter, criticising the idea of 'home rule all round' and arguing that the union had 'been a conspicuous success', was published in *The Times* on 19 September 1916.


7. To the Marquess of Salisbury

Blackmoor
Liss
Hants.
20 September 1916

My dear Jim,

Many thanks for your letter of the 18th inst.

I am afraid I did not make myself clear about the Parliament Act. Let me explain. If the Imperial Parliament remained exactly as it is we should have to consider the constitution of the House of Lords and its powers from rather a different point of view to what we should if it became the Parliament of the United Kingdom only just as we should have to consider the question of the Second Chamber for a Parliament for England; and again, the problem would be enlarged if we had to consider a new truly Imperial Parliament. I think that latter ideal will come sooner than you think if it comes at all; but that is only my opinion. I did not mean to suggest leaving the Parliament Act exactly as it is until all these problems have been dealt with. What I meant was that I could not indicate in my letter to you how I should deal with the Second Chamber because that problem was so affected by these even larger problems. Whether there are changes or whether there are not changes or whether those changes come quickly or slowly we cannot possibly sit down under the Parliament Act. The referendum is the least that we can go for, but I do not think that Bonar Law has a glimmering of sense or leadership about him in the matter, and G.N.C. is just as hostile to the referendum as he is to Women's Suffrage or to Devolution. He would not like to be told so but it is true that he has a far less flexible (using the term in its good sense) mind than you have.

Now as to the Welsh Church and the new Church constitution. If you read our Report carefully you will see that there would be no more difficulty in applying that constitution to the English dioceses alone than to the English and Welsh. If the Church in Wales were disestablished I imagine the Church in Wales would form a province of its own with its own Archbishop, and that its relations to us would be on the same lines as those of the Episcopal Church in Scotland only much more intimate.

You write:– 'Why should poor dear England be dragged about at the heels of these Scotchmen and Irishmen? And yet I cannot think that such an attitude is really gallant. These Welsh Churchmen and these Scotch owners of property have they not some claim upon us?' You are quite right in bringing this point forward, but in respect of the Scottish owners of property I have a quite definite view that we do them no good and are no help to them, and that they would do better for themselves in a Scottish Parliament than they ever will in the Imperial Parliament. More and more the attitude of even our own side is that Scottish matters must be settled by the votes of Scottish members. You saw that attitude plainly in our House of Commons men at the time when that really preposterous and execrable piece of legislation, the Scottish Land Bill, was under consideration several years ago. Scottish landowners get no show, or practically no show, in elections for the Imperial Parliament, but in elections for County Councils the same Radicals who beat them for Parliament are nowhere. I believe that in elections for a Scottish Parliament the lines of cleavage would be different and that all the legitimate rights of property would be safer in a Scottish Parliament than in the Imperial Parliament.

As regards Wales, what you say is very serious, but may not the same thing be true about Wales? We can make no serious impression upon Wales in elections for the Imperial Parliament, and I see no prospect of our being able to protect those interests which are to us most dear in the face of the opposition of 30 out of 33 Welsh members. I do not think those interests can be worse off in a Welsh Parliament and in my judgement the Welsh Churchmen and Welsh owners of property will be stronger proportionately in any Welsh Parliament than they will be in any representation of Wales in the Imperial Parliament. Yours ever

S

6/198

8.　To F.S. Oliver

49 Mount Street
W.1.
14 March 1917

My dear Oliver,

I have read and re-read your Minute on Ireland and the Imperial Conference[1] with great admiration, but I am not able to associate myself with all your arguments or opinions. I do not believe the reason of the shrinkage in the Irish population during the last ninety years to have been that given by you, nor that it is true that 'the bulk of the people will never be reduced by emigration, etc.'

If a country has no industry but agriculture there is a definite limit to the population it can carry, and it has to throw off its surplus population in swarms just like a hive of bees. I have myself seen these swarms leaving Norway for America. Ninety years ago the population of Ireland was greater than as an agricultural country it could carry without periodic famine or artificial support, and the probability is that it has still too many people for its cultivable land.

It is true that Irish agriculture is not intensive enough, and that much more could be produced from the soil for sale in England or elsewhere than is now produced, but the fact remains that the great majority of Irish holdings are still ludicrously and uneconomically small, and that the land could be redistributed into larger holdings and the farming become intensive with very little or no call for additional labour. The only chance for an expansion of the Irish population is by the establishment of industries. In what way can English rule be held to be responsible for the fact that industries have not established themselves anywhere except in Ulster? I do not think that any responsibility can be justly attached to it on that score.

But after all population is not the only test. Although the population has decreased the material wealth of the country has greatly increased by all the tests accepted in such cases, savings bank deposits, etc. You omit that fact from your statement entirely.

I think there is more truth in the 'double dose of original sin' argument than you are disposed to admit, only not in the sense which those words would naturally convey. I believe the form of government by which we try to govern the Irish, which is also the only form of government which we can confer upon them, and which is the only form of government for which they ask, parliamentary government in some shape or form, to be quite unsuited for them and, therefore, I am much less sanguine than you are as to the results of the prosperity of Ireland under any form of Home Rule. The 'Daily News' would consider this statement in itself to constitute an insult, but that will not be your view any more than mine . . .

. . . Having cleared the way by these reservations, and being permitted my digression let me say that I entirely agree with your central position, that the Irish question is an Imperial question; and that I hope that your definite proposals will be put forward at once. But do not think, even if they are accepted and acted upon, that the ranks of the Irish regiments will be re-filled; they will not, because too large a proportion of the Irish people are not in sympathy with Redmond but with Sinn Fein. I do not believe this is anything new; I do think that many, who have never been in sympathy with Redmond, thought they could achieve a situation of advantage through him and lay low. Their reasonableness (from the Irish, not the English, point of view) was never their strong quality and they were entirely thrown off their balance by the events of last Easter. If they should prove to be in the majority could Ireland be given any form of Home Rule consistently with the bare safety of Great Britain? The extreme difficulty of the present moment is that we cannot estimate the comparative strength of Redmond's followers and of the Sinn Feiners. To hand over the Government to the Sinn Feiners would be to sacrifice Redmond quite as much as England and Scotland.

Your suggestion for putting the Chief Secretaryship into commission in the meanwhile is attractive because it would not mean the setting up of an imperium in imperio. The Chief Secretary, though in commission, would still be subject to the orders of H.M.G. It would I think tend to bring out what the strength of the rival forces in Ireland really is. But are you quite sure that Redmond and Devlin would accept? I do not believe they would. They are I fear fatally pledged to the immediate establishment of an Irish Government and Irish Parliament which is utterly impossible during the war without jeopardising the whole cause of the Allies.

I have great personal sympathy with Redmond, he has behaved splendidly in the war; but he has great responsibility for the present 'devil's mess' as he had unlimited influence with Birrell. Yours sincerely

S

84/31

1.  A pamphlet by F.S. Oliver entitled *Ireland and the Imperial Conference: is there a way to settlement?* In it, Oliver argued that, whereas the idea of summoning an Imperial Conference after the war to seek a solution of the Irish question 'appears to be a sound one', this was 'a very different thing from rushing precipitately upon the special War Conference of the Empire and asking it to undertake a task which lies entirely outside its province'. Instead, the Conference should be asked if it considered desirable the idea of an independent commission to study the extent to which it would be necessary to amend the existing home rule act in order to fit it into a federal system; and also to examine the possibilities of setting up some temporary arrangement of the government of Ireland consisting of Irishmen of Unionist and Nationalist persuasion.

9.   From F.S. Oliver

8 Hereford Gardens
Marble Arch
London, W.
29 March 1917

Dear Selborne,

I have had a certain number of favourable responses to my pamphlet from some unexpected quarters. This is only symptomatic of the general desire to clutch at anything; but it behoves us to be on our guard.

I have rather a strong feeling that it may be desirable at some early date to launch a statement under your name, or possibly yours with one or two other well-known people, the object of which would be to put forward our financial ideas and switch the foolish creatures off 'Dominion' Home Rule. What I rather hope is that some tentacle has already come out, or will shortly do so, and pull you for this particular purpose in to the internal regions of power. If so, I hope you won't resist; and of course, you won't consider yourself in any way bound to tell me anything about it, because that might be embarrassing.

I have been thinking that when we settle down shortly to have the second reading of our measure, it might be a good thing to rope in a few more, whom we would like to carry with us. Of these, the one whom it would be most valuable to enlist the sympathies of is Salisbury . . .

. . . I enclose copies of two letters which may interest you. The first is from an Ulster Presbyterian, who happens, however, to dwell in England.[1] The second is from an Irish Member of Parliament in France. He ought not to be in France. He is older than I am and has had a devil of a doing for more than 18 months . . . A very gallant fellow called Stephen Gwynn. Yours sincerely

F.S. Oliver

*Enclosure*

24 March 1918 [wrongly dated]

My dear Fred,

I came here on the vigil of St. Patrick and luckily found the Brigade out for rest and have since got on better with my health than any time since January. St. Stephens, Westminster, was a poor sanatorium, largely owing to the matters your pamphlet deals with. I agree in the main with your views. Essentially I agree – and I urged last June – that to attempt a new settlement on the lines of the old Buckingham Palace discussion[2] – is to court disaster. I agree also – though I think you only imply this – that the important, the vital point, is to get something into immediate operation that will touch the Irish imagination.

For the rest, I am sick and despondent over the whole question. So many cowards have bedevilled and degraded it. The news of yesterday's debate[3] is less or more hopeful. But I find it difficult to hope.

If the chance of utilising the Imperial Conference be lost, as it probably will be, I see nothing ahead but sheer disaster. The trouble is that no one in Nationalist Ireland expects justice. Nor do I. One side has from historic causes (grown into social conditions) too many influential friends; the other has too few, and none of them courageous.

I continue to serve here but without expectation that anything of what I hoped will result from the service of those whom we asked to join for the sake of Ireland. England has so managed the affair that Pearse and his handful of half armed men have effected more against the Allies than all the Irish troops together in all their fighting have effected against Germany; and at the end of the war we shall probably find ourselves (if we are not so already) part of an army, part of whose task is to hold Nationalist Ireland down, whilst Carson issues the order. So I praise your efforts – but not hopefully. Yours etc.

84/40

1. Not attached
2. The Buckingham Palace Conference of July 1914, which lasted for three days, and which discussed the possibility of excluding some part of Ulster from the operation of the home rule bill.
3. A debate in the House of Commons which began on 22 March 1917, at the end of which Bonar Law declared that the government would make another attempt to settle the Irish question. The outcome of the government's rather tortuous discussions was the suggestion, on 16 May, that the Nationalists accept either home rule with the exclusion of six north-eastern counties of Ulster (as in 1916), or a 'Convention of Irishmen of all parties for the purpose of producing a scheme of Irish self-government'. This latter scheme proved acceptable to Redmond, the southern Irish Unionists, and the Ulster Unionists, though not to Sinn Fein, and the Convention began its deliberations in July 1917.


10.  From F.S. Oliver

Room 81 Second Floor
Foreign Office
Whitehall
S.W.
26 April 1917

Dear Selborne,

I have your letter of yesterday's date. No need to apologise.

No, I am not dining with Carson tonight, but I am more than delighted to hear that you are doing so.

He knows nothing of our financial plan – at any rate not from me – and therefore I presume he cannot have heard it from anyone else; but I have no secrets from him and if you judge the occasion favourable for opening the matter with him to-night, I have not the smallest objection. I told him we had a joint plan but that there was no use approaching him with it, until it had been boiled down to greater simplicity.

I feel it to be very important that Carson should be in sympathetic touch, direct or indirect, with the south of Ireland Unionists. (The enclosed letter[1] from 'A.E.' will explain to you some of my reasons. Please let me have it back when you have done with it.)

I forgot to tell you that Philip asked me through the telephone if our Federal proposals entailed cutting down the powers of the Irish Parliament as defined by the Home Rule Act. My reply was that for all practical purposes our proposals rather extended than cut down these powers; but that we *regarded the reservation to the United Kingdom Parliament of all unallotted powers, as absolutely fundamental.*

I shall be in my room at the Foreign Office, tomorrow, Friday, from 3 p.m. onwards and if you can spare time to come in and talk matters over, I will put down a list of the things I want to ask you about.

The most important of these, perhaps, is what pressure are we now going to try and bring to bear upon the government? and following from this ought we to make any effort to bring into our counsels (a) the south of Ireland Unionists, (b) the Murray Macdonaldites,[2] (c) the sympathetic but rather untutored unionists whom in the absence of Edward Wood, are apt to swing a little wide, and (d) any of the Irish Nationalists?

Don't bother to reply as I shall be at the Foreign Office in any case. Yours sincerely

F.S. Oliver

84/49

1. Lord Selborne's marginal note: 'I can't for the moment lay my hand on it'.
2. J.A. Murray MacDonald (1854–1939), Liberal M.P. for Falkirk Burghs, 1906–18, and Stirling and Falkirk Burghs, 1918–22, was a strong advocate of federal home rule. See, e.g., his letter in the *Glasgow Herald*, 13 June 1918.


11.   From F.S. Oliver

8 Hereford Gardens<br>Marble Arch<br>London, W.<br>6 September 1917

Dear Selborne,

I saw Carson yesterday afternoon and Stephen Gwynn later in the day.

Carson had seen Plunkett. He (C) differed from your view only at one point viz. he did not seem to think that things were really so far advanced as you thought.[1] On the other hand Stephen Gwynn (who is on the drafting committee) supported your view. On the whole I think Carson is right: for a long and very frank talk with Gwynn showed me how very far they are from having faced, as yet, their real difficulties. Both agreed as to Plunkett's 'wooliness' upon all matters of constitution and machinery.

Carson, who knows the general principle of our plan,[2] and Gwynn who knows only that we have a plan (without having any inkling what it is) agreed very eagerly that *it ought to be communicated at once*. The fact is, I suspect, that they have themselves no semblance of a plan whatsoever.

Carson told me that he asked Plunkett if they had discussed the Federal solution, and that Plunkett replied that in effect they had *not*. Carson then said to H.P. that he was 'rather surprised to hear that they had not examined the only principles upon which a settlement was possible' (that is encouraging).

I asked Gwynn for the names of the people to whom, if we decided to communicate, our memorandum might be sent with advantage. I set them out below:–

*Plunkett*

| | |
|---|---|
| *Midleton* | ) |
| Archbishop of Dublin (Bernard) | ) Southern Unionists |
| | |
| H.T. Barry M.P. | ) |
| Sir Alex MacDowall K.B.E. | ) Ulster |
| Londonderry | ) |
| | |
| Lord Macdonnell | ) a lone hand |
| *John Redmond M.P.* | ) |
| *Captain Stephen Gwynn M.P.* | ) |
| J. Devlin | ) Nationalists |
| The Bishop of Raphoe | ) |
| | |
| – Whitley (??) [sic] | ) Labour |

. . . The Committee which arranges for publication and circulation of documents consists of Lord Macdonnell, Barry and Gwynn.

If the above is in your opinion too long a list then the memorandum might go to the names underlined only.[3]

It should also go I think to Carson and Hopwood.

A covering note from yourself would be (in Gwynn's view as well as mine) a great advantage – 'Yourself several friends' etc – 'no mystery' – 'we think it inadvisable to circulate to convention on your own; but, if it were desired to do so by those responsible, no objection on your part; and copies could be supplied at once' (my secretary at Debenhams Mr. Sanderson has a stock) – 'no useful purpose at present in sending draft bill but that could also be supplied later if desired' – these are the rough suggestions.

Gwynn is even more emphatic than Carson about this – 'do it at once'.

There is one snag which of course we have always suspected viz – *Ireland* cannot wait until after the war but must have its plan now!! In this connection will you ponder the possibility whether the necessary bridge might not be built by means of that preposterous delegation to Westminster to vote on the reserved powers. Will you consider whether the intolerableness of this arrangement would not force England's and Scotland's hands and produce federal devolution in very short period automatically. I have not had time to weigh this and examine into it; but I have a vague kind of feeling that if the thing were done in the right way and the underlying principle clearly acknowledged, it *might* work . . . Yours ever

F.S. Oliver

84/55

1.  On 25 July 1917 the Irish Convention met for the first time in Trinity College Dublin. Sir Horace Plunkett was chosen Chairman, and Sir Francis Hopwood, then a civil lord of the Admiralty, was elected Secretary. The Convention followed Plunkett's idea of commencing with a series of general debates on Irish self-government. Visits were paid to Belfast and Cork. Good will was generated by the early discussions, but little progress was made towards formulating a detailed agreed scheme or even towards reaching agreement on the principles on which it should be based.
2.  A pamphlet by Lord Selborne and Oliver, produced for private circulation, entitled *A method of constitutional co-operation: suggestions for the better government of the United Kingdom*. In it, the authors recommended a federal organisation for the United Kingdom, on its own merits and as a means of settling Ireland. They proposed separate legislatures for England, Scotland and Ireland, to manage 'national' concerns, with a United Kingdom parliament for the common concerns of the three kingdoms. All powers not specifically allotted to the local legislatures would remain with the United Kingdom parliament, which would control customs and excise, postal services, the supreme court and the census. The Irish parliament would control taxation, and Ireland would be represented in the United Kingdom parliament on the basis of population. Subsidies from the United Kingdom parliament should be 'reduced as far as possible', though Ireland was to get substantial financial support in the first instance. Each of the three kingdoms was to be allowed to adopt that form of constitution which 'it may judge to be most harmonious with its traditions' and problems. Thus Ireland might have a single senate, but two separate lower houses, one for the north-east part of Ulster and one for the rest of Ireland.
3.  *i.e.* Plunkett, Midleton, Redmond, Gwynn.


12.   From Sir Edward Carson

Beach Hotel
Littlehampton
18 February 1918

My dear Selborne,

I enclose a copy of a letter I sent to the P.M. since I returned from Ireland.

I am sure any effort to force a 'settlement' will be disastrous. Yours ever

Edward Carson

Enclosure

Beach Hotel<br>
Littlehampton<br>
14 February 1918

*Confidential*

Since I have returned from Ireland, I have been thinking a good deal of the possibilities of a settlement during the war. It is clear to my mind that no settlement consistent with the interests of Great Britain can be devised which will satisfy the Sinn Fein or the extreme Nationalist Party who sympathise with Sinn Fein.

If, therefore, any attempt is made to bring Ulster into an Irish Parliament, to which they are averse, you will have both Sinn Fein and Ulster in opposition to the new Government, and I do not believe that any Government started under such circumstances would have the least chance of success. The promises made to Ulster when the War broke out were very distinct, and were frequently repeated by me when I was asking the people to join the Army, viz., that no attempt would be made to set up a Home Rule Parliament in Ireland during the continuance of the War, and indeed this was provided by legislation. I can assure you, that the Ulster people who have suffered severely in the loss of their men at the Front, will regard it as an act of treachery if the promises are broken and Ulster is put under a Home Rule Parliament.

Personally, I do not see how, under the circumstances, I could be expected to advise them to accept such a Parliament, nor do I believe I would have the least chance of persuading them to do so.

I have already, as you know, after great difficulty induced Ulster in the interest of the prosecution of the War, to accept a solution on the basis of the exclusion of the six Counties, which meant that the rest of Ireland could have Home Rule – such a solution preserved the Union for the vast majority of those who desired it.

The only other possible solution seems to me to lie in a system of Federation for the whole United Kingdom. Averse, as I am, from any change in the present Constitution with its single Parliament for all purposes, I do not deny that the Union, which I regard as the keystone of the British Commonwealth, may nevertheless be preserved upon the principles of a true federation.

In a true federation, it is essential, not only that there should be constitutional equality between the Nations which are to be the federal units, but also that the powers delegated and made over by the United Kingdom Parliament to the National Parliaments, should not be such as to hamper the actual and active supremacy of the former, and to set up impediments against the free intercourse of the federated kingdoms.

If such a policy were adopted, it is easy to see that a settlement of the Ulster difficulty could be found, either by making Ulster a unit or by providing for its particular needs within another unit.

The whole difference is, that in this case the Parliament of the Union would possess a real supremacy and not merely a titular suzerainty, and further, such a solution would not be in the direction of separation or secession, which seems to me to be of vital importance. It will be said that the Irish problem is so pressing that it cannot wait for a true federation of the United Kingdom. At any rate let us settle the lines upon which this true federation is ultimately to be made. When this is done, let the South and West of Ireland have their Act, with necessary safeguards, and let Ulster stand out until such time as England and Scotland can be brought in.

I have put this forward to show how untrue it is that Ulster presents a *non possumus* attitude. While I think all the discussions show that the Union, as it stands, is the best solution, I believe the true federation is the only other alternative. Yours sincerely

84/75b


13.   From Lord Hugh Cecil

20 Arlington Street
S.W.
14 March 1918

My dear Willy,

I do not think it quite so certain as you do that there will be a General Election in the autumn, supposing we are still at war. I agree, indeed, that such an election is at present what L.G. intends, and that he desires some sort of coalition or fusion with the Unionist Party. But, when it comes to the point, I think it will be seen that it is neither his interest nor the interest of the Unionist Party nor, on the whole, the interest of the country, to have a dissolution while war is still going on. I know that it would be a great advantage to get a new House of Commons with more self–confidence and more moral authority than belongs to the present out–worn assembly. But these advantages are outweighed by other disadvantages; – such as are the disturbance and excitement engendered by an election, the danger that purely temporary war issues would affect the election (like air–raids or rationing) with the consequence of disastrous pledges being given by candidates anxious for election, the temptation to the Government during the fortnight or three weeks preceding the election to do all sorts of foolish things for the sake of popularity. The really propitious moment for an election would be directly after the preliminaries of peace had been agreed to. Everyone would then be in high good humour, there would be no bitterness between parties nor between classes, the nerve–strain would be relaxed, and the election would almost certainly result in a parliament not very deeply pledged to anything but disposed to course of moderation. I believe that these considerations, though they may not be present to L.G.'s mind, yet will become clear to him when he gets to the point of deciding when he shall advise a dissolution; and that accordingly there will not be a dissolution until peace is made.

But, if there should be a dissolution in the autumn, while war is raging, I should be inclined to think that the wisest thing would be to maintain an attitude of great reserve, merely affirming – what everyone will admit – that we must carry out the policy of the war and support the Government in waging it. That will not be a matter of party controversy, because Asquith is quite certain to say it himself. Accordingly, if there were such an election, it would turn on other points. Some of them, as I have suggested, might be dangerous points; but what course it would be wise to take must be left to the moment to decide. Whenever the election is held I am in favour of taking the line of 'measures not men', to abstain from making any attacks upon any political leaders or any political parties, but to lay down political tenets largely of a platitudinous kind, like the value of liberty, the danger of Prussian bureaucracy in our Government, and the like, and to promise to support any Government which will act on such principles.

As you know, in my judgement, almost everything depends on the line that Austen Chamberlain takes. If he will take a line independent of L.G. it will be possible to keep up a distinct Unionist Party, not led by L.G.; and that Party must be ready either to act alone if it is strong enough to stand on its own feet. But, if Austen throws in his lot with B.L. and L.G. the rest of us will be but a remnant incapable of distinct political action and driven to be merely detached critics of men and things, – a depressing prospect. I remain, yours affectionately

Hugh Cecil

87/26


14.   To Austen Chamberlain

18 March 1918

My dear Austen,

I think that the Unionist Party is in great danger from Lloyd George and Bonar Law.

We are perfectly willing to support them in war and for the peace while they run straight, and at a dissolution during the war, where they do not seek a mandate for a future policy.

But that is just what I am afraid they will try and do. They will try and mix up a future policy with the war and a peace and so try to keep in their own hands the leadership of the Unionist Party after the war.

I do not suppose that you are prepared to stand down for either of these men after the war, and I believe that the men whom you would most wish to see following you, are fully prepared and indeed very anxious to do so. I *know* of no one, who would not except I suppose Walter;[1] but I put the matter in this form because I do not pretend to have ascertained the opinion of everyone.

But, if we are not to be rushed, you must be ready for action when the time comes and prepared with the heads of a policy which you will have ascertained to be agreeable to your friends.

Think it over, but not for too long. George and Law will try and stampede us. Yours ever

Selborne

87/28

1. Walter Long

15. From the Earl of Midleton

Peper Harow
Godalming
12 April 1918

My dear Willie,

You will have in your hands today or tomorrow the proposals made by the Southern Unionists[1] and those adopted by the Convention.[2] Our object has been to secure that these should in no way infringe the Federal principle. That is to say that whatever constitution is given to Ireland, should be capable of being worked into a Federal system.

One reason why we stood so firmly about 'customs' was that we did not wish Ireland to be able to drive a fresh bargain for herself, as the price of entering into a Federal system. Please let me know what you think of our proposals. They were not obtained without very hard fighting, and the tendency which Dillon shows, to establish himself with Sinn Fein in the resistance to conscription,[3] will seriously effect [sic] our power of further co-operation with the Nationalists. Yours ever

Midleton

3/156

1. The southern Unionists' proposals were laid before the Grand Committee of the Convention by Lord Midleton in November 1917. Their chief features were the reservation to the imperial parliament of the right to impose and collect customs duties, and the payment out of the receipts of an imperial contribution, but the concession to the Nationalists of full control of all purely Irish affairs including internal taxation. By February 1918, however, opposition to Midleton from other southern Unionists had begun to make itself felt.
2. In February 1918 Lord MacDonnell tabled a set of six resolutions in an attempt to provide a compromise solution, one of which suggested customs and excise should both remain under the control of the imperial parliament during the war, and thereafter until the question had been considered and a decision arrived at by the imperial parliament, the decision to be taken not later than seven years after the conclusion of peace. This resolution was carried on 12 March. Following this vote, the Convention considered the remaining aspects of the future Irish constitution, and by 22 March twenty-one resolutions, embodying a scheme for the government of Ireland, had been passed. This scheme is summarised by P. J. Buckland, *Irish Unionism One: The Anglo-Irish*

*and the New Ireland* (Dublin, 1972), p. 127. A report embodying this scheme was drawn up by Sir Horace Plunkett and approved on 5 April 1918.

3.  On 24 March 1918 the British government, faced with the heavy casualties and the critical situation on the western front, following General Ludendorff's offensive, decided to raise the age limit for liability to military service from forty-two to fifty. Shortly afterwards it empowered itself to apply the new conscription bill to Ireland by Order in Council. When the government's policy was expounded by Lloyd George in the House of Commons on 9 April the Irish Nationalist Members, led since Redmond's death in March 1918 by John Dillon, denounced it passionately, and eventually withdrew from the House in protest.

16.  To Austen Chamberlain

8 May 1918

*Private*

My dear Austen,

I sent out a circular to about 150 selected Unionist Peers sounding them about a federal solution. I received about 20 favourable and 2 hostile replies.

The balance are waiting; they are not hostile to the federal solution; but their attitude is this.

What is the position of Ulster? Under no circumstances will we take a hand in forcing anything upon Ulster. If both Irish Unionists and the Nationalists reject a scheme what can be the use of passing one into law during wartime.

And above all

Is it compatible with the safety of England and victory in the war to establish local government in Ireland the attitude of the Roman hierarchy, Dillon and Company being indistinguishable to us from the attitude of the Sinn Feiners? This being the position I came to the conclusion that none of these men would discuss the question, much less commit themselves at this stage. We must wait for the situation to develop.

Carson is the key to the situation and his manifesto in the *Times*[1] this morning seems to me to put the possibility of passing any bill now much more of bringing it into force, into the gravest doubt. Indeed what has just leaked out to us about the extent of German communication with Sinn Fein[2] makes the position gravely different to what it was even a month ago.

And now comes the Maurice crisis![3]

And now you ask me what happened last Saturday. I will tell you exactly.

I was at Blackmoor and went out riding after breakfast. When I came back at 1 p.m. the parlourmaid met me and told me that the P.M.'s private secretary had been on telephone [sic] saying that the P.M. wanted to see me and was sending his car for me.

At 3 p.m. she came to say that the private secretary was again on the telephone and wanted to know if the car had arrived.

I knew all about the Midleton negotiations so I had my suspicions.

I went to the telephone and gathered from the private secretary that it was about Ireland. I told him that I was not prepared to join the government but would await the P.M.'s message.

About 4 p.m. the car arrived, the car, the driver, and a messenger but no letter not a snap nor a line.

So I sat down and wrote to the P.M.[4] to say that I gathered that he was good enough to have some proposition in his mind for me about the government of Ireland but that I would be frank with him and must tell him that I was not prepared to join his administration or to take any responsibility for the results of the policy pursued in Ireland since the rebellion with which I had been completely in disaccord.

The car took this note back. I was not going to wrangle with the P.M. when no consideration on earth would ever induce me to join a government of which he was chief. Yours ever

S

AC 18/2/15

1.   A statement by Sir Edward Carson in *The Times*, 8 May 1918. It warned of the dangers of a Unionist party break-up over Ireland, of the dangers of establishing home rule in the present conditions, in the light of a 'Sinn Fein-German plot', all of which compelled him to appeal to the government to reconsider the matter 'before we have a fratricidal conflict at a time when our whole energies should be devoted to the prosecution of the war'.

2.   In May 1918 the government's agents in Ireland produced evidence of a 'plot' for another 'Sinn Fein' rebellion which should have German assistance. The evidence was later published as a command paper 'Documents relative to the Sinn Fein movement' Cmd. 1108 of 1921. The evidence was described by Hankey as 'of a most flimsy and ancient description' (Roskill, *Hankey man of secrets*, vol. i, p. 554). Alan J. Ward considers the authenticity of the plot in 'Lloyd George and the 1918 Irish conscription crisis', *H.J.*, vol. xvii, no. 1, pp. 107–129, esp. pp. 118–119.

3.   On 9 April 1918 Lloyd George said in the House of Commons that despite the heavy losses sustained by the British army in the Passchendaele offensive in 1917, the army in France was stronger on 1 January 1918 than it had been on 1 January 1917. He also explained that there was only a relatively small number of 'white' troops serving in Egypt and Mesopotamia. A few weeks earlier, on 23 March, Bonar Law denied in the House that an extension of the British line had been agreed at the meeting of the Supreme Allied War Council on 1 and 2 February 1918. On 7 May 1918 a letter from General Sir Frederick Maurice, who had recently been removed from his post as Director of Military Operations at the War Office, was published in *The Times* and the *Morning Post* claiming that these statements were incorrect. In a brilliant parliamentary performance on 9 May Lloyd George swept criticism aside, and a motion by Asquith calling for a judicial inquiry or a select committee of inquiry was lost by 293 votes to 106. However, Lloyd George's statement was in some important respects misleading (Roskill, *Hankey*, vol. i, pp. 522–3), and

Maurice Hankey himself described it as 'not the speech of a man who tells "the truth; the whole truth; and nothing but the truth". For example, while he had figures from the D.M.O.'s Department showing that the fighting strength of the army had increased from 1 January 1917 to 1918, he had the Adjutant–General's figures saying the precise contrary, but was discreetly silent about them' (p. 545). For an assessment of the significance of the 'Maurice debate' in Liberal Party history see Edward David, 'The Liberal Party Divided, 1916–1918', *H.J.*, xii, 3 (1970) pp. 509–33. Evidence supporting General Maurice's criticisms including extracts from his diary of 1 January–20 April 1918, is arranged and edited by his daughter Nancy Maurice in *The Maurice Case* (London, 1972).

4.  A copy of Lord Selborne's letter of 4 May is in 84/107. Lloyd George was seeking a replacement for Lord Wimborne as Viceroy. Selborne's name may have been suggested by F.S. Oliver. Austen Chamberlain knew about Lloyd George's proposal, warning him on 3 May that 'if you want Selborne, he is more likely to accept if approached directly by you than if sounded by anyone else. He likes the simplest and most direct methods' (L.G. F 7/2/11). Walter Long also agreed that Selborne should be approached (L.G.F 7/2/12).

17.  To Walter Long

31 May 1918

My dear Walter,

I have not hitherto troubled you with any letters about the Bill you are preparing[1] though I am greatly interested in the matter, because I knew that my contribution had been placed before you.

The political scenery has, however, shifted so much in this matter in the last few weeks that I make no apology for now taking up my pen.

On the one hand the conviction has become more widely diffused that that kind of devolution, which is called the federal solution, has become an absolute necessity owing to the appalling prospective congestion of parliamentary business if the needs of the Empire and the domestic concerns of England and Scotland are not to suffer fatally from neglect after the war.

On the other hand the Sinn Feiners, and the Roman hierarchy, and the Nationalists have so disgusted Englishmen and Scotchmen, that a great majority are prepared to concede the claim of the six Ulster counties to be treated as a federal unit and to say that, until the rest of Ireland has recovered its senses, it must be governed very much as a Crown Colony.

These considerations seem to me to make more important than ever the form of your Bill and its title. As regards the form I greatly hope that the first clauses will lay down the principles, on which various parts of the United Kingdom can be instructed to manage their own affairs without troubling the Imperial Parliament, and on which they can be financed in doing the work allotted to them.

I hope that by the next clauses Commissioners will be appointed to work out the details of their domestic constitution for England and Scotland and Wales.

The last part of the Bill would be devoted to the enactment for Ireland, of the constitutional details generally accepted by the late Irish Convention.

And now about the title of the Bill. I do very earnestly press upon you the extreme undesirability of calling it the 'Government of Ireland Act Amendment Bill'. Such a title is calculated today more than ever to arouse the resentment of all Unionists, and what excuse could you find for proceeding with a Bill with such a title, if all parties in Ireland unite to repudiate it as they probably will?

But if you call it what it really is 'A Bill for the Better Government of the United Kingdom' you can proceed with it just as you like whatever the Irish may say and it will be examined on its merits by all English and Scotch parties and without prejudice.

Indeed I do not see how by the practice of Parliament a Bill which dealt, however generally, with the principles of a federal solution applicable to the whole United Kingdom, could be covered by an Irish title. Yours ever

S

84/120

1. A committee set up under the chairmanship of Walter Long which began work on a home rule bill on 15 April 1918. It included four other Unionists besides Long (Curzon, Cave, Duke and Austen Chamberlain), and by late June it drafted a bill for a federal reorganisation of the United Kingdom.

18.   To the Marquess of Salisbury

17 June 1918

My dear Jim,

I feel like you acutely the danger of the situation into which the Unionist Party is drifting. It wants leadership very badly in both Houses and it wants to make up its own mind and adopt at least the framework of a future policy. For this purpose leaders, whips, and a group of followers who will stand together, act together, and support each other, are needed in both Houses; in the Lords we have the leaders but no whips and no group that is in the least reliable; in the Commons there would be no difficulty about the whips and the group if there was a leader.

Then on top of that comes what you call the Irish question. I do not call it the Irish question. I think I should feel more strongly even than I do about it if there was no Irish question with any taint of disloyalty about it; the existence of an Irish question with this taint is a difficulty to me, and not a motive of action. I entirely agree that under present circumstances self-government in Ireland is absolutely out of the question, unless it be for the six Counties of Ulster. I am quite prepared to rule the rest of Ireland as a Crown Colony for the present whether under the present constitution or under a revised constitution.

This brings me up against what for the sake of convenience we will call federation. There is no good in blinking the fact, this is a real and great difference between us; it is nothing less than a sorrow to me to differ from you about this, as I think it is the only question on the horizon as to which there is a difference of principle; but not only could I not consent to postpone the question of federation, I am pushing forward federation as in my judgment by far the most important thing now coming within the region of practical politics. I regard the introduction of the federal system as by far the most conservative thing that can now be done, far the greatest stabilising force possible to our constitution as it now exists. I know of no other means of making so secure what I most love and prize in the institutions and customs of my country. Further it would enable questions affecting the Empire and the whole United Kingdom, which are of the first importance, to be properly considered for the first time by a body elected for that special purpose, instead of being very ill considered, or constantly shelved, by a body principally elected for other purposes. I see no other means by which the questions of our future relations with the Dominions, of the Government of India, of foreign policy, of the reconstruction of the army, of the strength of the navy, of our economic and commercial policy, can receive any adequate consideration at all. Also I regard it as the only way by which the problem of reconstruction in domestic affairs can possibly be dealt with and, therefore, as the greatest safeguard against revolution. I think the only danger of revolution in this country will come from the impatience of the electorate with the proceedings of the House of Commons, but I think that a real danger, and I think that the federal solution would avert it. Lastly, I consider federalism as contributing that balance and check in a purely democratic system of government that is otherwise applied in the non-democratic systems. As I read the working of the constitution in all federal countries, even including Australia, this appears to be true, and I believe that these checks and balances can be obtained without reducing the power of the central executive authority beyond the point that is essential for good government. It is also worthy of note that in all these countries the Conservative Party seems to draw its principal strength from the subordinate legislatures.

I also regard the formation of an United Kingdom Parliament by the release of the Imperial Parliament from daily responsibility for the domestic affairs of England, Scotland etc., as a necessary step to the formation of a real Imperial Parliament, that is of one the normal functions of which would be to deal with the common affairs only of the whole British Empire.

You must remember that these are no new opinions of mine. I think I have not made any important (i.e. important to me as fully stating my views) speech in public on the Irish or Second Chamber questions since I came back from S. Africa without stating quite definitely that I regarded the federal solution as the only possible solution of our constitutional difficulties, and I remember quite distinctly discussing it with you before the war, particularly in a walk up St James's Street, when you asked me who, under my proposed system, would go into the United Kingdom or Imperial Parliament in preference to the English Parliament, and you were rather surprised when I did not hesitate in my choice and said that I would go into the United Kingdom Parliament.

I will now give the reasons why I do not agree with you that federation is at present inopportune on other grounds. The method of procedure under my plan would be to lay down definitely the division of powers, to say what powers are to be delegated to the Kingdom legislatures, the rest of course remaining exclusively with the Imperial Parliament. The Kingdom legislatures would of course have nothing to do with spheres of reconstruction that did not come within the powers allotted to them. With the allocation of powers would also come the allocation of revenue, which might, as you say, very easily involve a subsidy from the Imperial Parliament to the Kingdom legislatures, which would in point of fact be a subsidy from the English taxpayers to the taxpayers of the other Kingdoms; but such a subsidy is in fact paid today to their County Councils; I see no reason why it should not be paid instead, and on a larger scale, to their legislatures. This is the existing system in Australia, S. Africa, and I think Germany, and it works well. If industrial questions were reserved for the Imperial Parliament, industrial questions of reconstruction would not fall to the English and Scotch etc. legislatures to deal with; but, if power to deal with industrial questions was given to the Kingdom legislatures, it is quite possible that different labour laws might exist on the Tyne to those that exist on the Clyde. I do not see any insuperable objection to this. I do not pronounce finally on the point but I think a good deal might be said for making industrial legislation Kingdom and not United Kingdom business. The point must be threshed out when we consider the division of powers. I do not agree with you that reconstruction would not be assisted by federation; I am very convinced that it would be assisted.

Now as regards Church questions. I can most honestly say that I have never approached federation from the road of Church Reform. If that were facilitated in England it would in my judgment be a by-product of advantage, but it would have nothing to do with a conviction which as I have already said has its roots years back. I quite agree that the extension of the principle of the federal solution to the Principality of Wales, which I regard as inevitable, might make impossible that reconsideration of the terms of disendowment under the Welsh Church Act, for which I so intensely long. I should do my best to secure the reconsideration of that Act as part of the settlement; but I run a very great risk of failure. But, as I believe that the cause of religion would be more secure in the United Kingdom under a federal system without an amendment of the terms of the Welsh Church Act than it would be under our present constitution with an amendment of the terms of the Act, obviously I must run that risk. It is true that in the scheme, which you have seen, it is provided that Ireland shall not be allowed to establish a Church; that, as you observe, is quite illogical, and I have no wish to defend it on its merits; I certainly should not stand out for it; but, as it has been a condition accepted by all parties in Ireland, it seemed advisable to include it.

As regards Scotland you need not have the slightest anxiety; there is not the remotest chance of the Scots dis-establishing the Scottish Church under a federal system; the disestablishment and disendowment party has dwindled to nothing in Scotland; and almost the first Act of a Scottish legislature would be one to facilitate the Union of the Established and United Free Presbyterian Churches. Yours ever

S

7/33

19.   To Austen Chamberlain

49 Mount Street
W.1.
22 June 1918

My dear Austen,

I fully know the difficulties and the indifference about Second Chamber Reform in the House of Commons. Sandars tells me that Unionists have not really studied the Report[1] and without knowing anything of the difficulties of an alternative dislike election by the House of Commons.

Whittaker tells me that the Liberal attitude is not hostile, but indifferent.

Sandars also tells me that the Unionists are so sure of a Coalition majority at the next election that they will let the question stand over.

Now one of the greatest faults of the Unionist Party is its getting accustomed to the status quo and then waking up and finding that it has missed its chance and that irreparable harm is done. Look at the way they treated Old Age Pensions! I regard it as a very real danger that the Unionist Party will let this question stand over until a Labour Party comes into power – and then! Therefore, it seems to me, if I may say so quite frankly, that you will be missing a great opportunity which your position in the Cabinet gives you if you allow the federal solution[2] and the Second Chamber Reform both to slide. If neither the one nor the other was accomplished I should regard the position of the country as very dangerous – I should regard revolution as very possible.

I am sure that all this is present to your mind and I do not expect any answer. Yours ever

S

AC 12/214

1.   Lord Bryce's committee on the Second Chamber reported in 1918. It recommended that a Second Chamber should consist of two sections, one elected by a panel of members of the House of Commons, and the other

consisting of persons chosen by the Joint Standing Committee of both houses in the first instance, and thereafter by the House of Commons and the new Second Chamber. The new chamber was not to have any powers of amending or rejecting a financial bill, as defined in the recommendations, and adjustment of differences between the two houses was to be by a 'free conference' consisting of twenty members of each house appointed at the beginning of each parliament by the Committee of Selection in each house (the Joint Standing Committee of Conferences), and ten members of each house, added by the Committee of Selection on the occasions of the reference of any particular bill, to form with the Joint Standing Committee the 'Free Conference' on the bill. The Committee's recommendations were embodied in a 'Letter from Viscount Bryce to the Prime Minister', Cd. 9038 of 1918.

2.  On 26 June 1918 Selborne and Lord Brassey led an all party deputation to meet Lloyd George to promote the idea of a parliamentary committee to consider federalism, but a committee was never appointed.

20.  From F.S. Oliver

8 Hereford Gardens
Marble Arch
London W.1.
23 September 1918

Dear Selborne,

Many thanks for letting me see the interesting letter from your brother-in-law,[1] which I now return.

I have been thinking over the situation a good deal since we last met and Edward Cecil's views fall on more fertile soil than they would have done earlier perhaps. I will try and put my ideas out very briefly in the course of the next week or two, but in a nut-shell it seems to me that the wise course will be to leave Ireland out of the question altogether and go for Devolution in the law-abiding parts of the United Kingdom, as a necessity for reconstruction.[2] If Ireland is not fit to be trusted with its own affairs, or is discontented with the amount of powers proposed to be allotted to it, it will have to continue to be governed for the time being in the way which has always suited it best, i.e. the methods which Lord French is at present employing . . . Yours

F.S. Oliver

64/140

1.  A letter from Edward Cecil to Selborne, 5 August 1918 (84/136), in which Cecil doubted whether federalism would satisfy Ireland in her present mood, and warned that the federal system would not prevent Ireland 'blackmailing' the Imperial Government since Ireland would continue to be represented in the central parliament.
2.  A Speaker's Conference on devolution was set up in 1919, reporting in April 1920. It managed to reach agreement on areas, powers, financial arrangements

and the judiciary, but was divided on the character and composition of the local legislatures, being unable to agree on the principle of 'legislatures' as against 'grand councils'.

### 21. From the Marquess of Salisbury

21 Arlington Street
S.W.1.
24 February 1920

My dear Willie,

. . . Probably you would like to have a glance at the enclosed[1](1) in order to see that your preparations for the debate tonight, whatever their result, have been duly made and (2) in order that you should see the message from Lord Halsbury. As to this I have thought about our conversation the other day. I gather that your present mind is that the Home Rule Bill,[2] as being an improvement upon the Act on the Statute Book, should be allowed to pass and that if in that event the new Irish Sinn Fein Parliament made a declaration of independence the British Government would re-conquer Ireland. Frankly I have not made up my mind except to the extent of doubting whether, whatever heroic course we might advocate, we should get the Peers to follow us. But I should like to make two comments upon your position which I want you to consider.

First, the insubordination of the new Irish Government might not take that extreme form. They might simply ignore any safequards which were inserted in the Bill or any provision for Imperial Customs etc; and the

Second that in that event it is extremely unlikely that the British Government would interfere by force, even supposing you are right that in the face of a declaration of independence they would. If I am to speak the absolute truth I am not convinced that they would even in that last event, not at any rate for some time. There would be all sorts of negotiations which would be allowed to dribble away into nothing and the British Government without acknowledging the independence would abstain from enforcing control. And then there would be all the humiliation of a recognition of the Irish Republic by the United States and the British Government pretending not to see it. You will not forget will you that there is a section of opinion in the House of Commons which would let the Irish Sinn Feiners do *anything* they please provided only we are quit of the subject as they fondly imagine. Yours ever

Salisbury

7/82

1. A letter written by Willoughby de Broke (see no. 22, below).
2. In February 1920 the government introduced a new Government of Ireland Bill which provided for two home rule parliaments to be established in Ireland, one for Northern Ireland (the six counties of Antrim, Armagh, Down, Fermanagh, Londonderry and Tyrone), and the other for the remaining twenty-six counties (called 'Southern Ireland') with a 'Council of

Ireland' to discuss matters of common concern. The bill took its second reading in March 1920, and its third reading in November, becoming law on 23 December 1920. The Belfast parliament was accepted, reluctantly, by the Ulster Unionists, and was inaugurated in June 1921. The now dominant Sinn Fein party in the south of Ireland rejected the Dublin Parliament and the Council of Ireland, and continued to sit in its self-styled 'Dail Eireann' which it had set up in January 1919 following its victory in the 1918 general election. In 1920 a guerilla and terrorist conflict between the Irish Republican Army and the crown forces intensified.

## 22.  To the Marquess of Salisbury

27 February 1920

. . . I return you W. de B.'s letter. Halsbury and he would be quite justified in taking that course if they think it right, but I could not act with them.

Light ought to be thrown on the present and future situation by the debates during the passage of the Bill through the House of Commons, but for the present I would say that I do not agree with you in your view of the attitude of the British people towards Ireland. In my opinion the British people are quite determined to give these inscrutable Irish people the chance of working a Home Rule Bill; things having gone as far as they have, and taking in all the circumstances of the case with its world wide aspect they are determined to try this experiment out to the bitter end; but they will stand no nonsense afterwards. I do not mean by that that they will interfere if the Irish govern themselves badly, but that they will not stand any separatist action whatever, and no Government will be able to exist that does stand it. Nor do I believe that the Government of U.S.A. would recognise an Irish republic, or that the British people and therefore the British Government would not resent it properly if they did.

I regard the substitution of the new Bill for the old one as a real gain, and as one of the two has to be tried I prefer this one. It is not in the power of any human authority, except the Lords and Commons acting in unison to prevent this. If Halsbury was to succeed to-morrow in throwing out the new Bill the House of Commons would quite certainly let the old Bill come into operation with all its imperfections, or there would have been a General Election at which the British people would have declared by such a majority as has never been seen at any General Election yet, that they mean to make this experiment. Yours ever

S

7/85

## 23.  To Sir George Younger

27 February 1920

My dear Younger,
If you enquire you will find that before the War the Hampshire and Isle of Wight Provincial Division of the N.U.A. was one of the strongest and most

vigorous in England. Yesterday at its quarterly meeting it passed the following resolution unanimously, of which notice had previously been given by one of the members, and with which let me tell you I have nothing whatever to do.'That this Council views with greatest concern the rapid spread of Socialistic and Bolshevist principles, largely the result of Unionist apathy, indifference and neglect, and calls upon the Party Leaders to formulate a vigorous Policy calculated to appeal to the common sense and patriotism of the Nation'.

I believe that a year hence the organisation will disappear altogether. I cannot tell you with what feelings of depression I came away.

I can sum the situation up exactly. Hampshire is almost entirely Conservative not Liberal Unionists. Our people are very grateful for what the Coalition Government did in the War, but at the present moment they are profoundly unhappy. The future looks to them very dark and they want to know under what flag they are going to be led to meet it. In the storm of war many of the old political questions have disappeared, but not all, and in respect of these they know that before the war the Prime Minister and the Liberals who support him held opinions diametrically opposed to their own. If they and these Liberals and the Prime Minister are going to fight shoulder to shoulder against the forces of revolution they want to know on what principles these previous differences are going to be composed.

Since the War many other questions have emerged into the field of practical politics and they instinctively feel that before the War they would have given a different answer to these questions to what the Prime Minister and his Liberals would have given. If therefore they are to work together on these questions they want to know on what principles they are going to work.

Finally they say that they see no reason why a Coalition Government should not have a policy and announce it just as much as any other Government, and that there should be no difficulty in framing and announcing this policy, if once the principles had been agreed upon under which Liberals and Conservatives would agree to work together against Bolsheviks.

In conclusion I may say that not only is there no co-operation of any sort or kind between the Unionist Associations of Hampshire and any Liberal organisations whatever, but that all Liberal activities in the country are avowedly hostile. Yours sincerely

87/68

24.　From Sir George Younger

1 Sanctuary Buildings
Gt. Smith Street
S.W.1.
1 March 1920

*Private*

My dear Selborne,

I have yours of the 27th. I have already been informed of the situation in Hampshire, and I am glad to have your letter on the subject. I shall show it to Bonar Law today, as I imagine you will have no objection to that course, in order that he may realise the unhappy position which is developing outside. It is more pronounced in some cases than in others, but unquestionably it is becoming a little serious, and recently has been aggravated by the somewhat querulous tactics of Bob Cecil and others in the House[1] – they have been anything but helpful.

Yours ever

Geo Younger

87/70

1.　A reference to Lord Robert Cecil's attempts to bring down Lloyd George by constructing an alliance between anti-coalition forces, for which see Maurice Cowling, *The Impact of Labour* (C.U.P., 1971), ch. 3.

25.　To Lady Selborne

Mercers Hall
Ironmonger Lane
London E.C.2.
22 March 1921

My Beloved,

The Peers ran away again yesterday over my motion pressing the government to deal with the Second Chamber question this session. G.N.C. made a pompous speech about overwork, great deliberation required and bunkum of that sort and the Peers would only pass the motion in the meaningless form of 'earliest possible moment'.[1] The truth is that the fools or Lords predominate, and with G.N.C. they prefer to remain ermine dummies rather than stabilise the constitution. I thought that when they saw how closely the official programme of the Labour party touched their pockets they would wake up. But I was wrong.

Austen was unanimously elected head of the Unionist party in the House of Commons yesterday. Some of the M.P.s wanted to move that L.G. be elected forthwith leader of the whole Unionist party, and others wanted to propose the same thing for F.E., but Edmund Talbot squelched both movements by his tactics – no-one ever mentioned G.N.C. Cardinal Bourne went to Rome with a special box of proofs of the criminal nature of Sinn Fein. The box was stolen in Italy and everything else left. Is not that rather a proof of Northumberland's contention that the Irish rebellion is only part of a worldwide conspiracy (Bolshevist) against England? Your

S

104/26

1. Lord Selborne moved 'That this House urges His Majesty's Government to introduce their measure for the reform of the Second Chamber in time for it to be dealt with adequately by both Houses of Parliament during the current session'. This was amended by Lord Lansdowne, the amendment being carried (*H.L.Deb.*, 5s., vol. 44, cols. 690–731).

26.   To Lady Selborne

49 Mount Street
W
5 April 1921

My Beloved,

Today in both Houses the government took complete powers by resolution under the Emergency Powers Act passed last year to deal with the situation caused by this terrible coal strike and the risk of the transport workers and railwaymen, the whole Triple Alliance, joining in.[1]

The transport workers were to decide today and I do not know as I write at 7 p.m. what they have decided. The railwaymen meet tomorrow. I gathered from Curzon's speech in the House that the government thought the whole Alliance were going out.

England's shoulders need be broad and her people's hearts stout to carry such a catastrophe as this on the top of the Irish and the Indian troubles. But, thank God, our people's hearts are stout and if the government play their part truly I believe absolutely that the nation will support them and win a great victory for itself over these modern predatory barons.

But the cost in ill-will, in suffering, in loss of trade, in continuous unemployment, and in increased financial stringency will be simply prodigious. One man and one only stands to gain and that is Lloyd George. I acquit him of all responsibility for the immediate crisis, but I think his mishandling of labour questions during the last six years has much to do with the industrial atmosphere existing. But if he holds firm, and decisively defeats this attempt of a section of the nation to hold up the nation, he will dissolve at once and come back with a fresh lease of power – and all chance of reform of the House of Lords will again be relegated to the end of the next Parliament? and small that chance will be. Yours

S

104/50

1. In April 1921 the 'Triple Alliance' of railwaymen, miners and dockers threatened a concerted strike to support the miners in their dispute with the owners over new and reduced scales of pay, but backed down on 'Black Friday', 15 April 1921.

27. To the Marquess of Salisbury

13 June 1921

My dear Jim,

The only thing I can do is to give you my honest opinion and the reasons for it. You think that it is quite certain that the Government is toppling to its fall; I have no such confidence, and would remind you that the same impression has been held more than once previously during the last two or three years.

But the main question you and I have to consider is not whether a majority of the electors or a large number of Unionist electors has lost confidence in the Government, but whether the back-bone of the Unionist Party as reflected in its many local associations has lost confidence in the Government? I think you will agree that, if we collected together all the Unionist members of the House of Commons and asked them to shake themselves free of any allegiance to the Coalition Government, very few of them would agree to do so. But you think the Government has become so unpopular with Unionists generally in the country that in response to such a letter as is suggested, a large number of Unionist Associations, possibly even a majority, would declare against the Coalition Government and in favour of the views of the signatories of the letter. With great deference I don't agree. This Coalition Government has never been popular with the Unionist Party, but on the other hand the Unionist Party in every part of the country is practically unanimous in thinking that to-day there ought to be only two parties in the state, those who are in favour of the Labour Party or Socialists, and those who are opposed to them; and this conviction implies the willingness to co-operate with Liberals who are ready to oppose Socialists. You think that recent events have more than ever discredited the Coalition Government in the eyes of Unionists. That is not my experience from what I hear in the City, but I don't think the City a good guide in such matters. I attribute more importance to a tour I recently took through a large portion of Hampshire, Dorsetshire and Somersetshire, and there almost every Unionist I spoke to expressed warm approval of the way the Government have handled the Coal Strike and they seemed to me to be more favourably disposed towards the present Government than they ever had been before. Therefore I believe that, if we sent such a letter out to the Unionist Associations of the Country, we should meet with lamentable failure and evoke a very small response. I think the only result would be to create a division in the Party, which could advantage nobody except the Labour Party, and I think our influence with the Party would be destroyed. Therefore I could not sign such a letter nor advise you to sign it.

I don't think the same objection would apply to an appeal to the Unionist Associations in view of the critical position of affairs to exercise their right of demanding that the National Unionist Conference should be immediately summoned to discuss the situation. I forget the exact number at the present moment which can demand a meeting, I think it is 50

Associations of five provincial divisions, but you would find that in the rules. But I think that before doing so it would be a proper act of courtesy to ask Austen himself to summon such a Conference and only appeal to the Associations in case of his refusal. But, although I think this course is open to much less objection than the other suggestion, I do not advise it for two reasons. I am not at all sure that a sufficient number of Associations would respond favourably, and I am not at all sure that, if such a Conference did meet just now, that Conference would not end by electing Lloyd George as the Leader of the Unionist Party or of a new Party of which the Unionists were the principal part; and I should regard that as the worst thing that could possibly happen. After all if you want to feel the pulse of the Unionist Associations, you can do so at the Council Meeting at the Connaught rooms at 2.30 p.m. on Tuesday June 21st.

I am not disturbed by the fact that the men who are defeating the Government candidates are put up by Bottomley and such like. They will in due course fall into their places as very average Unionist Members of Parliament, and nobody suggests that Bottomley could form a Government; and that brings me to another consideration which seems to me to be of importance. Whatever support we got from the Party outside we simply could not form a Government, because we could find no Unionist to lead our Party in the House of Commons. There is nobody that I know now in the House of Commons outside the Government now that Bob has left us that could do it, and Austen and Horne are not going to throw over Lloyd George at this moment.

It is very unpleasant to have to wait and do nothing, but that is the natural result of our exile in the House of Lords. For the present there is nothing that I can see that we can do that is really for the advantage either of our party or, which is of much more importance, of the Country. Yours ever

S

7/103

28.    From the Marquess of Salisbury

21 Arlington Street
S.W.1.
6 July 1921

My dear Willie,

I will attend to your job at the National Union, but I cannot take much interest in it in face of the Irish situation.[1]

I saw St. John yesterday. I avoided a talk with him but I heard him talking to others. I should gather nothing much has as yet emerged from the negotiations. De Valera spoke at great length about Queen Elizabeth and Griffiths [sic] did not say a word. But obviously the journey of St. John and his friends to Canossa[2] is by itself of capital importance. It must seem to the Sinn Feiners that they have only got to sit tight to get what they want – whatever that may be. It is possible that the Government are acting under some secret understanding or at any rate information, but on the face of it what has happened is that they have asked rebels dripping with the blood of assassinated loyalists to negotiate with them. The rebels have refused and have sent for representatives of the loyalists to meet 'the President of the Irish Republic' in Dublin and the loyalists have gone with a commission from the Government. These are the facts as they appear and I expect that there is no understanding which might palliate them. Incidentally several leading rebels have been released, and the killing of the King's servants continues.

I have heard people say that driven to the last point we can always reconquer Ireland. I have however had a conversation with Carson – who has been to some extent taken into the confidence of the Government – and it appears that it would require 15 divisions. We only possess two weak divisions in Great Britain and Ireland, so that this seems to be impracticable. The Sinn Feiners are I believe advised by very competent soldiers, and they are no doubt aware of these facts. There appears to be no bottom to our humiliation.

Carson did not deny that something might be done by blockade, but he evidently had no confidence that the Government would do anything effective.

The practical questions seem to be:

1.   Have things been allowed to get to such a point that we must accept whatever terms de Valera chooses to impose? (He may be induced by Smuts to limit his demands).[3]

2.   If not, is there anything we the independent Englishmen can do and ought to do? I can for example conceive our asking the Government before they decide to surrender whether they will lay all the facts of the situation before a confidential body of representative men of all parties in England and Scotland.

3.   Shall we get into touch with Craig and find out what his attitude is and what his information is?

It may be that he could put a better face upon matters. Yours ever

S

7/106

1.   Following a conciliatory speech by King George V at the opening of the Northern Ireland parliament on 22 June 1921, the government on 24 June offered talks with Sinn Fein and with Sir James Craig. Terms of a truce between the I.R.A. and the crown forces were arranged on 8 July to come into effect on 11 July.

2.   A reference to St. John's role as a mediator between Sinn Fein and the British government in July 1921, and in particular to his decision to go to the Mansion

House, Dublin, in response to an invitation from de Valera, to participate in discussions between 4 and 8 July.
3.  Salisbury's guess was not far off the mark. General Smuts, in London for a conference of Dominion Prime Ministers, urged de Valera on 4 August to accept the government's offer of dominion status, made on 20 July.

29.  To the Marquess of Salisbury

House of Lords
29 July 1921

My dear Jim,
. . . As regards the Irish question I do not see it from quite the same angle as you do. I think that the government for the last four and a half years has mismanaged it beyond the possibility of exaggeration and the root cause of their mismanagement is the fact that they are a coalition. Desperate mischief was done in their first two years, Duke's regime,[1] and all that has since happened has flowed almost automatically as a consequence from that miserable period. I early came to the conclusion that an Ulster government and parliament could alone save us from the worst consequences of their policy, the independence of any part of Ireland, and I think we are now saved from that. Therefore to work with Craig is the key to my attitude. I think that a very large majority in the country are quite determined that the government shall have an unfettered chance to work out their policy to the conclusion of some form of semi-Dominion government for the South of Ireland if they can. I also believe that the great majority of Unionists and Nationalists in South Ireland wish for the same conclusion. What proportion of Sinn Feiners wish for it I have no idea. I could not have negotiated with the rebel leader, but I feel myself clear of all responsibility in the matter and I do not feel that the humiliation of such a negotiation rests on anyone except on the members of the government. I do not feel that any of it reflects back to me and England is so immensely great at this moment that I doubt whether the Dominions or foreign countries think that England is humiliated by it.

I do not think that we have the remotest chance of preventing or reversing the results of this negotiation because the nation in great majority is in favour of it. The time for our policy will only come if the Sinn Feiners are proved ad urbem et orbem to be utterly intransigent in their demand for independence, or if hereafter the form of government adopted now utterly breaks down. Then the position could be retrieved through the bridgehead of Ulster.

You and I think that the policy cannot succeed. Yet I would not say that in public for two reasons. The lesser is that I think more than you do that the rebels have had tremendous punishment. The greater because I think the Irish are a wholly irrational incomprehensible and contemptible race, and I do not regard it as wholly impossible that they may be slobbering the King with loyalty (!) before twelve months are passed.

Therefore I conceive that I can do no useful public service in Irish affairs at present except to support Craig and, if a plan is proposed, which I do not think can possibly work, to say so publicly and register my protest . . . Ever your affectionate

S

4th Salisbury, S (4) 97/90

1.  The Chief Secretaryship of H. E. Duke, 1st Baron Merrivale (1855–1939), who held office from July 1916 until May 1918, resigning because of the government's failure to declare that home rule was the corollary of conscription.

30.  From the Marquess of Salisbury

Hill Foot Hey
Woolton
Liverpool
15 November 1921

*Confidential*
My dear Willy,
I went back to Hatfield (for County Council) for the weekend. Yesterday I had a couple of hours in London and I went to see Bonar Law. I agree with you that his record is rather feeble, but I wanted to see him in order (1) to know where he stands (2) what the potentialities in the Irish situation are, or at least were when a few months ago he left the Government. I did not ask him about the letter in the Yorkshire Post[1] (which I read in the Morning Post) but I discussed the whole situation with him. The answer to the last question is that should the occasion arise the coercion of Sinn Fein is quite feasible. The answer to the first question is

1.  He is furious with the Government especially with the Unionist members of it for throwing over Ulster.
2.  He is trying to persuade L.G. to retrace his steps.
3.  If he does not succeed, as soon as the intentions of the Government are officially published he is prepared to try and rally the Unionist Party against them.
4.  He thinks he has strength enough to defeat these intentions but he doubts very much whether the new Government would have strength to coerce Sinn Fein. (I presume that this means that after an unsuccessful effort L.G. would come back again and have his way.)

The conversation on both sides was without prejudice, but I told him that I thought if he came out he would have very large support in the Party – not mainly because of Ireland, though the last three months have affected public opinion a good deal even upon Ireland, but because the treatment of Ulster comes on the top of great dissatisfaction on numbers of other points.

He asked me about the Liverpool Conference.[2] He was rather struck by the terms of the resolution which the Executive itself has inserted in the Report,[3] but he regretted that matters should come to an issue here. Whether it was that he hopes to persuade L.G. as I have mentioned and so avoid the split which the result of Liverpool may make inevitable or that he is afraid the Conference may come down on the side of the Government and make the position of Ulster worse, I did not quite make out. But there was a good deal of the Launcelot Gobbo in him all the time – a courageous and a shrinking Bonar Law, wrestling with one another all the time.

I told him that I did not expect too much here, that anything might happen, but that whatever it is to be nothing can be done to stop it at the last moment.

My impression is that Gretton's motion[4] will be carried easily even unanimously but that the discussion on it will take the wind out of the sails of Northumberland's which may very likely get shelved. The local circumstances of Liverpool may make a little difference. As you know the Party here is very Ulster. I learn that this fact is perturbing Derby very much. I suspect he will occupy a strong position on the fence, but the Liverpool contingent will be growingly anti Government.

Politics are odious, because as things stand there is no real issue to the Irish question.

But if Bonar Law comes again into the arena we have at last got a leader in the Commons even if we do not turn the Government out at this moment. Yours ever

S

7/112

1.  In November 1921 Lloyd George began to put pressure on the Ulster Unionists to come into an all-Ireland system of government, and was supported in his endeavours by leading Unionists such as Birkenhead and Austen Chamberlain as well as many of the party's rank and file and most of the Unionist press.
    On 10 November 1921 there appeared in the *Yorkshire Post* a long statement by an anonymous 'Unionist leader' who, remarked the *Post*, 'has the highest political qualifications to speak for the Unionists of this country'. The 'Unionist leader' protested against the attempts by the London press to lay all the blame on Ulster for impasse in the treaty negotiations, and reminded Unionists of their pledge that Ulster must not be coerced into an all-Ireland parliament: 'The Unionist case has always been that coercion begins not when you send troops, but when you pass an Act of Parliament which makes the people of Ulster rebels when they resist it'. The statement was reprinted in the *Morning Post* on 11 November, the *Post* commenting that 'to those who read with understanding it will be obvious that the author is indeed a Unionist leader'.
2.  The National Unionist Conference held in Liverpool on 17 November, at which the Irish negotiations were to be debated.
3.  The official resolution, moved by Sir Archibald Salvidge, the Unionist city boss of Liverpool, read 'That this conference expresses its earnest hope that, consistently with the supremacy of the Crown, the security of the Empire, and the pledges given to Ulster, and the safeguarding of the interests of the minority in the South of Ireland, a solution of the Irish difficulties may be found

in the Conference now in progress which will bring peace to Great Britain and Ireland and strength to the Empire'.

4.   A motion by Colonel John Gretton 'That this Conference places upon record its condemnation of the long-continued ascendancy of crime and rebellion in Ireland, and resolves that no settlement of the Irish question will be acceptable which does not absolutely respect the position acquired by Ulster and does not provide every safeguard that is essential for our Imperial security and the protection of the Loyalists in the South and West of Ireland'.

The motion was defeated, and Unionist spokesmen won a vote to continue the Anglo-Irish talks, but not to follow any particular line, except to promise that Ulster would not be coerced into an all-Ireland government. After this, Lloyd George turned his attention again to pressurising Sinn Fein, and on 6 December 1921 he secured their agreement to a treaty giving southern Ireland dominion status, with a boundary commission to make a final delimitation of the border of Northern Ireland.

31.   From F.S. Oliver

Edgerston<br>
Jedburgh<br>
Scotland<br>
23 June 1922

Dear Selborne,

I haven't answered your p.c. until now (1) because we have had our home full of guests and (2) because, until last night, I hadn't read the articles which you refer to in the *Round Table*[1] – the viands provided by that periodical have ceased for some years past to tempt my palate, so that it usually lies unopened on my table until the maid decides that it is sufficiently antiquated for the W.P.B.

The India article is poor stuff; but it does contain some information which bears an appearance of being material; and it didn't strike me as reaching quite the high level of nauseousness which we have come lately to expect from the R.T.

The Irish Article, however, is in their most characteristic manner. What they say about Ulster is untrue in fact, – it is not merely untrue, but untruthful; and I wish almost that the smug sophist who wrote it might see some one he cared about shot before his eyes.

But I am not going to address remonstrances. Life is too short. It would besides be quite fruitless. I ended my association last spring – it had become merely formal – by giving up my auditorship.

The news of Henry Wilson's murder[2] which came this morning has not surprised me. Whether grief, horror or black rage is uppermost in my mind I don't quite know: it is in a surge which makes correspondence rather difficult.

He was one of my closest friends. He had warned the Goat from the very first of the tendencies of his Irish policy. His view of it was simple – 'you are forcing the Irish people into a religious civil war, which is the most horrible of all wars civil or otherwise. Under your plan the Protestants will be 'done in' in the South, and the Catholics in the north: nothing in the wide world can prevent these results from flowing'. But they only said pooh! pooh! and tush! tush!

Something of course is going to happen in consequence of this latest murder – in *Eaton Place*!! but what exactly, I can't quite say: the nerves of the British people are terribly on edge. So, I fancy, are the Goat's. Austen has no nerves: he is only an eye glass. Yours

F.S.O.

84/163

1. Articles in the *Round Table*, vol. 12 (December 1921– September 1922). The article 'Ireland at the cross-roads' called on Ulster to be conciliatory and take 'some risks' on Irish unity for the sake of peace. It mentioned also the 'strong element of extremism' in Ulster 'exactly counterbalancing the extremism of the South'.
2. The murder of Sir Henry Wilson on 22 June outside his home in Eaton Square by members of the I.R.A.


32. From the Marquess of Salisbury

Hatfield House
Hatfield
Herts.
26 September 1922

*Confidential*

My dear Willie,

I was so much occupied with Gretton's tiresomeness[1] that I forgot to tell you about Bonar.

I saw him yesterday morning and had a long and friendly talk, but it was no go. He was thoroughly pessimistic but was not prepared to take any step to prevent disaster.[2]

He was really quite as convinced as we are that the Coalition is done for, but he saw no exit to the position except the break up of the Conservative Party. I could not quite make out whether he thought the break would come before or after the November Conference.[3] He discussed the proceedings at the Conference and anticipated we (the Free Conservatives) would be defeated there by speeches of Austen and A.J.B., and upon this defeat the breach would ensue. On the other hand he sometimes spoke as if the crisis would come before the Conference. L.G. had consulted him as to his (L.G.'s) position 'What did he advise him to do?' Bonar had advised him to get out, but Bonar told me he was sure he wouldn't, but he thought Austen was different and would not face the music. Austen when November looms near will tell L.G. he can't do it. This is of course quite different to the other idea – a great speech from

Austen which is to confound us. Anyhow the Party is to break up. Whether according to the second idea Austen would resign the leadership and carry part of our party into a Centre Party under L.G. or whether in order to avoid the November Conference there would be a Dissolution I can't say. I wish I had asked him whether he anticipated a Dissolution as the issue, but I forgot. I merely asked him *what* would be the issue and got no definite reply. The truth was that Bonar was much more interested in explaining that he himself could and would do nothing than anything else. He spent a good deal of time in explaining the hopelessness of the task before a Conservative Government if there were such a thing: What could they do about Ireland or about the French alliance or about Tariff Reform? The difficulties he was not prepared to face. Then he dwelt upon the impossibility on personal grounds of his appearing in opposition to Austen or A.J.B.

I told him, I need not say, of the peril to the Party of allowing things to drift. I explained the difficulty we had in holding our own men and in preventing Free Conservative candidates from opposing Co. Unionists. This point seemed familiar to him. I imagine it has been – naturally – the subject of conversation with Younger or L.G.

As I reflect upon all this the evidence seems rather to point to an immediate Election. I have seen some other confidential evidence pointing somewhat the same way. It would meet the Conference difficulty and would minimise the number of Free Conservative candidates.

I think this reinforces what I have said in my other letter about not chilling electoral zeal.

I am rather anxious. Yours ever

S

7/129

1. Colonel John Gretton, a strong opponent of the Anglo-Irish treaty and critic of the coalition. By July 1922 the leadership of the 'die-hard' Unionist movement had passed from Gretton to Lord Salisbury, because Gretton would not co-operate with Salisbury and because Salisbury was a more important political figure.
2. The 'disaster' was the decision by the Cabinet on 17 September to fight an early general election as a coalition.
3. The Conservative and Unionist Conference, due to be held on 15 November.


33.   From the Marquess of Salisbury

Hatfield House
Hatfield
Herts.
12 October 1922

My dear Willie,
I will certainly see Lady Edmund.[1] I will write her a line. It is almost incredible that there should be a fresh surrender![2] But after what has happened anything may be.

I was in London today to see Walter by appointment. On Tuesday he presided over some 40 Unionist back benchers at Sir William Bull's request. They consisted I gather almost entirely of 'ci devant' Coalitionists. They were in an awful state. Many of them still believed in L.G. but they were unanimous that in the circumstances he must cease to be Prime Minister. There was a proposal that a Committee should be appointed to confer with a Committee of ours, but finally it was settled that Walter was to have a talk with me.

We agreed that the P.M. must resign, that Austen would not do to succeed him, that the choice lay between A.J.B., G. Curzon and Bonar, that Bonar was the best. He asked me if I would serve in a Conservative Government under one of these and I finally replied that I would do so provided Austen and Birkenhead were *not* included, that some of my friends were included, and that the programme was satisfactory. I do not feel sure that we need pay much attention to all this latter part. We have not yet got rid of L.G.: and certainly we have not got rid of Austen and the rest of the chickens need not be counted. But the vital thing is that Austen and L.G., should be made aware of the feeling of this meeting of their supporters(?) [sic] and I therefore induced Walter to write a letter at once. Younger was at the meeting but Walter's written letter is a much more cogent weapon. So it was arranged that it should be written to Younger with an urgent message that it should reach Austen wherever he is forthwith so as to be in his hands before he speaks tomorrow. I suggested also that it should be shown to L.G. The letter of course which I saw after it was drafted only dealt with the necessity of L.G.'s resignation. Both Walter and I were afraid that the two leaders might say something in their speeches from which they cannot retreat. I would have run you to earth in London this afternoon but my cold was rather vile and I thought discretion was to come home. Gretton and I seem completely reconciled. Yours ever

S

7/135

1. Mary Caroline, daughter of Montagu Arthur Bertie, Lord Norreys, who married Lord Edmund Talbot in 1879.
2. On 10 October the Cabinet decided that an election should take place as soon as the crisis with Turkey, whose troops were threatening to enter the neutral zone of Chanak after defeating the Greeks, permitted. The prospect of an election caused consternation among many Unionists.

34.  From the Marquess of Salisbury

21 Arlington Street
S.W.1.
14 October 1922

My dear Willie,

Here is a note of B.L.'s attitude of mind.

It shows a very distinct advance on his attitude six weeks ago. He is fighting against the conclusion that he ought to intervene. But he is definitely against the Coalition and is driven to contemplate his return to the front. But he will avoid this if he can.

In the meantime his information about the improbability of a snap Election is very important.

I need not tell you I used every form of persuasion I could think of to get him to go further. Yours ever

S

*Enclosure*

Interview October 14 1922

1.  The disintegration of the Coalition has enormously increased since we last had a conversation, so that he no longer thinks we shall be unsuccessful in carrying an anti-Coalition resolution at the Conference.
2.  If we have patience he rather anticipates that there will be such a manifestation of overwhelming opinion in the Party that the P.M. and his colleagues will become convinced. There is a regular tide flowing.
3.  He has no course to suggest except to wait. There will be no snap Election. It would excite keen resentment in the Party and in this event he himself would go into active opposition. But in fact A.C. would not allow it. A.C. has written to F.E. that he has come round to the view that there ought to be no dissolution without a previous Party meeting.[1]
4.  In this meeting he (B.L.) would be obliged to advise that the Coalition must come to an end. He realises that a man placed like himself who gives such advice must be prepared if it is taken to accept office or retire altogether from the House of Commons.
5.  Except as above he is not prepared to be active. He will not take part in a meeting of Conservative ex Ministers, lest it should commit him to action. This is mainly due to personal reluctance to take office. He has not been vetted by his doctor lately (he proposes to make good this omission next week). For four years he was wretched. The difficulties in front of a Conservative Government are very formidable. He is entitled to enjoy life.
6.  He agrees that A.C. has burnt his bridges. In his view A.J.B. would

be the best choice as a temporary arrangement. He will not however ask him till the time comes. He thinks he would serve under him.

7/141

1.  On 15 October Austen Chamberlain bowed to Unionist pressure and agreed to a meeting at the Carlton Club of all Unionist M.P.s, to be held on 19 October.

35.  From the Marquess of Salisbury

Hatfield House
Hatfield
Herts.
18 October 1922

My dear Willie,

Your letter about Malcolm Fraser reached me this morning. I telephoned at once to Bonar. No change – boneless. He said he would be very glad to see me but that he should only be able to repeat what he said last time I saw him. However, I arranged to go to luncheon with him tomorrow. I thought that if it is to be any good there was more chance of this after we know what Austen has to say than before. I shall of course tell him all about Walter and his meeting and the substance of your letter (leaving out Malcolm Fraser's name perhaps). Then beside this I can tell him that Gretton went to the Central Office the day before yesterday and while there Leslie Wilson came in. There was general talk of the situation (Gretton assuring L.W. that all the bridges are intact and the gates open for a reunion of the Party up to now) and L.W. assumed almost as a matter of course that the Prime Minister must resign. The upshot is that *all* the party managers think that L.G. *ought* to resign, but that Malcolm Fraser – and probably Younger and Leslie Wilson in their hearts – believe that he is intent on breaking up the Unionist Party. I am to see Lady Edmund tomorrow morning and she may give me something more to stimulate Bonar.[1]

If I can make any impression my idea is to get Bonar to summon a meeting of Unionist leaders out of office. Walter Long, Derby, Devonshire, Carson, Lansdowne, St. John, Yourself and me – perhaps Younger. But I would like very much to have had your opinion on this before taking any definite step. I need not say I will communicate with you tomorrow afternoon.

I have called together our whole Group Lords and Commons for Tuesday at 2.30.[2] I have ominous symptoms of restiveness at their being kept in the dark.

At the meeting we might or might not at the proper stage admit reporters and state our position or we might read out a draft letter to the newspapers. But all this depends on Austen's speech and L.G.'s.

I have given up going to Newport.[3] Yours ever

S

7/137

1.  Law seems to have decided to attend the Carlton Club meeting by dinner time on 18 October, following pressure from many Unionist politicians, but almost changed his mind again at the last moments on the morning of the 19th.
2.  The fact that Salisbury was contemplating a further meeting of his 'group' after the Carlton Club meeting demonstrates that, like most of the government's critics, he did not expect the Carlton meeting to be decisive.
3.  A by-election was being fought at Newport, the loss of the coalition seat to an independent Conservative candidate being announced on the night of 18/19 October.

36.   From the Marquess of Salisbury

York Cottage
Sandringham
Norfolk
25 October 1922

My dear Willie,

. . . As I realise the upshot of all these events[1] I am depressed that our great comradeship is at an end. It may be this Government will be only an affair of weeks, but it may be otherwise and it is dreadfully sad that we shall not be working together. I do not of course criticise your determination, but it almost amounts to a tragedy.

You have been so awfully kind to me. Yours ever gratefully

S

7/146

1.  At the Carlton Club meeting on Thursday, 19 October, a majority of M.P.s voted in favour of forming a government of their own if they won a majority at the next election. Lloyd George thereupon resigned, and the King sent for Bonar Law. Law refused to see the King until he had been elected party leader in place of Austen Chamberlain. Salisbury, Derby and Curzon asked him to accept nomination at a Party meeting on 23 October. On the same day Law became Prime Minister. Lord Salisbury became Lord President of the Council in his government. In the election which followed on 15 November 1922 the Conservatives won a working majority of seventy-seven over the other parties.

37.  To the Marquess of Salisbury

49 Mount Street
W.1.
26 October 1922

My dear Jim,

Your letter of yesterday is a great pleasure to me. Thank you.

It has been a real happiness to me to have been of any help to you at all, and, it that is going to end now, it is a real sorrow to me. But many months ago I realised my choice. I had either to give up active politics or to let Blackmoor cease to exist as a home and rallying place for all my children and grandchildren.

I thought a great deal about it and prayed and came to a clear view of my duty, and not long after wrote and told you. Of course the existence of the National Assembly[1] and all that it will entail helped me in my decision.

But from that moment I took less and less part in public affairs. I gradually slid out. Because I felt that it was not right to take a lead if I was not prepared to take the responsibility. I am afraid that consequently I have not really been anything like as helpful to you as I might have been. Pray forgive me for that and make use of me whenever you can. Ever yours affectionately

S

4th Salisbury, S (4) 103/75

1.  The body set up by the Church of England Assembly (Powers) Act, 1919, on the recommendation of the Archbishops' Committee on Church and State which Lord Selborne chaired.

# Biographical Notes

Persons are found under their normally used or contemporary names, e.g. Lord Aberdeen is found under Aberdeen, and not his family surname, and Lord Halifax is found under Wood, E.F.L. Nicknames (e.g. 'Top' – Lord Wolmer) are found under the nicknames, with a cross reference to the real names and full biographies.

**Abercorn**, James Hamilton, 2nd Duke of (1838–1913), first President of the Ulster Unionist Association.

**Aberdeen**, John Campbell Gordon, 7th Earl, and 1st Marquess of Aberdeen and Temair (1847–1934), Lord Lieutenant of Ireland, 1886, Governor-General of Canada, 1893–8, Lord Lieutenant of Ireland, 1906–15.

**Acland**, Sir Francis Dyke (1874–1939), Liberal M.P. for Richmond division of Yorkshire, 1906–10, N. W. Cornwall, 1910–22, Tiverton division of Devon, 1923–4, North Cornwall, 1932, Financial Secretary to the War Office, 1908–10, Under-Secretary of State for Foreign Affairs, 1911–15, Financial Secretary to the Treasury, Feb. – June 1915, Secretary to the Board of Agriculture, 1915–16.

**Acland-Hood**, Sir Alexander, 1st Lord St Audries (1853–1917), Chief Whip of the Unionist Party, 1902–11.

**'A.E.'**, George William Russell (1867–1935), poet, writer and artist, a leading member of the Irish Agricultural Organization Society, member of the Irish Convention, 1917, editor of the *Irish Statesman*, 1923–30. A Protestant Nationalist and a mystic.

**Ailwyn**, Edward Fellowes, 1st Baron of Honingham (1855–1924), Conservative M.P. for North Huntingdonshire, 1887–1906, President of the Board of Agriculture, 1905–6.

**Ampthill**, Arthur Oliver Villiers Russell, 2nd Baron (1869–1935), Assistant Secretary at the Colonial Office, 1895–7, Private Secretary, 1897–1900, Governor of Madras, 1900–6.

**Asquith**, Herbert Henry, 1st Earl of Oxford and Asquith (1852–1928), Liberal M.P. for East Fife, 1886–1918, and Paisley, 1920–24, Secretary of State for Home Affairs, 1892–5, Chancellor of the Exchequer, 1905–8, Prime Minister, 1908–16, entered the House of Lords in 1925.

**Balcarres**, David Alexander Edward Lindsay, 27th Earl of Crawford and 10th Earl of Balcarres (1871–1940), Unionist M.P., 1895–1913, party whip, 1903–13, President of the Board of Agriculture and Fisheries, 1916.

**Balfour**, Arthur James, 1st Earl (1848–1930), Conservative M.P. for Hertford, 1874–85, for East Manchester, 1885–1906, and for the City of London, 1906–22, Chief Secretary for Ireland, 1887, First Lord of the Treasury and leader of the House of Commons, 1891 and 1895, led the

Opposition, 1892–5, 1906–11, Prime Minister, 1902–5, First Lord of the Admiralty, 1915–16, Foreign Secretary, 1916–19, Lord President of the Council, 1919–22 and 1925–9, British representative at the League of Nations, 1920–22. Lord Selborne's cousin.

**Balfour**, Gerald William, 2nd Earl (1853–1945), Conservative M.P. for Central Leeds, 1885, Chief Secretary for Ireland, 1895–1900, President of the Board of Trade, 1900–5, President of the Local Government Board, 1905, defeated in the 1906 general election.

**Balfour of Burleigh**, Alexander Hugh Bruce, 6th Baron (1849–1921), Parliamentary Secretary to the Board of Trade, 1889–92, Secretary of State for Scotland, 1895–1903.

**Barrie**, Hugh Thom (1860–1922), Unionist M.P. for North Londonderry, 1906, High Sheriff, 1918, Chairman of the Ulster Unionist group in the Irish Convention.

**Beauchamp**, William Lygon, 7th Earl (1872–1938), Lord President of the Council, 1910, First Commissioner of Works, 1910–14, Lord President of the Council, 1914–15, President of the Free Trade Union, 1916, leader of the Liberals in the House of Lords, 1924– 31.

**Bernard**, John Henry (1860–1927), Archbishop of Dublin, 1915–19, Provost of Trinity College, 1919–27, member of the Irish Convention, 1917–18, accepted the majority report in favour of Irish self-government.

**Birkenhead**, Frederick Edwin Smith, 1st Earl (1872–1930), Unionist M.P. for the Walton division of Liverpool, 1906, head of the Press Bureau, 1914, Solicitor-General, 1915, Attorney-General, November 1915, M.P. for West Derby division of Liverpool, 1918, Lord Chancellor, 1919, Secretary of State for India, 1924.

**Birrell**, Augustine (1850–1933), Liberal M.P. for West Fife, 1889–1900, North Bristol, 1906–18, President of the Board of Education, 1906–7, Chief Secretary for Ireland, 1907–16, resigned after the Easter Rebellion.

**Bledisloe**, Charles Bathurst, 1st Viscount (1867–1958), Conservative M.P. for the South or Wilton division of Wiltshire, 1910, founder member and hon. sec. of the Central Land Association, 1907–9, president, 1921–2, Parliamentary Secretary to the Ministry of Food, 1916–17, and to the Ministry of Agriculture, 1924, Governor-General of New Zealand.

**'Bob'**, see Cecil, E.A.R.

**Bottomley**, Horatio William (1860–1933) financier, bankrupt many times, founded *John Bull* in 1906, Liberal M.P. for South Hackney, 1906–12, 1918–22, made patriotic speeches in the Great War, found guilty of fraudulent conversion in 1922 and sentenced to jail, formally expelled from the House of Commons, August 1922, released from jail in 1927, died in obscurity.

**Bourne**, Francis Alphonsus (1861–1935), Cardinal Archbishop of Westminster, 1903–35, a strong critic of I.R.A. terrorism.

**Brand**, Henry (1841–1906), Liberal Unionist M.P. for Stroud, unsuccessfully contested Cardiff as a Liberal Unionist in the general election of 1886.

**Broadhurst**, Henry (1840–1911), Under-Secretary at the Home Office.

**Buckmaster**, Stanley O., 1st Viscount (1861–1934), Solicitor- General, 1913, Lord Chancellor, 1915–16.

**Bull**, Sir William James (1863–1931), Unionist M.P. for Hammersmith, 1900, and Hammersmith South, 1918–29, chairman, London Unionist M.P.s, 1910–29.

**Burns**, John (1858–1943), trade unionist and early member of the Social Democratic Federation, Liberal M.P., 1892, President of the Local Government Board, 1905–14, President of the Board of Trade, 1914.

**Caldwell**, Major General Sir Charles E. (1859–1928), Director of Military Operations, War Office, 1914–15.

**Campbell-Bannerman**, Sir Henry (1836–1908), Liberal M.P. for Stirling Burghs from 1868 until his death, Financial Secretary at the War Office, 1871–4, 1880–82, Secretary to the Admiralty, 1882–4, Chief Secretary for Ireland, 1884–5, Secretary for War, 1886, 1892–5, succeeded Harcourt as leader of the Liberal Party in 1898, Prime Minister from December 1905 until April 1908.

**Carmichael**, Sir Thomas David Gibson-Carmichael, Baron Carmichael of Skirling (1859–1926), Liberal M.P. for Midlothian, 1895–1900, Governor of Victoria, 1908–11, Governor of Madras, 1911–12, of Bengal, 1912–17.

**Carson**, Edward Henry, Baron (1854–1935), Solicitor-General for Ireland, 1892, M.P. for Dublin University, 1892–1918, Solicitor- General (England) 1900–5, leader of the Irish Unionists in the Commons, 1910, Attorney-General, 1915–16, First Lord of the Admiralty, 1916–17, member of the War Cabinet, July 1917–January 1918, M.P. for Duncairn division of Belfast, 1918–21.

**Cave**, George, Viscount (1856–1928), Unionist M.P. for Kingston division of Surrey, 1906, a seat which he held until he entered the Lords in 1918, Solicitor-General 1915, Home Secretary 1916–19, Lord Chancellor, 1922.

**Cawdor**, Frederick Archibald Vaughan, 3rd Earl (1847–1911), First Lord of the Admiralty, 1905–6.

**Cecil**, Lady Beatrix Maud, daughter of the 3rd Marquess of Salisbury, whom Viscount Wolmer married in 1883.

**Cecil**, Edgar Algernon Robert, 1st Viscount, of Chelwood (1864–1958), third son of the 3rd Marquess of Salisbury, Conservative M.P., 1906–23, Under-Secretary of State for Foreign Affairs, 1915–16, Minister of Blockade, 1916–18, Assistant Secretary of State for Foreign Affairs, 1918–19, Lord Privy Seal, 1923–4, Chancellor of the Duchy of Lancaster, 1924–7.

**Chamberlain**, Joseph (1836–1914), Mayor of Birmingham, 1873–4, Liberal M.P. for Birmingham, 1876, President of the Board of Trade, 1880, President of the Local Government Board, 1886, but resigned on the issue of Irish home rule, Secretary of State for the Colonies, 1895, resigned in 1903 to campaign for tariff reform and closer union among the colonies, forced by illness in 1906 to retire from active politics. Perhaps the second most influential figure in Selborne's political career.

**Chamberlain**, Sir Joseph Austen (1863–1937), elder son of Joseph Chamberlain, Unionist M.P. for East Worcestershire, 1892–1914, and West Birmingham, 1914–37, Civil Lord of the Admiralty, 1895–1900, Financial Secretary to the Treasury, 1900–2, Postmaster-General, 1902–3, Chancellor of the Exchequer, 1902–5, Secretary of State for India, 1915–17, Chancellor of the Exchequer, 1919–21, Lord Privy Seal and leader of the Unionist party in the Commons, 1921–2, Foreign Secretary, 1924–9, First Lord of the Admiralty, 1931.

**Chaplin**, Henry, 1st Viscount (1840–1923), M.P. for Mid Lincs., 1885–1906 and for Wimbledon, 1907–16, President of the Board of Agriculture, 1889–92, President of the Local Government Board, 1895–1900, a supporter of Tariff Reform.

**Chilston**, Aretas Akers-Douglas, 1st Viscount (1851–1926), Conservative Chief Whip, 1886–92.

**Churchill**, W.S. (1874–1965), Home Secretary, 1910–11, First Lord of the Admiralty, 1911–15, Minister of Munitions, 1917–19, Colonial Secretary, 1921–2.

**Colvin**, Ian Duncan (1877–1938), journalist, biographer and poet, leader writer on the *Morning Post*, 1909–37.

**Cooper**, Charles Alfred (1829–1916), editor of the *Scotsman*, 1876–1906.

**Craig**, James, 1st Viscount Craigavon (1871–1940), Unionist M.P. for East Down, 1906–18, Mid-Down, 1918–21, Parliamentary Secretary to the Minister of Pensions, 1919–20, Parliamentary and Financial Secretary to the Admiralty, 1920–21, first Prime Minister of Northern Ireland, and one of the members for Co. Down in the Northern Ireland parliament, 1921–40.

**Crewe**, Robert Offley Asburton Crewe-Milnes, 1st Earl (1858–1945), Lord President of the Council, 1905, Secretary of State for the Colonies, 1908, Secretary of State for India, 1910, Lord President of the Council, 1915, Ambassador to France, 1922–8, leader of the Liberals in the House of Lords, 1936–44.

**Crossman**, Sir William (1830–1901), Liberal M.P. for Portsmouth, 1885, became a Liberal Unionist and retained his seat until 1892.

**Curzon**, George Nathaniel, 1st Marquess (1859–1925), Conservative M.P. for Southport, 1886–98, Under-Secretary for Foreign Affairs, 1895, Viceroy and Governor-General of India, 1899–1905, member of the War Cabinet, 1916–19, Foreign Secretary, 1919–24.

**Desart**, Hamilton John Agmondesham Cuffe, 5th Earl (1848–1934), Assistant Solicitor to the Treasury, 1878, Solicitor to the Treasury, Queen's Proctor and Director of Public Prosecutions, 1894–1909, British member of the International Court of Arbitration at The Hague.

**de Valera**, Eamon (1882–1975) born in New York, brought to Limerick as a child, joined the Irish Volunteers in 1913, sentenced to death for his part in the Easter Rising of 1916, but reprieved, released 1917, Sinn Fein M.P. for East Clare, 1917, President of Sinn Fein and the Irish Volunteers, 1917. 'President' of the 'Republic of Ireland', 1919–22, rejected Anglo-Irish treaty, founded Fianna Fail party, 1926, President of the Executive Council of the Irish Free State, and Minister for External Affairs, 1932–7, following the enactment of the 1937 constitution became Taoiseach and Minister for External Affairs, 1937–48, Taoiseach again, 1951–4 and 1957–9, President, 1959, 1966.

**Devlin**, Joseph (1871–1934), Irish Parliamentary Party M.P. for North Kilkenny, 1902–6, and West Belfast, 1906–18, M.P. for Falls, 1918–22, and for West Belfast and Co. Antrim in the new Northern Ireland parliament, taking his seat in 1925–29, M.P. for Central Belfast, 1930–32, 1933.

**Dilke**, Sir Charles Wentworth (1843–1911), Liberal M.P. for Chelsea, 1868–86, returned to public life in 1892 as M.P. for the Forest of Dean and held the seat until his death.

**Dillon**, John (1851–1927), Irish Parliamentary Party M.P. for Tipperary, 1879–85, East Mayo, 1885–1918, chairman of the anti-Parnellites, 1896, Chairman of the Irish Parliamentary Party, 1918.

**Duff**, General Sir Beauchamp (1855–1918), Commander-in-Chief, India, 1914–16.

**Elliot**, Arthur Ralph Douglas (1846–1923), Liberal M.P. for Roxburghshire, 1880, Liberal Unionist M.P., 1886–92, and Liberal Unionist M.P. for Durham, 1898–1906, Financial Secretary to the Treasury, 1903, founder of the Unionist Free Trade Club.

**Ernle**, Rowland Edmund Prothero, 1st Baron (1851–1937), Conservative M.P. for Oxford University, 1914–19, member of departmental committee on the home production of food, 1915, and on the increased prices of commodities, 1916, President of the Board of Agriculture, 1916–19.

**Fisher**, Herbert Albert Laurens (1865–1940), joined the Lloyd George government as President of the Board of Education, December 1916, and was returned unopposed as Liberal M.P. for Hallam division of Sheffield. National Liberal M.P. for the combined universities, 1922–6, British delegate to the Assembly of the League of Nations, 1920–22, Warden of New College, 1926.

**Fitzalan**, Edmund Bernard Fitzalan-Howard, 1st Viscount (1855– 1947), assumed the surname Talbot in 1876 and until his elevation to the peerage in 1921 was known as Lord Edmund Talbot. Unionist M.P. for Chichester, 1894–1921, Chief Unionist Whip, 1913–21, last Lord Lieutenant of Ireland, 1921.

**Fraser**, Sir John Malcolm (1878–1949), adviser on press matters to the Unionist party, 1910, Honorary Principal Agent of the Unionist Party, 1920–23, Vice-Chairman of the Conservative Party, 1937–8.

**French**, John Denton Pinkstone, 1st Earl of Ypres (1852–1925), C. in C. Aldershot command, 1902–7, Inspector General of Forces, 1907, C.I.G.S.,

1912–14, C. in C. British Expeditionary Force, Aug. 1914–Dec. 1915, C. in C. Home Forces, 1916–18, Lord Lieutenant of Ireland, 1918–21.

**Giffen**, Sir Robert (1837–1910), economist and statistician, opponent of home rule. Assistant-Secretary to the Board of Trade, 1882–97.

**Gladstone**, Herbert John (1854–1930), youngest son of William Ewart Gladstone, Liberal M.P. for Leeds and West Leeds, 1880–1910, Home Secretary, 1905–9, Governor-General of South Africa, 1909–14, became a viscount in 1910.

**Gladstone**, William Ewart (1809–1898), M.P. for Newark, 1832, and sat almost continuously for various seats in the House of Commons until his retirement in 1895. Chancellor of the Exchequer, 1833, Junior Lord of the Treasury, 1834, Under-Secretary for the Colonies, 1835, Vice-President of the Board of Trade, 1841–5, Chancellor of the Exchequer, 1852–5, and 1859–65, leader of the Liberal Party, 1867, Prime Minister, 1868–73, 1880–85, 1886, 1892–4.

**Glenavy**, James Henry Mussen Campbell, 1st Baron (1851–1931), Unionist M.P. for the St Stephen's Green division of Dublin, 1898–1900, and for Dublin University, 1903–16, Solicitor-General for Ireland, 1901–5, Attorney-General, December 1905, and April 1916, Lord Chief Justice of Ireland, December 1916, created baronet, 1917, Lord Chancellor of Ireland, June 1918, member of the Senate of the Irish Free State, and its chairman, 1922–8.

**Goschen**, George Joachim, 1st Viscount (1831–1907), Liberal M.P. for the City of London, 1863–1880, for Ripon, 1880–85, and for East Edinburgh, 1885–6, became a Liberal Unionist in 1886, and sat for the Exchange Division of Liverpool, 1886–1900. First Lord of the Admiralty, 1871–4, and again, 1895–1900.

**'Grace'**, see Ridley, Grace.

**Grey**, Edward, 1st Viscount, of Fallodon (1862–1933), Liberal M.P. 1885, Under-Secretary of State for Foreign Affairs, 1892–5, and 1906–16, Ambassador to the United States of America, 1918–20, leader of the Liberals in the House of Lords, 1920–4.

**Grey**, Albert Henry George (1851–1917), Liberal M.P. for Tyneside, defeated in the 1886 general election when standing as a Liberal Unionist. Became the 4th Earl Grey in 1894, and served as Governor-General of Canada, 1904–11.

**Griffith**, Arthur (1872–1922), founder of the Sinn Fein movement, 1905, Sinn Fein M.P. for East Cavan, 1918, played a key role in the Anglo–Irish treaty negotiations, October–December 1921, and defended the treaty in the Dail, December 1921–January 1922.

**Gwynn**, Stephen Lucius (1864–1959), Irish Parliamentary Party M.P. for Galway City, 1906–18. Enlisted as a private, January 1915, and served in France with the 16th (Irish) Division. Member of the Irish Convention, 1917.

**Haldane**, Richard Burdon, Viscount (1856–1928), Secretary for War, 1905.

**Hall**, Sir Alfred Daniel (1864–1942), chief scientific adviser to the Ministry of Agriculture, and Commissioner under the Development Act, 1909–17.

**Halsbury**, Hardinge Stanley Giffard, 1st Earl (1823–1921), Conservative M.P. for Launceston, 1877, 1880, Lord Chancellor, 1885, 1886, 1895–1905, created earl in 1898.

**Hamilton**, Lord George Francis (1845–1927), Conservative M.P. for Middlesex, 1868–84, and Ealing, 1885–1906, Under-Secretary of State for India, 1874, Vice–President of the Council, 1878–80, First Lord of the Admiralty, 1885–6, 1886–92, Secretary of State for India, 1895–1903.

**Hamilton**, General Sir Ian (1853–1947), G.O.C. in C. Southern Command, 1905–9, Adjutant-General and second military member of the Army Council, 1909–10, G.O.C. in C. Mediterranean, and Inspector General, overseas forces, 1910–15.

**Hankey**, Maurice Pascal Alers, 1st Baron (1877–1963), entered Royal Marine Artillery, 1895, Secretary to the C.I.D., 1912–38, Secretary to the War Council, Nov. 1914–May 1915, to the Dardanelles Committee, May–Nov. 1915, to the Cabinet War Committee, Dec. 1915–Dec. 1916, to the War Cabinet, 1916–18, to the Cabinet, 1919–38, Minister without Portfolio, Sept. 1939–May 1940, Chancellor of the Duchy of Lancaster, 1940–41, Paymaster General, 1941–2.

**Harcourt**, Lewis, 1st Viscount (1863–1922), was his father's private secretary, 1881–5, 1886, 1892–5, 1895–1904, Liberal M.P. for Rossendale division of Lancashire, 1904–16, First Commissioner of Works, 1905–10, 1915–16, Secretary of State for the Colonies, 1910–15.

**Harcourt**, Sir William (1827–1904), Liberal M.P. for Oxford, 1868– 80, Derby, 1880–95, and West Monmouth, 1895–1904. Appointed Chancellor of the Exchequer by Gladstone in 1886, and 1892–5, leader of the Liberal party in the House of Commons, 1894–8.

**Hardinge**, Charles, Baron, of Penshurst (1858–1944), Viceroy of India, 1910–16.

**Hartington**, Spencer Compton, Marquess, later the 8th Duke of Devonshire (1833–1908), Liberal M.P. for North Lancs., 1857–68, New Radnor, 1869–80, North East Lancs., 1880–85, Liberal Unionist M.P. for Rossendale Division of Lancs., 1885–91, when he succeeded his father as Duke of Devonshire. Liberal Under-Secretary of State for War, 1863–6, Secretary of State for War, 1866, Postmaster-General, 1868–70, Chief Secretary for Ireland, 1870–74, Secretary of State for India, 1880–82, and for War, 1882–5. Broke with Gladstone over home rule. Independently supported Lord Salisbury's government, 1887–92. Lord President of the Council, 1895–1903.

**Henderson**, Arthur (1863–1945), Chairman, Parliamentary Labour Party, 1908–10, 1914–17, President of the Board of Education, 1915–16, Labour adviser to the government, 1916, Minister without Portfolio, 1917, Home Secretary, 1924, Foreign Secretary, 1929–31.

**Herbert**, Auberon Thomas, 8th Baron Lucas and 11th Baron Dingwall

(1876–1916), Under Secretary of State for War, 1908–11, and for the colonies, 1911, Secretary to the Board of Agriculture, 1911–14, President of the Board of Agriculture, 1914–15.

**Hicks Beach**, Sir Michael, 1st Earl St Aldwyn (1836–1916), Conservative M.P. for East Gloucestershire, 1864–85, and West Bristol, 1885–1906, Chancellor of the Exchequer, 1885–6, Chief Secretary for Ireland, 1886–7, President of the Board of Trar of the Exchequer, 1892–1902.

**Hobhouse**, Henry (1854–1937), M.P. (Liberal) for East Somerset, 1885–6, then sat as a Liberal Unionist from 1886 to 1902.

**'Hopie'**, See Linlithgow, Marquess of.

**Hughes**, W. M. (1864–1952), Prime Minister of Australia, 1915–23, member of the Imperial War Cabinet, 1917–19.

**Hyndman**, Henry Mayers (1842–1921), founder of the Social Democratic Federation in 1884.

**James**, Sir Henry (1828–1911), created Lord James of Hereford in 1895, Liberal M.P. for Taunton, 1869 and for Bury, 1885, Attorney–General, 1880–85, opposed home rule and refused to serve under Gladstone in 1886.

**Jellicoe**, Admiral Sir John Rushworth (1859–1935), Second Sea Lord, 1912–14, C. in C. of Grand Fleet, 1914–16, First Sea Lord, 1916–17, Chief of Naval Staff, 1917, Admiral of the Fleet, 1919, Governor-General of New Zealand, 1920–24.

**Kerr**, Philip Henry, 11th Marquess of Lothian (1882–1940), Assistant Secretary to the Inter-Colonial Council, 1905–8, editor of *The State* (a journal founded to assist the closer union movement), 1908–9, editor of the *Round Table*, 1910–16, a private secretary to Lloyd George, 1916–21, Secretary of the Rhodes Trust, 1925–39, Chancellor of the Duchy of Lancaster, 1931, Under-Secretary of State for India, 1931–2, Ambassador to the United States, 1939–40.

**Kitchener**, Horatio Herbert, 1st Earl, of Khartoum (1850–1916), Chief of Staff to Lord Roberts and appointed to succeed him as C. in C., C. in C. in India, 1902–9, British Agent in Egypt, 1911–14, Secretary of State for War, 1914–16.

**Labouchere**, Henry du Pré (1831–1912), Liberal M.P. for Northampton, 1880–1905, journalist, political gossip and go–between.

**Lansdowne**, Henry Charles Keith Petty-Fitzmaurice, 5th Marquess (1845–1927), Undersecretary for War, 1872–4, India, 1880, Viceroy of India, 1888–94, Secretary of State for War, 1895–1900, Foreign affairs, 1900–5, led Unionists in Lords.

**Law**, Andrew Bonar (1858–1923), businessman, entered politics as a Unionist M.P., 1900, Parliamentary Secretary to the Board of Trade, 1902, and leader of the Unionists, 1911. Colonial Secretary, 1915, Chancellor of the Exchequer and member of the war cabinet, 1916–18, member of the British delegation at the peace conference in Versailles, 1919, Lord Privy Seal, 1919–21, resigned because of ill-health but emerged to succeed Lloyd George as Prime Minister in 1922.

**'Linky'**, See Quickswood, Baron.

**Linlithgow**, John Adrian Louis Hope, 7th Earl of Hopetoun and 1st Marquess of Linlithgow (1860–1908), Governor–General of Australia, 1900–2, Secretary of State for Scotland in Balfour's administration, February 1905.

**Lloyd George**, David, 1st Earl (1863–1945), M.P. for Carnarvon Boroughs, 1890, President of the Board of Trade, 1905–8, Chancellor of the Exchequer, 1908–15, Minister of Munitions, 1915–16, Prime Minister, 1916–22.

**Londonderry**, Charles Stewart Henry Vane-Tempest-Stewart, 7th Marquess (1878–1949), Unionist M.P. for Maidstone, 1906–15, member of the Irish Convention, 1917–1918, Under Secretary of State for Air, 1920–21, leader of the Northern Ireland Senate, and Minister for Education, 1921–6, First Commissioner of Works, 1928–9, 1931, Secretary of State for Air, 1931–5, Lord Privy Seal and leader of the House of Lords, 1935.

**Long**, Walter Hume, 1st Viscount (1854–1924), Conservative M.P. 1880, Parliamentary Secretary to the Board of Agriculture, 1895, President of the Local Government Board, 1900, Chief Secretary for Ireland, 1905–6. President of the Local Government Board, 1915, Secretary of State for the Colonies, 1916–18, First Lord of the Admiralty, 1919–21.

**Ludlow**, Henry Ludlow Lopes, Baron, of Heywood (1865–1922), only son of Henry Charles Lopes, 1st Baron Ludlow (1828–1899).

**Lyttleton**, Alfred (1857–1913), Unionist M.P., 1895, Secretary of State for the Colonies, 1903–5, sanctioned the introduction of Chinese labour on the Witwatersrand, and sponsored a crown colony constitution for the Transvaal.

**Macdonnell**, Antony Patrick, Baron, of Swinford (1844–1925), joined the Indian Civil Service, 1864, Lieutenant Governor of Bengal, 1893, of North-Western Provinces and Oudh, 1895–1901, Permanent Under Secretary for Ireland, 1902–8, Chairman of the Royal Commission on the Civil Service, 1912–14.

**MacDowell**, Sir Alexander (d. 1918), Belfast businessman, a nominated member of the Irish Convention.

**McKenna**, Reginald (1863–1943), Liberal M.P. for North Monmouthshire, 1895–1918, Financial Secretary to the Treasury, 1905–7, President of the Board of Education, 1907–8, First Lord of the Admiralty, 1908–11, Home Secretary, 1911–15, Chancellor of the Exchequer, 1915–16.

**Maxwell**, General Sir John Grenfell (1859–1929), served for many years in Egypt, military governor of Pretoria, 1900–1, C. in C. Egypt, 1908–12, 1914–15, C. in C. Ireland, 1916.

**Mayo**, Dermot Robert Wyndham Bourke, 7th Earl (1851–1927).

**Midleton**, William St John Fremantle Brodrick, 9th Viscount and 1st Earl of Midleton (1856–1942), M.P. for West Surrey, 1880–5, and for Guildford, 1885–1905, Financial Secretary to the War Office, 1886–92, Under-Secretary of State for War, 1895, and for Foreign Affairs, 1898, Secretary of State for War, 1900–3, Secretary of State for India, 1903–5.

**Milner**, Alfred, 1st Viscount (1854–1925), active in forming the Liberal Unionist Association in 1886. Chairman of the Board of Inland Revenue, 1892–7, Governor of the Cape Colony and High Commissioner in South Africa, 1897–1901, Governor of the Transvaal and Orange River Colony, 1901–5, member of the war Cabinet, 1916–18, Secretary of State for the Colonies, 1918–21. Knighted 1895; created Viscount, 1902. The man whom Selborne regarded, above all others, as his political mentor.

**Monro**, General Sir Charles Carmichael (1860–1929), C. in C. Dardanelles, Oct. 1915, and of the Mediterranean Expeditionary Force, 1915–Jan. 1916, Commander 1st Army in France, 1916, C. in C. India, 1916–20.

**Montagu**, Edwin Samuel (1879–1924), Liberal M.P. for the Chesterton division of Cambridgeshire, 1906–22, Financial Secretary to the Treasury, 1914–16, Chancellor of the Duchy of Lancaster, 1915, Minister of Munitions, 1916, Secretary of State for India, 1917–22, author (with Lord Chelmsford) of the 1918 report on Indian constitutional reform.

**Morley**, John, 1st Viscount (1838–1923), entered the House of Commons as a Liberal in 1883, sitting for Newcastle-upon-Tyne, 1883–95, and for Montrose Burghs, 1896–1908, Chief Secretary for Ireland, 1886, 1892–5, Secretary of State for India, 1905–10, Lord President of the Council, 1910–14.

**Murray**, General Sir Archibald (1860–1945), Deputy and then Chief of Imperial General Staff, 1915, G.O.C. Egypt, 1916–17.

**Nash**, Vaughan (1861–1932), Private Secretary to Sir Henry Campbell-Bannerman, 1905–8, and to Asquith, 1908–12, Secretary of the Ministry of Reconstruction, 1917–19.

**Northbrook**, Thomas George Baring, 1st Earl (1826–1904), Under-Secretary of State for War, 1868, Governor-General of India, 1872–6, First Lord of the Admiralty, 1880–85, became a Liberal Unionist in 1886.

**Northcliffe**, Alfred Charles William Harmsworth, Viscount (1865–1922), newspaper proprietor, founded the *Daily Mail* in 1896, and bought the *Observer* in 1905 and *The Times* in 1908.

**Northcote**, Henry Stafford, Baron (1846–1911), Conservative M.P. for Exeter, 1880–9, Financial Secretary to the War Office, 1885–6, Surveyor General of the Ordnance, 1886–7, Governor of Bombay, 1900–3, Governor-General of the Commonwealth of Australia, 1903–8.

**Northumberland**, Henry George Percy, 7th Duke (1846–1918).

**Oliver**, Frederick Scott (1864–1934), entered the firm of Debenham and Freebody in 1892, author of many books and pamphlets on historical and political subjects, notably federal devolution.

**Palmer**, Robert Arthur Stafford, serving as a captain in the 6th battalion the Hampshire Regiment in Mesopotamia, killed in action 21 Jan. 1916.

**Parnell**, Charles Stewart (1846–1891), born in Co. Wicklow of Anglo-Irish landed family, joined Isaac Butt's Home Government Association in 1874, elected M.P. for Co. Meath, 1875, became chairman of the Home Rule party in 1880 after winning three seats, Meath, Mayo and Cork City, choosing to sit for the latter. Led the home rulers until the party split over the question of his continuing as leader after he had been cited in the O'Shea divorce case, 1890.

**Platt**, Thomas (later Sir Thomas) Comyn (1875–1961), served in the Foreign Office, 1906–7 and 1909–11, contested various parliamentary seats as a Unionist candidate between 1891 and 1929.

**Plunkett**, Sir Horace Curzon (1854–1932), founder of the Co- operative movement in Ireland, Unionist member for South County Dublin, 1892–1900, chairman of the Irish Convention, 1917–18, member of the Senate of the Irish Free State, 1922–3.

**Plymouth**, Robert George Windsor-Clive, 1st Earl of (1857–1923).

**Pretyman**, Ernest George (1860–1931), Civil Lord of the Admiralty, 1900–1903, Parliamentary and Financial Secretary to the Admiralty, 1903–6.

**Quickswood**, Hugh Richard Heathcote Gascoyne-Cecil, Baron (1869–1956), youngest son of the 3rd Marquess of Salisbury, Conservative M.P. for Greenwich, 1895–1906, burgess for the University of Oxford, 1910–37.

**Redmond**, John Edward (1856–1918), M.P. for New Ross, 1881–91, supported Parnell in 1890 and led the Parnellites until 1900, M.P. for Waterford, 1891, chairman of the reunited Irish Parliamentary Party in 1900, took part in the Irish Convention, 1917–18.

**Ridley**, Grace, third daughter of Viscount Ridley, Wolmer's wife.

**Ritchie**, Charles Thomson, 1st Baron (1838–1906), Conservative M.P. for Tower Hamlets, 1874, 1880, and for St George's in the East, 1885, 1888, Financial Secretary to the Admiralty, 1885–6, President of the Local Government Board, 1886, defeated in the 1892 election, M.P. for Croydon, 1895–1900, President of the Board of Trade, 1895, Home Secretary, 1900, Chancellor of the Exchequer, 1902, dismissed 1903, created baron, 1905.

**Robertson**, Field Marshall Sir William (1860–1933), C.I.G.S., Dec. 1915–Jan. 1918.

**Rosebery**, Archibald Philip Primrose, 5th Earl (1847–1929), Under-Secretary to the Home Office, 1881–3, First Commissioner of Works, 1885, Lord Privy Seal, 1885, Foreign Secretary, 1886 and 1892–4, Prime Minister, 1894–5, resigned from the leadership of the Liberal Party, 1896.

**Runciman**, Walter, 1st Viscount (1879–1949), Liberal M.P. for Oldham, 1899–1900, and Dewsbury, 1902–18, Parliamentary Secretary to the Local Government Board, 1905, Financial Secretary to the Treasury, 1907–8, President of the Board of Education, 1908, of the Board of Agriculture and Fisheries, 1911, and of the Board of Trade, 1914, resigning 1916, M.P. for Swansea West, 1924–9, St Ives, 1929–31, and as a National Liberal, 1931–7, President of the Board of Trade, 1931–7, Lord President of the Council, 1938.

**St Davids**, Sir John Wynford Phillipps, 1st Viscount (1860–1938), financier, chairman of the Buenos Ayres and Pacific Railway, 1900.

**Salisbury**, Robert Arthur Talbot Gascoyne–Cecil, 3rd Marquess (1830–1903), Conservative M.P., 1853–68, Secretary of State for India, 1866–7, succeeded as Marquess, 1868, Secretary of State for India, 1874–8, Foreign Secretary, 1878–80, became leader of the Conservative Party, 1881, Prime Minister and Foreign Secretary, 1885, 1886–92, 1895–1902.

**Salisbury**, James Edward Hubert Gascoyne-Cecil, 4th Marquess (1861–1947), M.P. for the Darwen division of North East Lancs., 1885–92, and for Rochester, 1893–1903, when he succeeded his father as Marquess of Salisbury. Under-Secretary for Foreign Affairs, 1900, Lord Privy Seal, 1903–5, Chairman of Tribunal on conscientious objectors, 1916–18, Lord President of the Council and Chancellor of the Duchy of Lancaster, 1922–3, Lord Privy Seal, 1924–5, leader of the House of Lords, 1925–9, President of the National Union of Conservative and Unionist Associations, 1942–5.

**Saltoun**, Alexander William Frederick Fraser, 18th Earl (1851–1933).

**Samuel**, Herbert Louis, 1st Viscount (1870–1963), Liberal M.P. for Cleveland division of Yorkshire, 1902–18, and Darwen division of Lancs., 1929–35, Postmaster-General, 1910–14, 1915–16, Chancellor of the Duchy of Lancaster, 1909–10, 1915–16, Home Secretary, 1916 and 1931–2, High Commissioner for Palestine, 1920–25, leader of the Liberal Parliamentary Party, 1931–5.

**Sandars**, John Satterfield (1835–1934), private secretary to A. J. Balfour, reckoned to be a power behind the scenes in Unionist policy-making.

**Sanders**, Robert Arthur, 1st Baron Bayford (1862–1940), Unionist M.P. for Bridgewater, 1910–23, Wells, 1924–9, Treasurer of the Household, 1918–19, Junior Lord of the Treasury, 1919, Under– Secretary of State for War, 1921–2, Minister of Agriculture and Fisheries, 1922–3.

**Scarborough**, Alfred Frederick George Beresford Lumley, 10th Earl (1857–1945).

**Selborne**, Roundell Palmer, 1st Earl (1812–95), Conservative M.P. for Plymouth, 1847–57, Liberal M.P. for Richmond, 1861–72, Solicitor-General, 1861–3, Attorney-General, 1863–6, Lord Chancellor, 1872–4 and 1880–85, created Baron Selborne, 1872, and Earl of Selborne, 1882.

**Sellar**, A. Craig (1835–1890), Liberal Unionist M.P. for Partick and a Party Whip, 1886–8.

**Simon**, John Allsebrook, 1st Viscount (1873–1954), Liberal M.P. for Walthamstow, 1906–18, Spen Valley, 1922–40, Solicitor-General, 1910, Attorney-General, 1913, Home Secretary, 1915–16, led the National Liberal Party, 1931, Foreign Secretary, 1931–5, Home Secretary, 1935, Chancellor of the Exchequer, 1937, Lord Chancellor, 1940.

**Smith**, Arthur Lionel (1850–1924), historian, Master of Balliol, and an active participant in the Workers' Education Association movement.

**Stamfordham**, Arthur John Bigge, Baron (1849–1931), private secretary to King George V.

**Strutt**, Edward Gerald (1854–1930), adviser to the Board of Agriculture.

**Sydenham**, George Sydenham Clarke, Baron (1848–1933), Governor of Victoria, 1901–3, member of the War Office Reconstitution Committee, 1903, Governor of Bombay, 1907–13, Chairman of the Central Tribunal hearing appeals from local committees administering the National Service Act, 1915–16, member of Lord Bryce's conference on the Second Chamber, 1918.

**Sykes**, Sir Mark (1879–1919), Unionist M.P. for Central Hall, 1911, served in the Great War, negotiated with the French over Palestine, 1916, attached to the Foreign Office as chief adviser on near-eastern policy, 1916–19.

**'Top'**, see Wolmer, Lord.

**Townshend**, Major General Sir Charles Vere Ferrers (1861–1924), Military Attaché in Paris, 1905, served in South Africa, 1909–11, served in the Mesopotamian campaign, April, 1915, captured Kut el Amara, Sept. 1915, but besieged by the Turks in Dec. 1915, surrendering in April 1916.

**Turnor**, Christopher Hatton (1873–1940), agricultural reformer, author of many books on land and food problems.

**Wharton**, John Lloyd (1837–1912), Conservative M.P. for Yorkshire, West Riding, and Ripon, 1886–1906.

**Whittaker**, Sir Thomas (1850–1919), Liberal M.P. for Spen Valley, 1892, and a member of the Bryce Committee on Second Chamber Reform.

**Williams**, Joseph Powell (1840–1904), Liberal Unionist M.P. for Birmingham South, vice-president of the Birmingham Liberal-Unionist Association and subsequently chairman of management committee, Central Liberal Unionist Association. Financial Secretary to the War Office, 1895–1900.

**Willoughby de Broke**, Richard Greville Verney, 19th Earl (1869–1923), Unionist M.P. for Rugby, 1895–1900.

**Wilson**, Sir Henry Hughes (1864–1922), Director of Military Operations, War Office, 1910–14, Chief Liaison Officer with the French, Jan. 1915, commanded the 4th corps, 1916, Chief of the Imperial General Staff, 1918–22, assassinated by Irish republican gunmen on the steps of his London home.

**Wilson**, Leslie Orme (1876–1955), Unionist M.P. for Reading, 1913–22, and South Portsmouth, 1922–3, Parliamentary Assistant Secretary to the War Cabinet, 1918, Parliamentary Secretary to the Ministry of Shipping, 1919, to the Treasury, 1921–3, Chief Unionist Whip, 1921–3, Governor of Bombay, 1923–8, of Queensland, 1932–46.

**Wolmer**, Lord, eldest son of Lord Selborne: Roundell Cecil Palmer (1887–1971), Conservative M.P. for the Newton division of Lancs., 1910–18, and the Aldershot division of Hampshire, 1918–40, succeeded his father as 3rd Earl of Selborne, 1942, Minister of Economic Warfare, 1942–5.

**Wood**, Edward Frederick Lindley, 1st Earl of Halifax (1881–1959), Unionist M.P. for Ripon, 1910–25, Under Secretary of State for the

Colonies, 1921–2, President of the Board of Education, 1922–4, and 1932, Governor-General and Viceroy of India, 1925–31, Secretary of State for War, 1935, Lord President of the Council, 1937, Foreign Secretary, 1938, nearly succeeded Neville Chamberlain in 1940.

**Wood**, Thomas McKinnon (1855–1927), Liberal M.P. for the St Rollox division of Glasgow, 1906–18, Parliamentary Secretary to the Board of Education, 1908, Under Secretary of State at the Foreign Office, Oct. 1908–11, Financial Secretary to the Treasury, 1911–12, Secretary of State for Scotland, 1912–16.

**Wyndham**, George (1863–1913), Chief Secretary for Ireland, 1900–1905.

**Younger**, Sir George, 1st Viscount (1851–1929), businessman and brewer, chairman, George Younger and Sons, President, National Union of Conservative Associations of Scotland, 1904, Unionist M.P. for Ayr Boroughs, 1906–22, Chairman of Unionist Party Organisation, 1917–23, Treasurer of the Unionist Party, 1923–59.

# Index